Rocket Surgery

D J Gilmour

Douglas J Gilmour has asserted his rights under the Copyright, Designs and Patent Act 1988 to be identified as the author of this work.

All rights reserved. No part of this publication may be reproduced, stored in a retrieval system or transmitted, in any form or by any means without the authors prior permission in writing.

This is a work of fiction. Names, characters, and incidents either are products of the author's imagination or are used fictitiously. Any resemblance to actual events or locales or persons, living or dead, is entirely coincidental.

Copyright © Douglas J Gilmour 2017

Front Cover: The Sugar Boat. All rights reserved by Inspired Ariel Images. For more information and some unusual and lovely images of Argyle and beyond visit iaimages.co.uk

Future's So Bright I Gotta Wear Shades lyrics © Warner/Chappell Music, Inc., THE BICYCLE MUSIC COMPANY

All proceeds from Rocket Surgery are going to the Alzheimer's Society in memory of my mother Marion Gilmour

I also need to thank Iain Macdonald for asking all the right questions, repeatedly, until I came up with at least some answers or he answered them himself.

About the Author, Douglas Gilmour grew up in Balloch, Helensburgh and the Isle of Lewis before a stint at Glasgow University. He then went south to seek fame and fortune. He is lucky to be married with two sons and is enjoying the pubs of the East Midlands.

First Edition 2022

About Rocket Surgery

Ben is walking out of Slough. As he does, he thinks about what has led him to this expedition. Of growing up on the west coast of Scotland and working in Slough. Of the human capacity for destruction both self and corporate. The value of friendships. The dangers of company rhetoric and the tricky nature of true love.

Rocket Surgery is being listed as a comedy, which may prove optimistic but it is adult in language and content and should not be read if that is likely to cause offence.

Some Reviews of Rocket Surgery

A great insight in to growing up in a small Scottish town in the eighties, whisks you through the University years and on to office work in the early nineties. It resonated strongly with me having done all three, humorous and engaging has to be recommended. The situations and characters presented were very tangible and rang true, many thanks for a good read, I look forward to the follow up.

Simon Foster

I really enjoyed this book. Like Iain Banks, Douglas has really captured what it's like to be a teenager in a small Scottish coastal town in the 1980's: and has vividly evoked memories of my experiences in the 70's. The later experiences in the world of work are just amazing: I worked for staid giant corporations and the frantic world of call centres, synthetic management concern, ersatz enthusiasm and sackings was a complete revelation to me. Christmas is Cancelled had me agog - never come across that before! PS: I'm the author's brother, but don't let that put you off. It really is a good book!

David Gilmour

Fast moving and entertaining journey into adulthood, work, friendship and love. Being a fellow Scotsman living abroad a lot of references and details ring true. Passionately and cleverly written

Moray Robertson

Insightful humour. I loved this book. It lampoons business culture and modern thought trends. There is wry humour and comedic metaphors.

We meet the protagonists when they are young and wild only to follow them into the seeds of career building. There were so many clever bits that I wanted to read out loud. I looked forward to picking it up to read a bit more.

Rosemary Blake

A wry, authentic and witty observation of life and early adulthood. Bringing back memories of growing up in Scotland in the Seventies and Eighties: a well-written, wry, entertaining, and at times laugh-out-loud, account of youth, holidays and surviving teenage foibles and corporate adult life. And for a good cause

Raymond Smears

An emotional rollercoaster of the best and worst of human behaviour. The rollercoaster of life's gains and losses. Of childhood friendships we all valued and then cast aside. No doubt we will all relate to the ill choices we all make re friendships, relationships and work dynamics. An emotional read and I can't wait for the sequel.

Karen Yates

ROCKET SURGERY

PROLOGUE

Ben takes another swig from the pint of water on the shelf in the hall. It is his fifth and his stomach is beginning to hurt. 'I'm too sexy for my shirt' drifts in from the kitchen with the first of the morning sunshine. Ben camps it up to the mirror, he back-combes his long, thin, blonde hair and mouths 'lovely' to himself. His reflection flutters its eyelashes in appreciation. Ben smooths his white T-shirt and stands by the door. A sealed packet of Benson and Hedges slides into its usual pocket, keys into the other. Another half-empty packet is propped up by the folded back lid. Ten filters, still in their perfect three deep formation, peek out at him. He pulls one out, lights it and takes a final big swig.

'Drinks too wet without one.'

The lighter drops into the pouch already marked out for it in stressed denim, 'Five pints of water without going for a slash,' the smoke billows out of his mouth as he talks. 'Gotta be a record,' he looks round the flat with only a single chair in the centre of a bare room and tugs the door to.

The sun still has that clean look of an early morning in Slough. Later it starts to look red and uncomfortable as all of the pollutants (physical and spiritual) below begin to knock out its earlier optimism. It will be a saddened and world-weary star by the time it sets, dark in an orange sky above the Thames Valley. Now, though, it is beautiful- just as he had been at the start of things. The six starlings that constitute the wildlife of the street are deep in conversation as Ben bounces down the steps. This is their moment when they can catch up on the news without shouting. In another hour Windsor Road will be fulfilling its function as a car park extension from Windsor to Slough. The M4 at the end of the street is already supplying the backing track of roaring tyres, while the forty-five second cycle at Heathrow and the fast trains to Paddington take it in turns to raise the sound level just beyond the level of tolerable.

Ben, though, is oblivious to all of this; he has been here too long. Returning from his travels around the UK it is everywhere else that is really quiet. He stoops to check the laces of his fourteen hole Doctor Martin boots in traditional black. Ox blood red would be better but he hasn't had the spare cash for a long, long time. He breaths in deeply, spreading his arms wide. He can feel the mass of water moving uneasily in his stomach. Ben has memorised the route. It takes about thirty minutes in the car, at an average say of twenty miles an hour, so ten miles.

It is no longer than walking to Glen Fruin and flatter, so it shouldn't be a problem.

Ben remembers climbing over the Hill to Glen Fruin. The Hill doesn't have a name. As children they had checked on a dozen maps to see if they could find out what it was. In a land where every ridge and rock manages a name of a budding Rob Roy extra, the two thousand five hundred foot mountain that separates the Fruin and the Clyde remains the Hill with No Name. Ben wonders what is the hill equivalent of a cigar and poncho? From the top of the Hill you can see north to Ben Lomond, west to the Arrochar Alps and east to the Gargunnock hills. To the South, beyond the sparkling Clyde and the Sugar Boat stands Goat Fell on Arran and the Paps of Jura. Thoughts of the Paps of Jura reminds Ben of Clorinda.

Clorinda Ferguson. Red hair, the tightest of jeans, a chest that deserved a mapping expedition all of its own. Released early from his Aunt's shop, Ben and Clorinda had climbed the Hill and only then thought of Craig's Pool. The pool was where the Fruin Burn deepened and slowed for a while on its way through the highlands to the sea. The water, ice cold despite the heatwave, always posed a tricky problem. Stay below the water as much as possible and experience the first stages of cryogenic freezing. Stay above the water and the vicious Argyll Cleg would strip the flesh from an exposed limb in seconds. Or at least give you a nasty nip. No costumes? No problem, they stripped off and dived in. The prospect of snogging Clorinda provided a brilliant solution to the bitter cold. Her body stretched the surface tension of the still pool, rolling onto her back and gliding to the gravel of the far bank. Ben, teeth flashing, slid after her, only his eyes above the surface, the Jaws theme running in his head.

A squeal of dusty breaks made them both turn in the water. A yellow Escort Mexico pulled up at the car park about a hundred yards from the pool. A short, fat man in a brown shirt rolled out with four kids boiling out behind him. Something frightening rocked the car as it shifted out of the passenger side. Ben straightened slightly to get a better look, it must have been female once, but there could be two, maybe three of Clorinda there. Ben looked back at the man scratching the underside of his gut and stretching. The dark circles in the nylon shirt took the scent out of the heather from here. Behind him Clorinda swore.

'Aye. Frightening what can happen if you don't take care of yourself. Nice car though.'

'Eh? The clothes you bloody idiot!' Ben started towards the pile but he realised that despite contact with the wintry water, he was charging towards four kids with his tackle stiff enough to double as a towel rail. The children looked rather taken aback, as did the nylon-clad driver.

'Hey. You. What the hell do you think yer doin?'

'I. It's not. Shit!' Ben gathered all that he could from the shore and splashed back across the river. About two thirds of the way across he had to swim. One armed but fast, as the lumbering Ford owner closed. Clorinda was shouting abuse equally at both men from the dangerous shelter of a gorse bush. Ben hauled himself up the bank and kept on running across the grass and heather to the yellow flowered spiky cover. The pair pulled the wet clothes into two piles as the man stood up to his not inconsiderable waist in the water inviting Ben to pop back for a chat. With the gorse to their backs they dragged on what they could and squelched up the hill. They were still laughing when they reached the top. Holding hands as they looked out over Argyll. She hung her bra on a battered rowan, followed by Ben's shirt. He stretched, conscious of his easy muscularity.

I looked fine and dandy in those days, fine and dandy. Had it all then, Ben thinks as he walks. A straight 'A' kid with nine 'O' grades, five Highers and an offer from Glasgow University in his pocket. All this and a kiss from Clorinda too. A song pops into his mind 'I'm doing all right, getting good grades, The future's so bright, I gotta wear shades!' Of course, Ben reflects, that's really when it all goes wrong.

The White Heather Club

Chapter One December 1983

It was cold. Ben pulled the collar of his flying jacket up and was glad of the fur against his face. Genuine 'Beaver' the man in the Army and Navy Store had said. Ben still wasn't sure if he'd been trying to crack a joke but he didn't look the type. Irrespective of the rodent content, several sheep and a cow had undoubtedly died to make that jacket. It was so heavy that his shoulders had hurt for the first three weeks after he had got it. Ben had carefully gone over every inch of the second hand jacket with Leather Food and polished it. This, to Ben at least, was a thing of beauty. He was glad of it tonight, had been cold all day and getting colder.

They had started early. Drinking that is, with it being Hogmanay'n all. They had started when the pub had opened. A splendid establishment called the Guilford Arms which had a round table sunk into the floor, closed off from the rest of the bar. They could drink there without attracting attention. This was vital given that most of those around the table were still to make it to eighteen. The staff were happy enough for the early business as long as the lads kept a low profile. It was a win-win.

At some point, and Ben was hazy about when, they had decided that a chippie was in order. Within moments they were standing in the cold Edinburgh air, stuffing chips down their throats with murmurs of 'it'll soak up the alcohol'. Ben doubted that it would. There had been much confusion caused by the offers of 'salt and sauce'. Tiny had had to ask the rather grumpy looking man behind the counter three times to repeat the question and Ben still didn't get it till they were outside. Salt and vinegar would the honest accompaniment in any Christian country. These East Coast folk and their strange ways. Ben looked at his companions, Tiny, Rhino and Angus. He was thinking that they were the finest that Helensburgh could offer. Indeed the finest that the West Coast could offer and therefore by clear implication, the world. But he suspected that the only people who would share that view, other than himself, would be Tiny, Rhino and Angus. They looked across a big bit of grass to what appeared to be a hill that had got lost and wandered into town. Perhaps it was attracted by the lights.

'What is that?' asked Tiny.

'Arthur's Seat,' chimed the rest of the group.

'Sleeping elephant,' he said looking quite distant.

'Bet you get a good view from the top,' said Rhino.

Ben looked up at it, 'It's not that big. We could be up there, watch the sun go down and be back before the celebration starts.'

Tiny's face lit up, 'That would be brilliant!'

'I'm game,' Ben shrugged.

The group finished stuffing what was left of their chip suppers into themselves. Ten minutes later, after a brief discussion, they decided that the path was for girls and they weren't girls, they were men, real men. Being real men, they would climb straight up the crag. Thirty minutes after that as they jammed their fingers and toes into small cracks in the rock face, Ben wasn't too sure he wanted to be a real man any more.

He looked across the struggling team, 'This is a shite idea.'

Tiny smiled back at Ben and taking one hand from the rock face waved at the air behind him.

'It'll be a fucking amazing view!'

Angus had found a burst of energy and surged on ahead, a fag hanging out of his mouth. 'It'll be fucking amazing if none of us get killed,' Angus responded.

With alcohol coursing through their veins they reached the top in, apparently, no time at all. Ben and Angus had arrived ahead of the other two and it was interesting to watch the surprised look on those sensible people who had used the spiral path up to the top of Arthur's Seat as the four youths hauled themselves into sight and collapsed on the broken rocks. Angus had already skinned up. He took a long draw and then held it out to Ben, 'Fancy a wee shmoke?'

Ben smiled and took a can of Carlsberg out of his jacket pocket, 'I have my drug of choice.'

Rhino hauled himself into view like a pustulant seal rolling along on his stomach. Usually Rhino sported the traditional Scots skin colour, light blue. Now he looked decidedly green against the pale sky. His few remaining plukes purple against his washed out face as he held out his hand. Angus pulled the joint out of reach.

'Fuck off Rhino, you're going to spew your ring in a minute. No way am I going to waste this on you.'

Rhino managed a faint, 'bastard,' and rolled on to his back, 'I'm fucking dyin here.'

Tiny was striding about the top of the hill, his tweed jacket held tight around him against the cold.

'This isn't Arthurs Seat you know,' Angus said, looking at the bigger hill behind them, spiky with all the walkers crowded around the top, 'It is brilliant though.'

Ben looked west towards the setting sun. You could see to the south the Pentland Hills, a dusting of white frost that the low winter sun had failed to disperse. Looking to the north, peak after peak piling on higher than the other. Someone had drawn a ruler straight line across the huge bulk of the Highlands, above it the snow, brilliant yellow turning to gold above the darkening hills. Westward, Ben Lomond and home. All around them the jumble of stunning old Edinburgh and rather a disappointing new Edinburgh. Ben took a pull from his can and passed it to Angus.

'Lovely. That's 1983 gone then.'

'Did sir think it a good year?' Angus aped an imagined wine connoisseur; it passed since none of them had anything to compare it with.

'Aye. Not bad. Some good parties. Doing my Highers kind of took the fun out of it.'

'You did alright.'

'Straight 'A' kid,' Ben confirmed. Angus passed the can back and managed to say the word 'Bollocks' in a burp.

'Nice.'

'Thank you. You could be at University now. Why did you stick around for Sixth Year?' Angus asked. Ben was quiet for a moment, he had thought the same himself several times. It had seemed a good idea at the time but now? He should have had an offer from Glasgow but had heard nothing. Only Paisley Tech had come back, offering him a conditional. Maybe there was some kind of list of folk that really shouldn't be allowed in anything more than a Tech. It had to be said though he hadn't pushed that hard to find out what had happened.

'Too young man. I would have just turned seventeen,' Ben looked over his can at the setting sun, 'Plenty of time. And besides would I want to miss out on all of this?'

Angus smiled and didn't need to call him a liar.

Was Ben frightened to leave Helensburgh? This was Sixth year. 'O' Grades and Highers had been done, Universities applied for and conditions set. Now was the time to go back and fill in the gaps, to cushion the shock of tertiary education, to prepare to be responsible for your own learning. Christmas was out the way, this was the start of the final run to the exams in May. He had a sense of standing at the edge of the ski jump, another shuffle of the feet and he would be off sliding, slithering down the ramp, unstoppable, faster and faster then out into the wide blue sky, the noise, the rush the fury, the sudden silence. Life beyond school, University, a job, kids, being old, death. It all felt very abstract. Not to say unlikely. 'Scary,' he said quietly

'Aye.'

The pair looked round. Tiny was in the Crane position watching the last sun of the year. Ben thought about copying him but with the Special Brew kicking in, he realised he was too drunk to stand on one leg. Angus was sitting cross-legged radiating coolness. Rhino, as forecast, was throwing up over the edge of the crag they had climbed.

'What a class act. You are a credit to Helensburgh,' Ben carefully eased himself over onto all fours and then stood up, 'Come and we'll go.'

'Or we will finish up in the dark.'

They rolled down the hill, by unspoken agreement taking the path this time without questioning each other's sexual orientation. Steady streams of people were going the other way. To Ben's ear those with posh accents were carrying picnic baskets and lanterns up to the top of a hill, in the dark, and nobody questioned why.

Such is the structure of the city of Edinburgh that the four heroes were soon back in the bustle of the city. Around them people were united in one purpose: to drink as much as they could before the pubs shut. The lads had sorted their carry-outs while still reasonably with it and set to that general purpose with a will. By half past nine the pubs began to close. A curious tradition, to remove all the bars at the heaviest drinking night of the year. Ben had been told it was so that the bar staff could get home or to a party.

Ben, Tiny, Rhino and Angus worked their way up to the Royal Mile. Overshot for an unplanned drink in the Halfway House and finally joined the throng around the Heart of Midlothian. The Heart itself was shiny with the frozen spit of those who had passed by. Spitting on the heart was a sure sign of luck for the year ahead, or of a bad upbringing, depending on your belief structure. Rhino and

Angus disappeared for a while but returned with grins like Cheshire cats and a bottle of wine.

'We've been invited to a party,' Angus had to shout above the increasing noise of the crowd. Rhino looked quite forlorn.

'What just you two?'

Angus shook his head.

It was Rhino that spoke, 'All of us. Just bumped into Chris's big sister, she used to go out with my brother and recognised me.'

'What's she doing in Edinburgh?' Tiny asked. At that point both Rhino and Angus burst out laughing.

'Student nurse! And she's invited us back. She's over there. We've to meet her and her pals after the bells.' It was really hard to make out the words now as the cheering, shouting and the occasional scream increased in volume. Somebody said it was nearly midnight and the crowd began to count down, great clouds of steam rising up like smoke signals from the mass with each numbered end of a year.

'Two! One! Happy New Year!' Ben found himself being kissed and hugged by everyone around him. He saw Angus drain half the bottle of wine before handing it to him and then throwing his arm around Ben's shoulders.

'Happy New Year man! Finish that and we'll go and catch up with the others!'

Ben looked around. Right enough, he didn't know any of the friendly faces. He upended the bottle and drained it in one shot. He started to follow Angus's stressed brown leather jacket through the crowd. He turned and staggered against him.

'They said they would meet us over by that tower.' Angus pointed but Ben didn't really see where he was pointing to. He tried to nod and smile but he boked, the wine making a surprise return visit to his mouth. Taking its chance, the ground rolled from under him and Ben went down to a small cheer from those nearest. A small calm voice, a product of too many Public Safety Information Films, popped into life.

'You're going to get stood on if you don't start moving Ben.'

From all fours he managed to get back up and reeled through the crowd till he found a wall with his head.

So it was cold now. The ground had settled down after a while and stopped trying to throw him off. Being on his own in the crowded Royal Mile seemed a less good place to be. Tiny had been holding the carryout so there would be little point in trying to crash a strange party with no drink to contribute. Ben followed the path of least resistance down the hill from the Castle to Leith. The flat they were meant to be stopping at was round here somewhere but Ben really couldn't remember where. The singing and the cries of welcome to 1984 had become sporadic and finally ceased. A cessation of hospitalities. Time for bed. Ben came to a halt outside a corner shop, sober enough to realise that he was too drunk to find the flat tonight.

There were some breadbaskets stacked up against the shop wall. Big blue plastic frames. Ben took one after the other and laid them out in the street. Three long, two wide and two deep it looked pretty comfortable. The main thing, Ben remembered from his Bullet Magazine 'Survival the Fireball Way' training, was to stay off the ground. Although it was freezing the air was perfectly still. As long as he wasn't in contact with anything cold he would be fine. He hoped.

Ben looked at his watch. It was black with no numbers. Only the multi-coloured words 'Don't' 'be' 'too' 'late!' placed evenly around the otherwise featureless face. An unexpected Christmas present from a girl at St Mungo's. He had been trying to get off with a girl called Clorinda but the watch came from Ruth. Confusingly Ruth had been too cool to talk to him since but Ben was sure there was some kind of message there. The little hand had passed 'be' and the big hand pointed to 'too'.

Ben stuffed his hands back into his pockets. They went through torn material and into the lining. Ben laughed to himself as he pulled out a crushed packet of ten Regal Dinky and his last can of Tennents. Things were looking up. His Zippo scratched into life. Ben listened to the tobacco burn in the silent cold air, tapped and opened the can. He hoped the guys were having a good party, wherever they were. He clinked the can against invisible glasses and took a long draw from the crackling cigarette.

'Happy New Year,' he quietly toasted absent friends.

Rocket Surgery

Chapter Two

The return to school filled Ben with dread. Not that there was any issue with getting 'done' anymore. This was Sixth Year. Everyone with low IQs, and knuckles scraped from being dragged along the ground were two years gone. Things had subtly changed in the last couple of years, Ben mostly. A little more confident; Ben could no longer stand in for Bambi and had lost the sign that said 'kick me' on his back. Or the sign that said 'spit in my open mouth', the one that said 'cut the straps from my Adidas bag' and even the one that must have said 'Please set fire to my jacket.' C&A for some reason had seen fit to make the cords of snorkel jackets out of fast burning fuse wire. Spontaneous Human Combustion wasn't the mystery that most people thought. They just hadn't paid attention to where the victims' mothers shopped. Ben had maintained an aversion to blue nylon parkas ever since.

The casual violence of the previous years had faded so slowly that it had not left a clear event to mark its departure. Obviously the clear-out of Fourth Years had helped a lot. But even in Fifth Year he remembered Rhino slugging it out with Tiny for some reason on the Link stairs. Very Seventies structure, all glass and square edged aluminium. After Rhino and Tiny had thrown each other around a bit there had been blood all over the place. Looked really nasty by the time the teachers finally battled their way through the baying crowds to stop the fight. Mr Reid had been the first there. Where other teachers feared to tread, Mr Reid would be there, arms flailing like a combine harvester, clearing a path to the combatants. Tiny had made the mistake of throwing a punch back at the unexpected teacher and quickly found himself considering the prospect of a short and inglorious academic career. Rhino took his cue and exited with Ben down the Link Stairs two at a time.

But all that was behind them now. Sixth Year. Maturity. The first week back at school had been dominated by heavy snow. Tiny, the classroom lawyer, had insisted that if the bus couldn't make it as far as the stop then he wasn't required to go to school. Much to his disappointment all of the buses made it every day.

Tiny had developed his interest in law about the same time it had developed an interest in him. He and Rhino had somehow sourced a small keg of gunpowder. A short but spectacular period of practical experimentation followed, peaking with an attempt to blow up a safe at the railway station. Foiled by the failure of their shaped charges, the pair blew their way into a less robust garden nursery, stole two chainsaws and proceeded to wipe out most of Helensburgh's ornamental forestry before being finally run to ground by several very cross parkies. Thirty-two charges and some surveillance by the Police followed shortly after. It was generally agreed that Tiny's sense of shocked innocence persuaded the Panel to let them off with a 'stern talking to.' Not blessed with an angelic face, Rhino had sensibly been right behind Tiny, where he was harder to see.

On the bus Ben kicked two kids off the back row and lit up a fag. He watched as the pair shuffled down the aisle looking for some First Years to intimidate. Tiny was on the row in front, already fast asleep. Ben sat back in his seat and tried to relax, stamping the snow out of his climbing boots. He wasn't really looking forward to going in. The break had not improved his relations with the rest of his year. It was this cold war of mutual contempt that generated his dread.

Contempt was hard work. It was subtle, all pervasive. It was best illustrated by their position in the Gallery. The Sixth Year Common room was a long thin affair stretched out along the length of the school gym hall. It had its own kitchen and a row of comfortable seats built into the wall. The great and the good of Sixth year had taken up this central position. The clever people tended to gather by the kitchen, which left Ben, Tiny, Rhino and Angus, being classed as neither good nor clever, with the small space by the fire escape. On the positive side it afforded a floor to ceiling window to stare out at the low Scots winter sky. The fire escape had proved useful should the teaching staff require to be avoided and it was a good twenty feet from the nearest other table, minimising chance contact with those blessed with greater life chances and a more positive outlook. Rhino was already there playing Nuclear War with Rae and Sandy who, although firmly in the clever group, had a rebellious itch that Ben, Tiny, Rhino and Angus were able to scratch.

Nuclear War was a cheerful little card game where each player tried to protect their population from nuclear attack by the other players. By the looks of things they had left the Cold War of propaganda and secrets to knobble the other players, and were in the final stage of the inevitable Mutually Assured Destruction. On the artwork was a red button with 'Press to Test' written on it. Tiny walked over, his finger hovering over the illustration and smiled.

Tiny and Ben had brought up coffees for everyone and three of them lit up. As the last of Rhino's population were wiped out by a surprise virus counterattack, Stuart, head of the Sixth Year Council, strolled up bringing his easy smile and rolled neck Pringle jumper. He'd come to Helensburgh from the

North, possibly Tillicoultry- near Stirling, at the start of Fifth year and been seen as a bit of a loner. At some point this had changed to popular but Ben hadn't been paying attention so didn't know when it had happened, or indeed why.

'All right lads. I thought we'd agreed at the last council meeting that we weren't going to, you know...' Rhino was on his feet accelerating towards Stuart's face on a collision course.

'What Stuart? What are you trying to say? Am I hassling you? Do I come over there and and hassle you? Do I? Do I tell you how to live your life?' Rhino sat down. Stuart, dumbstruck, looked at Tiny and Ben who were both grinning. Rae and Sandy were trying to look concerned.

Rhino got back on his feet, 'Fuck off man. Get the fuck out of my face. What? What? I mean what the fuck have I done to you that gives you the right to stand over me like this with your fucking,' he poked Stuart's knitwear, '£50 bloody golfing jumpers.' The Councillor backed up doing a good impression of a collie savaged by a sheep.

'Go. Get the hell back to your bit of space. Leave me to mine.' he turned and sat back down. Tiny shuffled all the cards back into the pack and smiled at Ben. Rhino was too absorbed to notice them for a while.

'Bloody hell. Got a bit wasted at the weekend. Haven't really calmed down yet,' he picked up a Pepsi cup and began to tear it into strips, 'What about you two?'

'Went up Ben Bowie with Tiny,' said Ben.

'You wouldn't be able to keep up with that 185cc he's got now?' stated Rhino.

Ben shrugged, 'My bike is a lot lighter so on the snow it was no problem. What about you Rhino?'

'Played my saxophone, smoked a little with Angus. Nothing much.'

Tiny started dealing out the cards into five piles. Rae was looking at Tiny, 'We better go,' she said.

Sandy a little slower to agree, stood up, 'Yeah. Classes. Thanks Rhino. I'll get you next time.' The pair headed back down the Gallery.

'What you doing playing with them?' Tiny asked.

'They are all right Tiny. You should ease up on them. Whereas Stuart by dint of choosing public office deserves everything he gets.' Rhino said. He picked up the cup he had been tearing into strips. It now stood on twenty legs, he folded one leg out at ninety degrees to the rest creating a white, red and blue dalek. He opened the window and dropped his creation onto the flat gravel roof of the sports department.

'Fly, my beauty, fly,' Rhino whispered. As the cup blew across the roof, the individual strips of cup clipped the stone chipping on the roof felt. It created an intricate dance, a score of tightly choreographed feet gliding away in a style that Fred and Ginger would have been proud of. Rhino pulled the window shut and the three stood watching.

'What's up? Girls' cross country?' Angus peered over the top of Rhino.

'Lo. I have created life!' As he spoke the cup slammed into a skylight. It span away disorientated. One of the legs snagged between two chips. 'Fuckety fuckety fuck,' whispered Rhino as quietly as before. Caught, the dalek struggled in the wind, tugging desperately to free its limb. 'I can't watch,' Rhino turned his back on the window. The other three couldn't not watch.

'It's stuck good and proper.'

'I think I can hear it squeaking,' Angus winked at Ben, 'Help me. Help me.' he said in a tiny voice.

Rhino turned back to watch his creation as it fought for its freedom.

'I have to go and help it.'

Before anyone thought to stop him Rhino was out of the window and walking slowly across the roof. He pulled his foot back, the roof-felt must have started to give way under him.

'That wood's rotten. He'll go right through,' Angus stuck his head out, 'all fours Rhino, spread the weight out as much as you can.' The steam in his breath curled away slowly.

Rhino zipped up his combat jacket tight and restarted. This time, crawling out towards his baby. Ben became aware that most of the common room had gathered to see what was going on. Stuart was clearly worried, torn between the desire to say something and the desire not to get another mauling while everyone was in earshot. Discretion and all that, meant that he melted away to the back of the crowd. He was all right Stuart, really, Ben thought. Contempt had probably run its course. Rhino covered the last piece of roof carefully. The cup, unsure of Rhino's intentions, struggled even more frenetically, perhaps fearing recapture. Rhino stretched out a hand and with a gentle tug, set it free. Released, it span off across the roof and out of sight. Someone, probably a civic minded clever type, shouted 'Reid' from the kitchen end of the Gallery.

Angus stuck his head back through the window, 'Wee man, Reid. Get your arse in here.'

Rhino paused looking to Ben for confirmation and was up sprinting straight back towards the window. He skidded to a halt at the frame and was hauled up by Ben and Angus.

'I'm risking my life for it and the bugger didn't even say thank you.'

'That's children for you. Take the best years of your life and... sir!' Reid was standing behind them with a vampiric swiftness. The window was swinging on the hinges. It banged just in case Reid hadn't noticed it was open, and the teacher stepped towards it, taking a long look outside.

'There would appear to be items out there that shouldn't belong to any pupil of this school.'

Angus, Ben and Rhino couldn't help but look. The roof around the window was a mass of cigarette douts as well as piles of other detritus that had managed to be blown there but not off again.

'Right enough sir.'

'And you were just about to volunteer and clean up somebody else's mess. Good man Mr Roberts.'

Rhino looked panicky, 'It wouldn't be safe sir. Going out the window like that.'

The teacher smiled, 'You're beginning to sound like Tiny, the school advocate, Mr Roberts. A slight man like yourself would pose no threat to the structure of the building,' the smile faded away, 'bin bag from the kitchen. That roof cleaned by lunch time or the three of you won't see the sun set. Am I understood?'

'Yes sir,' The three chimed.

'And Mr Williams-'

Ben jumped, 'Yes sir?'

'Your shoe appears to be on fire. A repeat of this and the lot of you are banned from the Gallery and lose all Sixth Year privileges. Happy New Year Gentlemen,' Mr Reid swept up his imaginary cloak, strode back down the Gallery and out.

Ben looked down at his feet. Smoke was curling around his boot. When he lifted up his boot he realised that the cigarette, instead of being put out when dropped and stood on, had neatly fitted between the tread.

Ben looked at Rhino in a state of shock, 'Must be still full of Christmas cheer. Off you go then Rhino.'

'Absolutely not. You can fuck right off. I've already been out. You two can do it. I'll go to the kitchens though.'

Ben and Angus climbed out on to the roof, Rhino passed them out some black bags. He pointed towards the skylight, 'Don't go near there, I thought I was going to go through on the way back.' The two began to pick their way gingerly out from the window collecting cups, fag packets and filters. In half an hour they had finished and stopped to admire their handiwork. They waved cheerily at Tiny and Rhino, cosy and warm on the right side of the glass, who raised their coffee cups in return. Ben looked out towards Ben Bowie and the hills into Glen Fruin. The sky was a brilliant blue, not even a contrail marring its perfection. The hills always looked more impressive when the snow was on them.

'Shplendid,' Ben said in his best Sean Connery. He reached into his pocket and pulled out a packet of fags. Angus took one and they shared the peace of the moment on top of the sports hall.

Tiny pushed the window open and shouted, 'Fourth Year girls on the trampoline.'

Ben and Angus stubbed out the fags and flicked the butts over the edge of the roof in line with the new policy of keeping the roof clean. They pushed through the two bags of rubbish and Rhino pulled him through and they both got Angus.

'Well boys. I hope you've learned a lesson,' Rhino earnestly scolded them both as they dusted themselves off.

'Fuck off Rhino,' He swore.

'Rhino, Angus. Economics, she'll go mad if we are late again.' Ben grabbed his bag. Without checking to see if he was followed, he ran along the Gallery and out onto the stairs scattering First Years as he fled.

Chapter Three

Ben was alone. He was aware of the buzz of the mighty 50cc Trail Bike underneath him. He could hear and feel the water reluctantly getting out of the way of his tyres. It was getting hard to make out the road through the heavy rain and the gathering gloom of a winter's afternoon. People shouldn't miss him though. He had bright yellow oilskins and a matching full face helmet. It was cold enough that the oilskins had set in position around him. His steel toe cap boots finished off his protective shell. There may be more water in the air than in the loch but this boy was going to arrive dry. Ben felt like a knight in armour or one of those Civil War blokes in a buff coat. That is, he tried to feel that way but the slow progress of his steed tended to kick him out of the daydream. He settled for feeling dry and delighting in the sense of the storm battering ineffectively against him.

It had taken the best part of hour to go round Arrochar and climb Glen Crow. He had come off the main route and dropped onto an old military road built two hundred years earlier to pacify the troublesome Highlanders after Charlie fled. Not that they all had needed pacifying. Ben's own ancestors had, by family tradition, seen the French agitator for what he was and fought alongside the Lowland Scots and those few English that had come along to see if they could take the credit. While the new road began the climb up to the pass as you turn west into the Glen, the old road wound its way along the bottom as if hopeful that the climb at the end could somehow be avoided. At the head of the U-shaped valley, the road realised its folly and began to wind its way back and forward against the almost sheer ascent. Ben stood on the pegs, letting the bike move about him as the track began the climb. Turn and climb, turn and climb. On horse or foot this path had been exhausting hence the name of the road, 'The Rest and be Thankful'. Turn and climb, turn and climb. The weather closed in around him. Mist and rain greyed everything out.

The two stroke rasped free of the ascent, they had reached the top. Ben eased the bike over the mounds of earth and tarmac spoil that had been piled up to prevent cars doing what he had just done. Ben was breathing hard as he pulled his helmet off. The cold air hit his scalp, damp with sweat. Pulling the bike onto its stand and tugging his soaked gauntlets off, he dug inside his jacket for a cigarette. He listened to the tick of the engine cooling. The rain clouds had lifted a bit at the top of the pass, allowing ragged glimpses of the bulk of the mountains gathered high around. Black rock gleamed through the thin soil.

Here the air from the bottom of the Glen followed the path he had just completed, forced ever higher the moisture in the air began to condense. At the top of the valley was a ridge of rock judged too hard to mess with by the glaciers. It jutted out over the valley edge and back over towards the car park. The rising air struck this ridge and condensed, creating a ghostly feathered plume streaming up over Ben's head. He realised it had stopped raining at some point.

Ben sat in the lee of the rock and smoked his fag. Two caravans climbed the main road, those caught behind apparently choosing death rather than continue at the tourists' enforced slow pace. At least he had been able to climb in his own way, slowly, without being swept off the side of the road by some caravan crazed Cortina. There was a hint of sunlight for a moment, the light caught on the waterlogged hillside, glistening rock and sparkling burns. But as soon as the moment arrived it was fading and the cloud closed in again. Ben decided it was time to go. He took the new road down. It was long, straight and downhill all the way. Lying flat on the tank, throttle wide open, he almost broke the national speed limit.

With one eye on the clouds, Ben rode back through Arrochar and on down the loch side. Rhino lived in a static caravan behind his mother's house. It had brilliant views out over the loch and the mountains. Ben had checked to see if Rhino had been in on the way up. It was the rule never to check at the house. Ben had known Rhino for six years and had never once been inside the home itself. If Rhino was in the caravan he was in, if he wasn't he wasn't. On the way up he wasn't. Now on Ben's return from the mountains the caravan lights were on. Two o'clock and the daylight was already starting to fade.

'If I was a vampire', Ben thought, 'I wouldn't bother with southern Europe. Make yourself at home here, wait for winter and you would clean up, the humans wouldn't stand a chance.'

The caravan was a big thing. It gave Rhino and his big brother a decent sized bedroom apiece, a small kitchen, a living room and a toilet. However since it was a chemical toilet and no one wanted to clean it, it was strictly for emergencies only. Ben parked up and knocked on the door. Within moments the faintly weasely face of Rhino appeared at the door.

'Come in. Close the bloody door you're letting out all the heat,' Rhino looked up at sky, his face soured, 'Miserable fucking weather. It gets you down. Do you not think so? In the name of the wee man there's water everywhere!'

As Ben began to peel off his layers, trapped rain streamed out of the hard folds of the oilskin. Ben pulled off his boots but kept his thick climbing socks on.

'A cup of tea or would you prefer something stronger?' Rhino asked not waiting for a response, 'I think it's getting colder. Gets to me, this constant fucking dark. Do come in my man. Do come in. Would you like a cup of tea?' he repeated the question.

'Tea would be brilliant.'

Rhino closed one eye against the smoke curling into it as he filled the kettle and put it on the stove. Ben leaned against a kitchen unit and looked around for an ashtray before flicking his ash into the sink.

'I was planning to start work on my dissertation. 'Gormenghast'. How the hell am I going to write four thousand fucking words on Gormenghast? Have you read it? It's a mad book. I started reading it and wondered what the hell it was doing to my mind. It was changing how I saw the world around me. I started looking at people and seeing the characters from the book in them and it wasn't pretty. I don't think I am going be able to finish it and stay sane. I mean how the fuck am I meant to do an essay on a book that should carry a mental health warning! For fuck's sake! What goes through the minds of the bloody teachers?' The kettle started to whistle on the hob, matching the stridency in Rhino's voice. He switched suddenly, his voice deep, a smile on his lips, 'Maybe they do it deliberately. What are you doing yours on?'

'Images of death and depression in Sylvia Plath's poems and the Bell Jar.'

Rhino couldn't talk for a minute as he spluttered and coughed, 'That's a classic. There is no way you came up with that one. Who the hell did?'

Ben didn't really want to talk about it and shook his head, 'Miss Paterson gave me till the end of October to come up with a theme. I didn't, she did.'

Rhino was still laughing as he passed him a cup of tea, 'What's your poison tonight Ben? I have the finest imported resin, or for the more adventurous we have a reasonable stash of speed?'

Ben pulled a bottle of whisky from inside the lining of his leather jacket, 'I still prefer a more traditional approach to losing consciousness. After that tea has thawed me out.'

'Good man yourself. Well since its Christmas time, nearly, I was planning to watch the Great Escape and maybe drop a tab.'

Ben settled down on an open frame chair in front of a cream coloured machine with black keyboard, 'Before you do could you get this machine up and running? Elite, please.'

Rhino bent over the BBC Micro. It had been designed as an educational computer and would teach a generation how to programme and thereby foster an explosion in British software development. But to Ben it was the mysterious gateway to another world, another galaxy in fact. Here he could pilot a small ship from space station to space station. Take on missions and passengers, run guns or medical supplies as the opportunities arose. Here with a bottle of whisky, twenty B&H and a good ship, lay the jump to Nirvana. The small black and white telly blinked and focused itself on the job in hand. Lack of colour made it hard to tell the good guys from the bad guys but that just made it all the more like real life.

Ben had suppressed his blink reflex so well that his eyes had dried out. He looked at his watch. It had gone past 'too'. He saved the game and sank back in the chair, enjoying the soothing sensation of lids over pupils. The images of the last half hour still burned on his eyes. Fleeing a bounty hunter from system to system. It was meant to be that you could play without fighting. Ben doubted it. There always seemed to be somebody out to get him.

While he had been away the room had changed. Tiny was curled up in front of the television with Rhino's cat on his lap. Rhino had set up a hookah on the floor.

'Pull up a piece of floor.'

Ben folded his long legs beside the diminutive Rhino and took the pipe from him.

'Did you beat off the Cylons?'

'Wrong Universe. Cylons are Battle Star Galactica whereas...' Ben stopped, he could sense Rhino's boredom building up already, 'What are we watching?'

Rhino lit up a fag to keep himself going till the hookah came back.

'We are watching Rollerball,' Rhino pronounced each word clearly and brightly, 'What Tiny is watching, only he knows.'

Ben looked over at Tiny. His eyes were open and his hand gently stroked the cat but Rhino was right, what he saw wasn't in this room. Ben looked at the hookah, 'Good stuff man.'

Rhino shook his head, 'Not this. Tiny's being doing speed and acid all week. Thought I would set this up to calm him down but he said he didn't want to mellow yet. Must say it's nice when your friends pop round for a wee natter. Between him in his current state and you plugged into your alternate reality, it's been hard to get a word in edgeways. Who says the art of conversation is dead. Have a beer?'

Ben looked down. One hand held a hookah, the other a fag, 'Like, not enough hands man.' He went to hand the hookah back, 'Be a shame to waste it.'

The VHS sounded like tape munching was always on its mind but the film made it through unscathed. It was the full version of Rollerball, with the violence and the philosophy. The quartet watched in silence and various degrees of clarity as a party of shiny people piled out of a house. They laughed and drank. One of the women pulled out a blaster and started blowing up a line of poplars.

'It's like a St Mungo's party,' Rhino commented.

Ben shook his head very slowly, the words trickled out, 'Don't remember that bit. You know, with the gun,' Ben added a gun shaped hand for the hard of thinking, 'But I wouldn't be surprised.'

The movement appeared to trigger his body back up to a functional level, 'Gotta go for a piss.' Ben bounced down the corridor and through the door of the caravan. He kept walking for a moment. Rhino always got violent if anyone did a slash on the outside of the caravan so Ben started to piss into a bush he had bumped into. The rain had gone, the black sky was studded with stars, frozen, sparkling through the bare branches of the trees above him. He could see his breath against the light from the slowly closing door. His bladder was still a long way from empty as he saw the chink of light from the caravan narrow and disappear with a click. The stars looked brighter now they didn't have any competition. Ben could make out the black line of the mountains through the black trees against the black sky.

Something was picking its way through the woods. It was wild out here, fox, badger. Did they hibernate? Wolf, they didn't hibernate, last one shot in 1786 though so that would be really unlucky to get eaten by one now. Must be a werewolf then, Ben thought logically. The hairs on the back of his neck rose as the temperature fell away and he shivered. Whatever it was it was coming closer.

There was a werewolf sneaking closer to him and he was standing there with his dick in his hands. He willed himself to stop pissing, stuffing his dick back into his jeans slightly too early. He swore softly. Whatever it was stopped. All was still. Ben slowly started to turn and realised that he wasn't sure which way the caravan was. A heavy branch snapped close by to his right. There must be two slowly circling him

'Shit!' Ben stumbled back. This place would be perfect cover. They would never find his body out here. Even if they did find his remains they would just put it down to another midgie kill. Something caught his ankle and he screamed as he fell. The wolves rushed in, he could feel their hot breath panting on his face. What were they waiting for, were they laughing? Ben's bright future was about to be taken away from him and they thought it was funny! Ben tried to scream again but nothing would come out. He lay frozen as a snout gently nuzzled his chin out of the way and the teeth caressed his neck. The werewolves breath was hot on his skin. With slow, unstoppable force the jaws closed, the pain was overwhelming. *This is it,* Ben thought, *I only have until the blood in my brain runs out. The stars are fading...*

The door opened, light tore apart the darkness. From amidst that blinding arc Rhino's haloed head appeared.

'Ben what the hell are you doing out there? Fuck it's cold!'

Ben looked up at the now illuminated trees from where he lay, 'Man. That was rough.' He rolled over and walked towards the light. He was so glad to see Rhino he wanted to give him a hug.

Rhino's face wrinkled, showing his teeth, 'You aware your prick is hanging out?'

Ben stopped and looked down, 'Still there then? I've got plans for you.' Ben looked up from tucking his privates away and smiled warmly at his accidental rescuer. Unsettled, Rhino slid backwards into the caravan, his shadow followed, slightly out of synch.

On the threshold of sanctuary Ben was hit by the carefully hoarded warm air. It had been filled with so much smoke over such a long period that it was almost completely free of oxygen. Bens lungs, still enjoying sudden reprieve from death and the fresh air, refused to swap. Coughing, Ben wondered if instead of ripped apart by lycanthropes they would be simply found to have asphyxiated at some point in the night. Be nice and warm though. Tiny had slid to the floor and was whimpering. Rhino tried to uncurl him a little, calling Tiny's name but there was no response. He only coiled tighter and started to cry. Rhino looked up at Ben, 'Wonder what's eating him?'

CHAPTER FOUR

They had stalled at the bottom of the drive. Ben, Tiny, Rhino and Angus stopped at the sight of the house. At some point in its past, Helensburgh had been the prosperous retreat of the Tobacco Barons and ship magnates of Clydeside. Their legacies, in part at least, were huge square houses in large square gardens looking through vast square bay windows to where their ships had once returned with leaf from the colonies. Most of these houses had been split up into two or three maisonettes, the grounds supporting another two or three more modern and modest homes with curving drives. But a few were still intact. This was one.

'You sure this is the right place?' Ben asked.

Angus passed him a bottle of cider, 'What time is it, maybe we're too early?'

Ben looked at his watch, 'The big hand is pointing at 'don't' and the little hand is pointing at 'late!'.'

'What happened to that Casio 'can land a man on the moon' computer thing?' asked Rhino.

'Way too fragile to be out on a party.'

'That watch is cooler,' Angus said with the confidence of someone who knew about these things. Ben raised an eyebrow.

'Oh yeah,' Angus looked over at Rhino and pointed up the gravel, 'Just follow the sound of the pounding music. I am willing to bet a sum of my own money that this is where Chris's party is going to be.'

'Or is,' corrected Ben, 'I don't think I ever really appreciated how loaded Chris must be.'

'He hides it well,' said Angus running his hands through his black curly hair, 'He's always been-' Angus bounced with nervous energy, 'You know, normal.'

'How come he didn't go to St Mungo's?' asked Ben.

'Didn't want to,' said Angus. He and Chris had been close friends all the way through school. They'd stayed in touch despite Chris going to Herriot Watt at the end of Fifth Year and being a year older. 'His big sister, the one you didn't meet Ben, did go but left at the end of Fourth year. She is the nurse. His wee sister Clorinda did go though, to St Mungo's. And she is just right.'

'Wonder if Clorinda has any friends at this party?' asked Tiny, he had started to carve his name in one of the pine trees with his six-inch lock knife. They all carried them, though the only thing that most of them had cut was badly cooked sausages when they camped up in the hills. Tiny looked like he'd been hung from a piece of elastic and twanged. Rhino had taken to hiding in one of the rhododendron bushes. Angus looked across at Ben.

'Somehow I don't think we need to worry about that guys.' said Angus. He lit a cigarette and strolled on up to the house looking perfectly at ease.

'Why not?' asked the bush. Angus and Ben laughed.

'Let's just find Chris and then we will see what happens from there.'

Tiny looked up from his carving, 'I think I'll give it a miss lads,' he said to howls of protest, 'it's not ma scene, posh birds. Stuart will be there, I'll be forced to hit him,' pressed his lips together as he shrugged, 'be messy in front of everyone.'

'Not if I get there first' said the emerging Rhino, 'Come on it will be fine.' They argued for five minutes. Ben realised that Tiny wasn't just stalling so that he knew they loved him, he really didn't want to go.

'Tiny man, up to you. Come on,' he said to the others. He could feel the cider kicking in and he didn't want to lose momentum. Rhino held the centre point between the group as it stretched towards the house. His face contorted as he tried to decide what to do.

Tiny folded up his lock knife, 'You go on. I'll see if I can get a lift back to Garelochead and pick up my bike. I'll be fine.' He disappeared out of the dim white light of the mercury street lamp.

'Hang on!' Rhino shouted as he ran to catch up with Ben and Angus. The front door was open; a large dark wooden staircase dominated the hall. It felt like there should have been some suits of armour playing gate guardians. Maybe they hadn't liked the music and gone off to find something less contemporary. Chris was there with a glass of whisky and his arm already round Ruth McCarthy. He waved the glass at Ben and Angus.

'I was beginning to wonder if you gentlemen were going to make it through the door.'

'Bit of a crisis with Tiny,' said Ben. Chris raised an eyebrow. 'Small crisis,' said Ben indicating with thumb and forefinger. He tried really hard not to look at Chris's arm wrapped snake-like round Ruth. 'Tiny even.' She probably hadn't noticed what Chris was trying to do yet. Otherwise she would have done something surely, moved, punched him, that kind of thing.

'Hello Ruth,' said Angus.

'Hello.'

'You look great,' Angus added looking quite pleased with his suave patter. Ben had to say that she did look great. Stunning in fact. Bit of a blow that Chris had moved in so fast. Complete bloody disaster. She hadn't looked at him yet. Her dark eyes were fixed on Angus rather disturbingly.

'Thought you fancied Clorinda, Angus?'

Ruth mirrored Chris' deliciously evil smile. 'Is that true Angus? I always thought us St Mungo's girls were too posh for your tastes,' she took a long sook from her tin of Carlsberg.

That was it; Chris was plying her with drink. The swine. Meanwhile Ruth continued

'Stuck up bitches who wouldn't know real life if it bit them on their arse.' I think the phrase was,' she was still smiling as she quoted. Seventeen going on twenty five. She looked at Ben and said something but Ben missed it. Chris was laughing too, he slid Ruth closer across the polished wood step. Now she had her arm round him! They hadn't looked at each. Everybody was cool. Ben better be cool too. Random acts of violence weren't cool, he was pretty sure of that. How could this happen at the start of the party? Ruth's lips were moving again.

'I said you're very chatty tonight Ben.'

'Aye.'

'Like the jeans.'

Ben looked down at his red jeans and black Dr Martins. He looked back up not sure if she was taking the piss. Then he noticed Chris was allowing himself to look cross for a second as he stared at his audience. He mouthed 'fuck off' but the word that came out was.

'Drink?'

'Aye,' said Ben, 'where?'

'Follow the yellow brick road,' Chris pointed towards the kitchen in an echo of ZZ Top and turned towards Ruth. Ben got the feeling that the audience was over. He boogied off to some Brian Ferry, Rhino followed doing a good invisible sax impersonation.

The beer was in the kitchen right enough, as were Clorinda, Judith and Alison. They were sitting on thirty-six shrink-wrapped packs of beer representing a volume of accessible drink that Ben had never really believed existed up till now.

With Ruth seemingly out of reach, all he could hope for was one of the three girls to pin him against a wall and demand a snog and his life would be complete. He sat down next to Judith and Rhino tucked himself into the gap between Ben and the rough plastered wall. During the disturbance there was a complex silent exchange between Clorinda and Judith that Ben didn't have enough X-Chromosomes to follow.

'Good party,' Ben said to Judith. She nodded in a distracted way and turned back to Alison who appeared to be having a bad time. Tears were beginning to gather like a summer thunder cloud on a blue sky. Ben felt urge to run before the lightning struck. Too late. She was staring at Ben.

'It's all my fault,' Alison said, 'I knew he wasn't sure if he wanted to keep going out with me. I wasn't sure.'

Judith was concerned and supporting, 'You were Alison. You loved him. He said he loved you. I don't understand how it ended up like this. He's your friend Ben. Do you know?'

Ding, the penny dropped. They were at a St Mungo's party, Alison, Tiny not wanting to come in. Got there in the end. He usually did.

'You're Alison that used to go out with Tiny!' Ben saw as the words 'used to' span round in front of his mouth with blue strobe lights and flashing neon arrows. Somewhere in silence someone hit a very large gong. But maybe he'd got away with it. Both girls looked as though he had stabbed them. Apparently not then. Rhino beside him had started to drum the floor with two wooden spoons. 'I mean, you are the Alison that's going out with Tiny. I sort of hadn't put the two together for some reason.'

'Because we're not together,' Alison blubbed. Judith managed to convey *throw this girl a lifeline or die* in a look.

'That's not the case,' Ben emptied the can and took another from under Judith, 'Tiny is just trying to sort out who he is at the moment. Who he is going to be? What does he want from life? You know?'

Alison was getting blotchy now, 'That's bullshit.'

'I don't know who I am,' Rhino looked up from his drumming but kept the beat going perfectly. He looked up, meeting Alison's hatred by proxy with a blank innocence that Tiny would have been proud of. 'How can I? I am at the centre of my being. I have an infinite world of possibilities around me.'

He looked around to emphasise the point, 'Every decision I make, every step I take and the infinite becomes finite. Every choice limits my next choice until there is no choice and I'm a fucking bank clerk or sweeping the streets for the Donald Duck Club. Can't go back. Only forward. That's the way time works. The choices only get less.' He took a drag from his joint and passed it to Ben, indicating it should go to Alison. Ben managed a casual draw and passed it along. Judith had swung just so slightly away from Alison. She was frowning.

'Show me a man who has made no mistakes and I will show you a man who has done nothing. You have to make decisions.' She stated

'Precisely,' Rhino looked to Ben who crashed the fags round to supplement the one joint. Ben was still trying to figure out what Judith's perfect man and the slob had to do with each other. Rhino seemed to be following this much better than him. 'If you are willing to make those decisions now then you are committing yourself to a course, to an end that you cannot yet know. But you set off with confidence? How can you know yourself? How can you be sure that your actions now will result in the person that you want to become?'

'But,' said Judith, 'if you are right, then once you know yourself then you can be sure what you are doing is right.'

'And not before,' Rhino added. The small man smiled the smile of Buddha and took his roach back. 'You must discover who you are first then everything else will follow.'

Judith was nodding, 'And you think this is what Tiny is going through?' she asked both of them.

Ben shrugged. He was sure there must be something sensitive that he should say at this point. He looked to Rhino for support but lucidity had passed and he was drumming the floor again but looking at Judith, smiling in a vacant away. Rhino did respond, but distantly,

'He's just completely lost the plot on speed and acid that's all.'

Judith looked back to Alison for a reaction but she was too wrapped up to hear anything from the outside. Judith cocked her head back at Ben.

'Is he really that bad?' Judith asked. Ben emptied his tin and pulled another one past Rhino.

'He's has found a great big red button marked 'Self Destruct' and he can't help pressing it,' replied Ben who felt horribly sober and took half the can in one slug. 'Frequently.'

'Shame - he's really nice,' Judith smiled.

'A lot of people think that. Something I have to work at,' Ben pointed at Judith with the hand holding the can.

'Why? A lot of people think you're nice too,' she pushed back her jet black hair out of her face and pulled a Silk Cut from behind her ear. Ben lit it and smiled back. 'Well, not that many obviously, but one or two.'

'Glad to hear it,' Ben smiled his best smile. In another room they were playing Blue Monday by New Order. Judith saw his eyes flick to the door and back.

'Do you like this one?' she asked.

'Absolutely brilliant! They were playing it in every bar we went to in Edinburgh.'

'I like Edinburgh. When were you through?' asked Judith.

'New Year, stayed at Chris's, mostly, apart from when sleeping rough. Never seen anything like it.' Whoever was nearest the hi-fi had turned it up. The pounding base line was calling to him like no song ever had before.

'Want a dance?' Not quite a snog, but close enough. Ben watched Judith glide out of the chair and towards the door. Ben turned to Rhino, he had paused, his drumsticks hung in mid-stroke.

'Look after the beer will you Rhino. I gotta go boogie.' Laughing at himself he strutted out the door and into the dark and the music.

An hour or two later and Ben, Rhino and Angus had washed up on the front steps. The cold damp Helensburgh air had hit them like a wall when they had first come outside. Now they were enjoying a cigarette and the whining noises in their ears. Rhino had found an actual saxophone in his travels and began to play it over the Hot Chocolate echoing though the hall. He winced and stopped.

'What's up?' Ben asked.

'You can fuck off for a start,' He swung a half-hearted punch at Ben but the sax got in the way.

'What have I done?' asked Ben.

Rhino ignored the question and turned to Angus, 'I'll paint the scene for you gentlemen. I'm there nestling in amongst Clorinda, Judith and Alison. Three of the loveliest women that have ever graced this planet.'

'Which one's Alison?' Angus asked.

'Bit tubby and smells of hand cream.'

'Oh aye, used to go out with Tiny.' Confirmed Angus.

'Funny, you know that and shit for brains here knew that but it seems nobody told Alison. Which is the point. Judith is doing her best to comfort her and numpty here is doing all the 'I really understand' stuff and the pair of them were completely ignoring me.'

'I'm sorry man I didn't think you would mind.'

Rhino waved the apology away, 'It was perfect. Her blouse had crumpled up because the way she was sitting and I could see right past her buttons to her breasts man. They were perfect. They were inches away. I could see them rise and fall as she breathed. They shook when she laughed man. They just shook like two buckets of seaweed. It was incredible. And then this tube goes and asks her for a dance. Blows the whole thing.'

Angus raised an eyebrow at Ben, 'Judith? I thought you were after Ruth?'

'I was but she doesn't seem to have taken her eyes off Chris all night. They are probably going to end up in a bedroom here tonight and I'll be down here with Animal,' He pointed at Rhino, 'Though not in a biblical sense. Thought you were after Clorinda?'

Angus lit a joint and passed it along, 'Normally I wouldn't outside but Chris has crashed me a ton of stuff so what the hell. Clorinda? Definitely. Best looking woman in the year. But it feels like the whole party is watching the pair of us. Got to play it cool, and I'm not part of a bloody circus. You don't need to worry about Chris by the way.'

Ben drew breath to ask more but somewhere close by they could hear the familiar roar of a badly muffled 185 approaching far too quickly. In swept the rider, the bike over so far the stand was striking sparks on the road and then sending gravel flying. He tore up the path, and managed to stop in a speedway slide of grit and oily smoke. The rider jumped from the bike letting it fall unnoticed behind him. Tiny, for it was he, pulled his helmet off and carefully stuffed his gauntlets inside before letting them also crash to the gravel, unobserved by himself if not by his apprehensive audience.

'Guys that was brilliant. I've got to tell you. It was incredible. What's the time? Quick tell me what the time is.' His hands, still in fingerless gloves, were shaking as they pulled a packet of fags from inside his leathers. Ben looked at his watch out of reflex. It took a moment to make sense of what he was looking at.

'Somewhere between 'Don't' and 'Be'.'

Tiny was hopping from foot to foot. More people were drifting out, wondering what the noise was about. Ben saw Ruth and Clorinda amongst the St Mungo's folk looking on in blank incomprehension at what the Comprehensive Chimpanzees were up to in the garden.

'That's a shit watch Ben. You need something that can actually tell you what the fucking time is, time is?' Tiny repeated.

'Twenty two minutes past two. Hey that's neat,' Rhino grinned up at Tiny but got no recognition.

'That means I did Garelochead to here in seven minutes.'

'Can't be,' the gang said as one.

'No seriously. I hitched back to your caravan Rhino to collect my bike. Saw you'd left a tab there for me which was great man. Really great of you to think of me like that.' Rhino looked as surprised as everyone else. Charity was not meant to start at home. 'So dropped the tab and set off for home. Suddenly it was like really clear. Don't know why I'd never seen it before. There in the road was the slot. It was like Scaletrix man. And I knew man. I knew that all I had to do was put the wheels in the slot and that was it.'

'What was it?' asked Rhino, looking oddly uncharacteristic as he struggled with guilt.

Tiny had lit another cigarette and now had one going in each hand.

'I couldn't drop the bike. Once that bike was in the slot I knew there was no way I could fall off, no matter how fast I went. The track went both ways. One way off into the mountains, looked good with the bright moon, the wet roads. But I knew the other would take me back to Helensburgh, I just wasn't sure where. I had to find out. Had to be something good. So I turned the bike around and wound the throttle back all the way. I was right man. It really didn't matter how fast I went it was just there,' he held out one of his open hands, parting the road in his mind. 'Brilliant.'

Rhino looked like he wanted to be somewhere else.

'You got to stop leaving that stuff lying around man,' Angus said what they were all thinking.

'Bugger off Angus.'

They looked like they were squaring up for a fight. Ben took a step forward and then noticed that Ruth and Clorinda had left the steps.

'Shit. Think we've blown it?' asked Ben. Angus snapped out of the argument and looked round at the three other space cadets.

'I didn't think we had anything to blow?'

'Clorinda will be disappointed when she hears that.'

Angus shrugged, 'If we have then there is only one reasonable course of action left.'

'Oblivion?' Ben asked. Angus nodded.

Behind them Tiny started shouting, 'Which one of you fuckers dropped my bike? I cannot believe you would do that. And my bloody helmet is scratched to fuck!'

Angus and Ben relaunched themselves into the exhausted party like men reborn. Free of the expectations of success they danced, chatted and drank with confidence. Ben felt a power run through him that he had never felt before. He caught himself in the mirror, wild eyes, red from constant smoke peered back at him from behind wild straggly hair which he pushed back as best he could. Judith was a definite maybe.

'Damn I look good.' The mirror laughed with him. Angus skidded into sight at the end of the hall. He ran straight past him with 'Go!' his only comment. Somewhere at the bottom of the stairs Ben could hear Tiny shrieking.

'Spiders!' their friend shouted in need.

Sounded like someone, maybe Alison, trying to calm him down, Rhino as well, guilt and compassion in the same night? Ben was on more familiar territory as he spun on the spot and legged it away from the noise and after Angus. The pair rounded another corner laughing as they slid on the polished wood and crashed into the wallpaper. They accelerated into the door at the end of the passageway. And stopped dead.

Ben can see that scene as clearly walking through Slough as he had that night. It was Chris' Mum and Dad, his wee brother Peter and the baby of the family, Jo. They were huddled up on the sofa with something on the telly. Bottle of wine and one of those huge two litre bottles of coke sat on the table beside empty crisp packets. Chris had said that the Granny flat was off limits, the family must have been holed up here all night. What hit Ben like a sledge hammer was looking into the eyes of Chris's dad and seeing absolute terror.

There was a horrible shriek behind them, Tiny crashed into them so hard that he rolled over the top and landed on his back. He was scrabbling at his jeans and screaming as high-pitched as a child. Angus had caught his stomach on the table and was groaning. He pulled himself up and lurched to the window. Rhino and Alison appeared and knelt beside Tiny, trying to calm him and keep his jeans on in equal measure. Ruth joined Ben.

'Hello Mrs Ferguson, Mr Ferguson,' she said brightly as Tiny's screaming subsided into sobs. They smiled back but seemed incapable of moving. As did Ben when he felt an arm slide round his hip. 'Brilliant party. Thank you. We'll just get out your way.'

Chris's mum smiled, glad of the hint of normality and opened her mouth to reply.

'I'm going to be sick!' Angus announced as he reached the window and fumbled with the catch. With a triumphant look he slid the frame back only to be faced with another window. Secondary glazing was beyond him and he banged his head hopelessly against the unexpected glass and vomited, filling the cavity between the two panes. The result was a brief, purple aquarium. Angus slid down the wall trying to catch the recycled diesel as it washed back out and down the wall.

'Don't worry Mrs Ferguson. We'll get that cleaned up right away,' Ruth sounded like a nurse that had wandered onto a bad night in the psychiatric ward. 'Alison, and-' she pointed at Rhino, 'and you, Thing. Can you find somewhere quiet for Tiny? Come on Ben let's find some cleaning stuff from the kitchen.' They went down the stairs two at a time sniggering all the way. They found Chris and skipped the sniggering bit while they told him what had happened. As they went on to the kitchen Chris started clearing the house immediately and, in some cases, forcibly.

Within seconds, or so it seemed to Ben, the pair were back in the flat making it smell strongly of disinfectant by scrubbing the carpets and the walls. The room was empty now, the family presumably having been found a safe house for the night. After Ruth and Ben had cleaned up, they sat on the sofa getting their breaths back. Chris popped by looking very scary but stopped when he realised the positive nature of their actions. All of the shouting stopped and it felt like they were alone in the house.

Ben looked at Ruth, his head felt heavy and slow. She looked absolutely fabulous, bit too close for his eyes to focus on but nevertheless absolutely fabulous. The first half of a sentence couldn't quite get passed his lips. She leant heavily against him. Her head on his chest, he could hear his own heart pounding.

'...surprise,' he managed.

'I've been waiting for you to talk to me all night, all year really. Gave up in the end and thought I'd better just pin you down myself.'

'Chris?' was the only clear word amongst the mumble.

She laughed in a way that made Ben thrill.

'We were just mucking about. He's really after Judith. Thought you knew that? Anyway I knew when I saw you wearing my watch tonight. I knew you were mine, even if you were too shy to say it,' she held his chin in one hand and kissed him, a slow, sticky kiss.

'...Brilliant.'

Chapter Five

The sun had risen in the East. It was raining in Garelochead. He would miss the deadline for his dissertation. Ben knew all these things to be inevitable and true. He drove as close to the caravan as he could so that he didn't have to walk through all of the water-filled ruts. Since his centre stand had snapped off, Ben had to lean the bike up against the GRP panelling of the caravan. The noise disturbed the Thing from its layer. Rhino's face, as cheerful as ever, appeared at the door. He squinted at the relative brightness of the low, rain heavy clouds between the black green pines.

'Ben.'

He sounded disappointed.

'Mind the wall with that bike, you can spit through it,' he sank back into the shadows, the open door the only invitation. Ben pulled the door to and picked his way to the kitchen. He handed Rhino a cigarette and light one himself off the gas ring trying not to set his hair on fire as he did so. He unzipped his flying jacket and pulled out a handful of A4 sheets heavy with ink. They crackled as he tried to flatten them.

'Images of Death and Depression in Sylvia Plath's novel the Bell Jar,' Ben took a step back and ran his free hand through his hair. He pointed at it, 'All done bar the typing. I really appreciate you letting me use your typewriter.'

'No problem.'

Rhino sniffed the milk carefully and then poured some into the two cups, 'Well actually there is. I'm still doing mine but its fine. We can take turns.'

A momentary flicker of concern crossed Rhino's face, 'Actually I only started mine today but I dropped some speed. It's brilliant. I've done so much, so quickly, you wouldn't believe it. The ideas just pour out, it really does it make it very simple. It took me a while but it's all clear now. I think you should have a look and see what you think. Or maybe you should wait and see what it looks like when I've finished. That's probably better. Do you want some? Speed that is.'

Ben shook his head and smiled, 'No thanks Rhino, a cup of tea will do fine.'

'What is the Bell Jar anyway?'

'It's a metaphysical glass bowl that separates her from the world. But she doesn't realise it. She thinks the world is going mad but actually it is her that is changing. It's a really good book. You could borrow it.'

Rhino laughed as he filled the kettle, 'I have enough problems with Mr Peake. Sounds like you should lend it to Tiny.'

While Rhino sorted out the tea Ben went back to the bike and pulled his sleeping bag and two hundred Benson & Hedges out of the box on the back carrier. The gold bar spilled its wonderful light around the car park as he walked back to the caravan and closed the door on the now faded world.

Ben wasn't too sure how much time had passed. They had sat silent apart from 'Supper's Ready' repeating on the turntable and the steady thump of the typewriter. With a continuous supply of tea Ben managed to get his four thousand words revised and typed. He had filled and emptied the pub ashtray twice. He coughed and chain-lit another one. He had crashed a hundred fags to Rhino and was looking nervously at his last packet. Hadn't started smoking them yet but it wouldn't be long. Ben got up from the desk and peered around for something to tell him the time. In the bedroom he found Rhino's huge digital alarm clock. He couldn't see that well, his eyes appeared to be determined to close in reaction to the smoke and the hours of staring at his copy. He craned his neck forward to get a fix on the slowly spinning tumblers.

'5:47 Oh shit,' Ben shambled back into the living room. Rhino had taken up the empty chair and was typing furiously. Ben rubbed his eyes and made for the door to see how the rain was getting on. The air outside was cold, still and damp. He filled his lungs and it felt like he was drinking rather than breathing. He reflected on the last twenty hours. It was an amazing feat. There they were, having hopelessly screwed up all year and yet they were both going to be able to hand their dissertations in on time, more or less. A triumph!

He left the door open as he went back in. Rhino could curse but the oxygen content really had dropped to dangerous levels. He put on 'Selling England by the Pound' and the kettle. Rhino had stopped typing. He shuffled the papers and handed them to Ben.

'Done it. What do you think?'

'Do you want me to read this now?'

Rhino ran two cups under the tap, 'Somebody needs to proof read it before I hand it in.'

Ben went back to the living room and curled up on the sofa. Three paragraphs in Ben began to realise that there was a problem. He kept reading through till the bottom of the second page. Sped read a few and then went straight to the conclusion. At some point his coffee had gone cold. Ben looked up. Behind Rhino's expectant face the sky was beginning to lighten. He looked shockingly childlike, innocent in a way that would have done Tiny proud, earnestly waiting for his due praise and for a moment Ben decided that he couldn't say anything.

'Well what do you think? Brilliant, isn't it.'

'Rhino there are a few bits that still need to be worked on. Look, you start your argument at the start of this but by the end you're on something completely different. You're talking about the architecture of Gormenghast and its impact here which is fine but you never finish the thought. This bit is all about Saruman, that's Lord of the Rings. Different book.'

'It's about fucking dysfunctional people and I'm drawing from other media.'

'Fucking dysfunctional is about right. You don't make the connection. From page three on you don't even manage to hang on to one sentence. On the bright side the conclusion is really good. It just doesn't have anything to do with the rest of it but it is really good.'

Rhino came forward, the child crushed. His hand was outstretched for his work.

'You ever seen the Shining?' asked Ben.

'You're fucking kidding me.'

Ben handed it over. Rhino started reading it through as though for the first time, which in a sense it was, 'Shit, shit, shit.' He looked the clock on top of the fridge. 'Not going to get it sorted in time. The school bus will be here in an hour. What the fuck am I going to do?'

'See if she'll give you another extension.'

'Aye right enough. And maybe she'll write it for me to save me the bother. I need some more speed. You come and give me a shout when the bus turns up.'

Ben managed to sleep on the bus. Once they got to school Angus, seeing Rhino's plight, rolled them a couple of joints, and they relaxed up against the back fence of the school playing fields while they took the piss out of Rhino. It was an open spot but one that gave a great field of view in which to identify approaching ne'r-do-wells and teachers. Some Fourth Years had managed to get close enough for an audience.

'Why the hell won't you give us a shot?'

Rhino took a long drag and passed it to Ben.

'Abso-fucking-lutely no way. I can't be seen leading minors astray.'

There were four of them, all easily taller than Rhino or Angus and two were more massive than Ben. The four had been building up to this for the last couple of weeks. Now they looked like they were desperate enough to try something. The end of break bell sounded adding to their pressure.

'Come on man give us a break. Look when we get something, we'll give you what we have.'

Rhino was laughing but Angus looked thoughtful, 'Have you got any money?'

The Fourth years' piggy eyes narrowed further as they looked at each other. Their spokesman nodded.

'We've got £2 between us.'

'That won't get you anything,' Rhino was packing up and still laughing. Ben was joining in.

'Tell you what lads. Special introductory offer,' Angus pulled out a small brown cube between two fingers. He held out the dice for inspection. 'Straight forward Red Lebanese. Very pleasant, as these two gentlemen will testify. Easy to use, just crumble a little of it up with some tobacco and away you go.'

Ben and Rhino were still smiling and passing the joint between them. The roach was getting hot. The Fourth Years were straining at the leash of their impoverishment.

'Where will we get tobacco from?'

Angus held up the blue and white packet of Regal Dinky.

'Fags.'

'How much?'

'£5 for the set.'

'Fuck off.'

'Okay,' Angus swung his Adidas bag on his back and, taking the almost finished rollup from Rhino, began walking across the playing field back towards the school.

'Hang on.' There was more muttering. '£4 and that's all we've got.' Angus tossed the cube and fags across and took the money. They ran off leaving the three Sixth Years to saunter towards the rain stained concrete buildings.

'You looked two look wasted. Which presumably means I do? Do you think we're too high to go to Economics?'

Rhino ignored Ben and was looking shrewdly at Angus, 'I haven't sold you any Leb. What did you sell them?'

Angus looked like he was going to explode, 'Clay from the tennis court. I've been carrying it round for days wondering if I could get away with it.'

'They'll go mad.'

'They'll get high on the tobacco and not know. I have saved them from themselves. One day they will thank me. Spicy buns and coffees on me then.'

'Time for Economics,' said Ben. Rhino started towards the Gallery.

'Mrs Paterson has given me till tomorrow morning to get my dissertation in. Send my apologies.'

It turned out that Ben and Angus were too stoned to get through Economics and were kicked out of the class after half an hour by a mystified teacher. They were still giggling when they got back to the Gallery. There was no sign of Tiny and Rhino was working harder than he ever had in his life and therefore no fun. With exams only a month away there was only one thing to do. Bunk off school and get the train up to Glasgow, problem was it decided to stop at Partick. When it was clear that the driver had wandered off to see if he could find anyone the pair finally abandoned the train and headed for the underground, much to the relief of their fellow passengers.

Glasgow Underground had just resurfaced, as it were. It looped around the west of Glasgow, a new bold urban transport system for the eighties.

'But why is it orange?' Ben asked as the plastic train hurtled out of the dark, filling one side of the tunnel.

'Somebody really wanted to piss off Celtic,' Angus got on and swung round to sit. They had the carriage to themselves.

'Really?' Angus' response was lost in the hiss of the doors closing. They revealed the carefully scraped letters exhorting anarchy. All eight doors in the carriage carried the same anti-establishment message; 'Block~~ing~~ the doors, cause~~s~~ delays and ~~can~~ be dangerous.'

They got off at Central Station and walked the three hundred yards to Treasure Island. The first impression was a wall of sound. The ten button bandits lined each side of the entrance hall, blasting out light and noise, drawing the punters in with the promise of easy money and suspension of reality for as long as the coins lasted. Angus and Ben walked straight past. Tiny had memorised the sequence to jackpot on most of the machines. Without him it would be only be luck if they won. They were here for games of skill not chance. A depressed looking waif peered through the smoke of her booth checking the denomination of the pound notes before sliding ten tens back towards the lads. Coins heavy in their pockets, they took their time walking round the arcade taking in the new games and how they were played. They paused to watch the old favourites and see if their names were still up in the Halls of Fame. There were a few names they recognised.

Treasure Island had a new machine, 'Robatron', typical Williams, overwhelming sound, violent colour scheme, two joysticks side by side, one to fire one to move. Neither Ben nor Angus had ever seen anything like it. The speed of the action, the incessant blasting, rescuing families before they got squished. It was incredible. Ben realised it was time for a break when he started expecting the people around him to exploding as he came back with more change. He stepped outside and was impressed by the quality of the graphics till he remembered it wasn't a game he was watching, it was real life. Hours had passed. Oddly at that point a huge black battleship landed in front of him. Chris Ferguson unexpectedly leaned out of the window.

'Want a lift?' It was his dad's Rover SD1 3500, Black, twice the size and three times the power of anything else in the city.

'Oh aye. Angus is inside I'll go get him.'

He jogged back through the light and sound and found Angus surrounded by hordes of the things. All the neds that had spent their money, or never had any in the first place had gathered around Angus as he played the Robotron machine like a cathedral organ. He was in undiscovered country.

'Angus! Got to go! Chris will give us a lift back home.' Angus turned to the snot nosed urchin without two bob to his name standing blank-eyed next to him.

'Don't fuck it up.' Without a backward glance he walked away from the machine and the crowd and jumped up the six stairs to join Ben.

'Got his dad's car.'

'Huzzah!'

Ben climbed into the back of the Rover. He felt the leather seats and looked at the square weirdly attached steering wheel. Both firsts for Ben.

Chris took a long look at Angus, 'You going out with my sister?'

A lie danced obviously over Angus' face, 'Aye,' he confirmed eventually.

'You be careful.'

In what way Chris never defined. But Angus looked like a man determined to be careful in all the ways he could think of and if he thought of a few more he would be careful in them too. In a moment of inspiration Angus pulled out one of his trademark immaculately rolled joints and Chris put on Jean Michelle Jarre, Equinox. After that the journey home was swift and pleasurable. The third roll-up took them to Loch Lomond side. Chris was obviously enjoying himself and carried on up the loch side to Tarbet and then through to Arrochar.

'If you go back to Garelochead I could collect my bike.'

'Down Loch Long in this thing? It's wider than the road in some places,' Chris slide the joint from one side of mouth to the other, his white teeth flashing in the unexpected sun. 'Why not?' The engine roared and the black car leapt forward, dashing down the ever narrowing road. Soon the mountain closed in on the left and loch beckoned on the right. The car crouched, jumped and twisted round the bends. Ben's mind became a succession of images as they dove and climbed, the sump gouged danger spots, the frozen face of terror of the couple in a Viva, the bus that was so so wide. Somebody screamed and Ben suspected it might have been him. They flashed out of the glen and up onto the relative width of Whistlefield and the open sky. It felt like they could touch the clouds as, like a black artillery shell, they marked their trajectory back down into Garelochead.

Chris pulled up at the end of Rhino's house. Angus and Ben fell out of the car still laughing at the joy of being alive. Chris grinned and sped away in a spray of gravel.

'Absolutely mad,' Angus held his hand out, 'look I can't hold it still.'

Ben was stretching, taking as deep breaths as he could, 'I think I'm going to throw up.'

'Smoke too much?'

Ben pointed an imaginary gun at Angus., 'That'll be it. I'll get my helmet off Rhino and I'll take you back to Helensburgh.'

'Slowly.'

'The only way with my trusty...' Ben stopped as the two came round the corner. They could see the caravan. Someone had splashed blood and feathers over the front, the door had been kicked in but a mattress was providing the last line of defence. Bits of broken furniture stuck through the gaps on each side.

'Not good,' whispered Angus. The two advanced cautiously. Ben saw that Angus had his rather neat black-bladed knife held low and realised that he had his own lock knife out, 'one could say spooky.'

'Spooky,' Ben circled left round the side of the caravan and Angus round the right. They met at the back and shrugged. The rest of the van looked fine. All the damage was focused around the door. The two returned there. 'Rhino.'

'Rhino!'

There was some movement in the dark. 'Rhino,' Ben stopped shouting and talked to the mattress. 'It's us Rhino. Angus and me. If you're in there let us know you're all right.'

He turned to Angus, 'Think we could cut our way through the wall?'

'Touch the fucking wall and you're dead.'

Ben smiled in recognition to Angus, 'Not that bad then. Rhino, you okay?'

'What the fucking hell do you think? I've been fucking attacked. Attacked in my own house. What the hell is the world coming to?' A stream of blasphemy followed. The mattress lurched forcing the two back into the car park. The swearing and cursing continued till, with a flip Rhino, emerged looking more mole-like than ever.

'You on your own?' Angus and Ben grunted positively and pulled Rhino through the rest of the wreckage. Ben crashed fags to the other two and lit his own last. They blew smoke into the cool evening air. Rhino seemed unwilling or unable to talk. They tried waiting.

'Give up Rhino, what happened?' asked Ben.

'Tiny.' They waited while he dragged heavily on the fag. 'Turned up this afternoon. Started telling me that he had been trying to kill himself. Did you guys know this?' Ben and Angus shrugged. The idea didn't seem to be a shock to either of them. 'News to me. Told me that on Sunday he had walked into the Clyde and only just stopped before the tide took him away. Yesterday he had to throw his knife away in case he cut himself. He was doing the thing with the hand,' Rhino mimicked his right hand trying to attack him. 'Today he came to hurtling across the car park at the Rest and be Thankful. He managed to jump clear. Left his bike at the bottom of the glen and hitchhiked back here.'

'Why here? Is he all right?'

'No problem at all. Bike completely fucked by the sound of it but I'm sure his Mum will buy him another one. Why here? I'll tell you why here.' Rhino took another cigarette but his hands shook too badly to work the lighter. 'On his way back here he realised what was happening.'

He met his rescuers' eyes for the first time, 'It was mind control. Tiny wasn't committing suicide. I was controlling his mind and making him kill himself. Nobody would know. The perfect crime.'

'Ah,' Ben said.

'Well Tiny arrived here and explained all this to me. There's a lot more that I can't really remember he was talking so fast in a tranquil stream of consciousness kind of a way, you know. Anyway it all seemed very logical. I said there was no way that I would do that. Then he explained to me that I probably didn't even know that I was doing it. 'Monsters from the Id', he said. But he really didn't want to die and he could only think of one solution.'

Rhino took another cigarette from Ben and lit it from the one he already had. He ran his fingers through his hair as he stared at the gravel at his feet.

'It was to kill me,' Rhino looked up again. 'He seemed calm enough. He was quite sorry about it but it was the only thing he could do to save himself. I bundled him out of the caravan and closed the door. I think he was surprised, given how reasonable his argument had been that I wasn't happy to go along with everything and just die on the spot. When he realised I wasn't, he started to kick the door in. I threw everything I could find into the hall. I was scared man, really scared. Tiny was outside screaming that he would get me because it was either him or me. He killed a chicken then. Cut its head off and threw it against the caravan. It kept running off and he kept catching it and throwing it back. Eventually the poor thing died and he just stood there looking at it and crying. He ran off with the chicken about half an hour ago.'

There was a crunch of gravel which made all three jump. Ben saw a black shape in the half light and went to shout, overwhelmed by his own sense of personal safety but realised it was too short for Tiny and, under all the jumpers, looked a bit girl shaped.

'Alison! Hello. If you're looking for Tiny I think you've just missed him.'

Alison, her face twisted in concern walked right passed Ben to the wrecked figure of Rhino looking like a hermit crab between shells.

'You alright Lachlan?'

Rhino smiled weakly. This took the weirdness of the day in an unexpected direction. She took Rhino's arm and for a moment Ben thought she was going to hug him. That was a lot bit weird. Ben and Angus felt the shift from would-be rescuers to definite intruders in a few seconds.

'We'll head back home then if you're going to be okay. Can we borrow a lid for Angus?'

Rhino nodded, 'Aye sure I'll go and get one.'

Probably for the first time Rhino faced the wreckage of his home, 'Man my brother is going to kill me.'

Chapter Six

The sun was shining down on the school. This was nature's usual cruel way. Exams had not so much loomed but more snuck up from behind and tapped everyone on the shoulder when they were all relaxed and least expecting it. The result was baking tarmac, dry grass and dying moss, unburdened by the youth of Helensburgh. There was a keen sense of what might have been in the class. Miss Paterson radiated it.

Ben and Rhino had been in to see Miss Paterson before the exam. It had only been six years since she had been in the same position herself and she acted as one of the few who understood what they were going through. She had tried to give them some good last minute advice. She sat on one of the desks, a slightly short tartan skirt rode up over thick, possibly knitted black tights. Her legs swung back and forth, quite hypnotic, especially once it had occurred to Ben what those tights were wrapped around.

'I hear you are going out with a couple of St Mungo's girls.' Both boys looked pale at this creepy crossover in their well delineated lives. She laughed, looking more Elven than ever, 'Better be careful with them. There is always trouble when St Mungo's girls go out with boys from this school. Especially with the exams coming. You have to keep your concentration. Not that you had that much to start with. You're clever enough you just need to apply yourselves. Now I do sound like a teacher,' she said more to herself, 'which means not thinking about Ruth or,' she turned to Rhino, 'Alison.'

Something was very wrong with this conversation. Ben and his friends had specialised for years in being the boys that other parents would be happy for their sons to hang around with. 'Ben's such a nice boy,' they would say as they left the house. Not realising within minutes those nice boys and their own little darling would be burning flotsam on the beach or experimenting how much sugar and fertilizer it would take to blow up a traffic cone. They were firm believers that information was king and that Parents, School and Social life were much better kept in perfect isolation. Better for everyone involved.

Miss Paterson carried on as if she was unaware of the impact of what she had said. Ben didn't hear most of the pep talk as he tried to figure out what mechanism had permitted what was clearly was a massive breech of security.

'If you had applied yourselves through the year with the same diligence that I have seen for the last four weeks you would all be assured of 'A's. As it is I think you'll be lucky if you get a pass. But you can still do that.'

'How did you know that Miss?'

'I have observed you through the year. You are capable of walking this. Whether you do or not is up to the pair of you.'

Ben shook his head, 'No Miss. About us and, you know...'

Miss Paterson laughed and held her legs out in front of her.

'Judith is my wee sister. You numpties didn't know did you?' she swung off her desk and looked up at the Sixth Years towering above her. Ben was struck by the reason why he hadn't seen the resemblance before - he had always seen the teacher, not the woman. Her smile made it clear she was in total control.

Miss Paterson at least recognised some innate talent, however unfulfilled. The Headmaster had been less optimistic with Ben when reviewing his options.

'I don't know why you are wasting my time Mr Williams. You have no talent, limited ability and little prospect of getting to University.' Ben sat back in a state of shock. 'You have wasted every opening this school has tried to make for you.' Harsh but fair, Ben thought. Though it was the first time someone had actually said it to him. The headmaster sensing the paralysis on the other side of the desk leant forward, 'What exams are you about to sit?'

'English SYS, Higher Economics, Higher Maths and French 'O' Grade, again.'

It was the Headmaster's turn to be taken aback.

'But you haven't got the grades to do this, you haven't even done the 'O' grades for these. I don't understand how you have managed to get into these classes? This is ridiculous. Are you trying to be funny? I assure you young man that this is no joke, particularly in your position.'

Ben felt the tension fall from him as understanding dawned; he stood up, leaning across the desk reading the file name upside down, 'This is for Jim Williams sir. Jim is called Jim so that he would have reasonable chance of spelling it. I'm Benjamin Williams.'

Elongating his name to emphasis the extra syllables, 'Anything else? Sir.'

Vindicated he left the room without another word. As he walked out the door it felt like that the outer office was too small to contain him. He was Benjamin Williams. The Head's secretary jumped. He must have said that out loud. He gave her his best winning smile and walked out into the sun-filled quad, his arms stretching out from building to building. He looked down on the roofs of the school and laughed his titanic laugh. I am Ben Williams!

He put his ego back in its velvet box and took the route through the canteen to get to the gallery. It was dark with the lights off, especially after the bright glare of the quadrangle. Something was moving in the in the kitchen but it was hard to make out what. A thing that didn't want to be seen. For a second Ben thought of Alien. Maybe the thing was right, he didn't want to see it either. He thought of the spidery thing with the hands and long egg depositor. There was a pop and hiss and something caught the top of his head. Ben just about wet himself.

'You mad bastard what was that?' he shouted into the dark.

'Flying Dalek,' said a voice, unmistakably Rhino, from the poorly lit kitchen. There was another pop and this time Ben managed to duck as a Pepsi cup whistled over him and banged loudly against the canteen window. Ben slide across the floor to the worktop. He felt he should have something proportionate to hit back with, possibly a flamethrower.

'Rhino, hit me again and you're in trouble.'

'Ooo, scared,' said Rhino, obviously not. He sounded close. Ben wondered if he could get through the entrance to the kitchen without getting cupped again. As he eased silently round the cupboards he looked into the base of a loaded Pepsi cup and knew the game was up.

'You win. I give up. What the hell is it?'

Rhino snapped the gun up into the air, his face a picture of triumph, 'Simple. Pepsi cup jammed on the end of a CO2 fire extinguisher, here. Give it a quick blast with the trigger here.'

Rhino would have made a splendid, if slightly disturbing, air hostess.

'The pressure builds up until it's enough to blow the cup off the scoop and Bob's your aunty. Daleks get a new edge.'

'Give us a shot.'

'Fuck off and find your own.'

The water extinguishers with their straight forward hoses were a clear non-starter. They found two powder extinguishers but the cups didn't fit and they guessed they might be a bit messy in combat. Luckily there was another CO2 extinguisher by the deep-fat-fryers. Suitably armed they duelled back to the Gallery. By the time they had got back to the Sixth Year common room, both had burned their hands on the frozen nozzles of the extinguishers. Ben tossed Rhino a lit fag and read the label.

'It says here that you should be careful not to touch the black bit as it is likely to freeze and 'May result in injury,' he ended with a quote.

'No 'May' about it. A bloody dead cert I'd have said,' Rhino tried to shake some warmth back into his left hand. 'Bit spooky about Miss Paterson being Judith's sister. Do you think she'll give us better marks?'

'No,' Ben laughed the smoke out of his nose and mouth, 'We'll be lucky if she doesn't hold our papers back.'

They sat in silence for a moment listening to the tick of the extinguishers as they thawed in the May sunshine. The open window let in a cool breeze.

'You ready for your exams?'

Ben could feel the normal bravado building but it left as suddenly. He shrugged, 'Mostly. I've left it all too late like Miss Paterson said but I've worked it out. I've got three nights on each subject before the exams start. Then two nights each between each exam apart from Maths but I think I'm fucked on Maths anyway.'

'Shit.' Rhino didn't elaborate and Ben didn't want to spoil the moment. 'Do you need maths to get in to Glasgow' asked Rhino.

Ben frowned, 'Something went wrong with the UCCA forms. It looks like I'm going to Paisley Tech.'

'A fine establishment I understand, ' said Rhino in his Lord Provost voice.

'Oh hell aye. Better than nothing.'

This took the conversation where Ben didn't want it to be.

'Have you seen Tiny, since you know, me and Angus were round?' Ben asked. Rhino didn't answer for a while.

'Cool. He's backing off on stuff. He realises that he's been overdoing it. Probably the exams. They've made us all a bit crazy.'

The part of Ben's brain that was responsible for picking topics of conversation was clearly away on holiday early this year without letting the rest of his head know.

'How are you and Alison getting on?'

Rhino took even longer to answer this question, 'Fine.'

Ben managed to stifle the next question for fear of personal injury and the pair settled into companionable silence watching the smoke trickle out through the open window. Rhino picked up one of his stack of Pepsi cups and chuckled.

The next time Ben saw Rhino it was the day of the Maths exam. In between the sun had beaten down relentlessly day after day, Ben and Ruth had made various attempts at studying together. Studying together alone. Studying together with other people present so that nothing would happen. Studying together but only seeing each other at pre-agreed break points. No matter the combinations, the results had been, in an academic sense, a complete bloody disaster. On the other hand they were some of the happiest times that Ben had ever experienced. The onrushing avalanche of exams adding an exquisite edge to the whole proceedings. Life was about to come to an end and that meant what little left to them had to be lived to the full. Everything had to be experienced now since the moment would soon pass. The sun would set and the shadows would creep out and smother them in despair. Somehow he felt that if could achieve paradise with Ruth he could side step the onrushing tsunami that would crush all else. All that had meaning would be washed away but somehow they would be free. He had explained it to Rhino and Angus that morning over spicy buns and coffee.

'Do you know you're talking bollocks?' asked Rhino.

Angus laughed but interjected, 'No I know where he is coming from. It's like if you have her then nothing else matters. Not the exams, not a job, parents, they are out of there somewhere.' He was waving his arms a lot, 'If you have her, and she has you, and you're happy, you have everything.'

Ben sat back in his chair his arms wide at the vindication of his argument. He opened his mouth but Angus continued, 'But you're right Rhino. It is total bollocks. You don't pass your exams boy then only way you're going to work will be with a Donald Duck Club logo on the back of your Donkey Jacket and there is no way that is going to cut the mustard with a lady from St Mungo's.'

Ben was about to ask for the proof of this cynicism when he saw a trail bike tearing across the asphalt sports field at what appeared to be full tilt.

'Crazy Tiny at 12 o'clock,' he said quietly.

Angus looked at his watch, 'It's half past nine, that watch of yours really is useless isn't it.'

'Over there, you Muppet,' he indicated the figure in the full-face helmet now circling back out of sight. 'Shall we go see what he does? But not too closely,'

Ben added. The three walked out of the gallery and down to the front of the New Building trying to hurry fast enough not to miss the action but not so fast that they would blow their cool by hurrying.

The school office looked like an ant's nest somebody had stirred up with a big stick. Teachers and pupils were stumbling out into the unfamiliar daylight, swarming around looking for something to attack. Ben could hear the distinctive soft roar of the 185cc four stroke but couldn't see it.

It was Rhino that spotted it first.

'And there.'

He pointed to the front of the New Building. Somehow Tiny must have managed to ride the bike up the internal flights of stairs, along a hall, between the classes, back down the central stairs and now, without pausing, launched himself into the air from the top of the broad entrance stairs landing with a hell of a thump back in the playground in front of the school office. With a whoop Tiny pulled the bike round in a tight circle and sped away back under the link stairs and the Main Gates leaving dazed children scattering like wildebeest across the tarmac. It was all over. The oily smoke hanging in the air was the only proof that it had really happened.

'Impressive,' said Angus. 'Massively stupid but impressive.'

'Reid doesn't look too happy.'

Indeed the Assistant Head was descending the main stairs clearly furious and looking for something to hit. Unspoken Angus, Rhino and Ben decided it wouldn't be them and quietly melted back into the New Building.

Chapter Seven

Ben stood naked in front of the full length mirrors in the master bedroom. He adjusted his sunglasses. 'Looks damn good. Tall and fair in a country that mostly isn't,' he said to himself. 'A fine catch, if I say so myself.'

Fresh out the shower he turned so that the sunlight could catch the water drops on his skin. Bit like Michelangelo's David only with a proper sized willy. The summer had read the script properly and really got the hang of things now. It had been hot all week. This was the fourth day in a row where he had been forced to look, obliquely, at Clorinda in her bikini.

He was trying to get right in his head how her legs joined her body. They started at her waist, that wonderful waist that then just like, flowed down leaving her body as perfect arcs. Ruth was great, clever, funny, very together but the way Clorinda was put together... Ben looked at himself in the mirror again. In comparison to either he just looked like the Gingerbread man. Two legs stuck on where the body ended with no sense of art at all. He pulled on a pair of shorts and went down stairs to the fridge. It was one of those big ones you see in American films with plumbing and an ice machine in the front. This was Clorinda's house, or rather her parents'. They were at work right now, presumably working very hard to pay this lot off. Four chilled cans of Carlsberg in his hands he left the cool marble kitchen and walked into the baking heat of Helensburgh.

Angus, Clorinda and Ruth were stretched out on rugs on the grass. Clorinda had produced a portable telly from somewhere and the three were watching Wimbledon on the smallish black and white screen.

'Why is it called Love?' Ben asked as he approached the trio. Clorinda rolled over to look at him. He stopped in his tracks as she turned, the way her hips and legs changed shape as she moved, each angle better than the last. They seemed to flow, curves and re-curves like golden dunes sweeping in across the tartan rug above the parched grass. Ruth had a pair of really big Seventies sunglasses which made her expressions pure guess work.

'No that doesn't work with those on,' he said assuming that had been her 'stupid' look. He handed a tin to Ruth, resisting the temptation to chase a bead of sweat on the small of her back. He had been kissing her there only half an hour before.

'Of course it is called 'Love' because...' she paused.

Clorinda sat up, head to one side, listening, 'Shh.'

'What?' There was the sound of a heavy car on gravel.

'Shit it's my Dad. You tidied up upstairs, right?'

Ben pictured the wet towels on the floor. The duvet piled up by the bed, itself a mass of distorted linen, 'All sorted.'

Clorinda laughed, 'You are such a bad liar!' she pointed at Angus, 'you two get upstairs and sort both the rooms out. Shift!'

She clapped her hands chasing them like two chickens towards the white pebble-dashed house. Angus and Ben ran up the stairs, Angus dived into the spare bedroom and Ben into the master bedroom. Clorinda had said something about she couldn't in her Mum and Dad's bed. He flipped the double mattress and pulled the sheet tight. The duvet snapped back into place. He was picking up the towels when his eyes met Angus's across the hall. He was grinning like an idiot as well.

'Absolutely incredible. Is this real?' Ben asked.

Angus was tugging on a pair of jeans, 'Make the most of it sunny boy. You have now had the briefest of glimpses of what you could win.'

Ben grabbed the towels and stuffed them into a wicker Alibaba basket. As he left he saw the ashtray by the bed and emptied the douts into his hand.

He followed Angus as they ran back down the slick wooden stairs. They turned left and out to the back garden throwing the ash and filters under a rhododendron. This place was so familiar to them now. Hard to think of these as the same stairs where he had thought he had lost Ruth to Chris at that party.

There were two men in the back garden talking to Ruth and Clorinda. One Ben recognised as Clorinda's dad. He looked across at the door and saw the two young men leaving his house. He looked comfortable and relaxed. No look of fear today or, luckily, recognition.

'Hello Mr Ferguson. I'm Ben,' Ben held his hand out. It hung there for a moment before the surprised father rescued it.

'Ben. We've met before?' It was only half a question.

'You have probably seen me about with Chris. I used to play a lot of Risk and Tunnels and Trolls with him. But must have been before you moved here.'

'Trolls?' Mr Ferguson looked confused for a moment, 'This is my partner David. David Evens. Angus and Ben.'

David was rather too obvious in his appreciating the sight of girls in swimwear. Ben felt uncomfortable but Clarinda's dad appeared to be oblivious. David made an easy smile and shook both hands, 'All right lads.'

'What were you lot up to before we disturbed you?' Mr Ferguson asked.

Clorinda pointed towards their sunbathing spot, 'Watching the tennis.'

David was laughing.

Clorinda put her hands on her hips and asked, 'What?'

'It's a hard life,' said David, enjoying their sense of annoyance. Clorinda's dad took a sharp intake of breath keen to change the subject. Ruth had pulled one of the towels from the sun screen round the telly and wrapped herself in it. She was frowning at David.

'How would you…' Mr Ferguson's words were slightly too loud, too fast, 'like to come to Campbelltown with us next weekend? We'll go on the Friday and back on the Monday. The Mull of Kintyre is just incredible this time of year.'

Clorinda pulled a face and looked over at Angus, 'Go all that way just as cover for you and your pals playing golf? No thanks.' Clorinda's face was transparently hit by an idea, 'We could stay here with Mum?'

'No way.'

Any plans Mr Ferguson had for keeping the peace appeared to been thrown out of the window by that comment. 'After what happened in March? No way young lady. I thought I had made it perfectly clear to you and your brother that there were to be no more parties in this house.'

Clorinda looked distraught.

David turned to Angus and Ben, 'Do you play golf?'

Angus nodded, 'Played a bit at the Council course.'

'Good enough. What about you, Ben?' asked David.

Ben wondered if Crazy Golf champion at Butlin's Skegness counted, 'I have played a bit. Also.'

Ruth laughed but David carried on, 'Excellent. You two come as well then. I think there will be quite a crowd.' He turned to Mr Ferguson, 'Peter? John and Iain were talking about inviting their kids. We get a mini bus. Iain's house could hold twenty as long as people aren't too fussy where they sleep.' He turned back to Ruth, 'Are you fussy where you sleep?'

Ruth stepped closer to Ben, 'Very.'

'It'll be good. It's not Campbelltown itself. Our friend Iain has got a house near Machrihanish. Dead handy for the golf course. Great beach. If we take two mini-buses that would give us plenty of room for beer.'

He was talking to Mr Ferguson again. He couldn't seem to maintain a conversation with Angus and Ben, Clorinda or Ruth for more than one sentence. The pair started to walk towards the house. David turned back to Angus and Ben, 'Are you two going to come then?'

Angus took half a step forward and then realised what he meant. He looked to Clorinda for guidance but the oracle wasn't giving anything away, 'Yeah? Sounds like a good idea.'

'Excellent,' laughed David. He clapped Mr Ferguson's back as they disappeared out of the glare of the sun, 'I'm really looking forward to this.' There was silence for a moment.

'Creep,' Ruth managed to put a lot of venom into that word. 'He couldn't take his eyes off us.' She looked up at the sky, catching Ben out of synch, 'What makes men think they can stare at us like that?'

Ben shook his head in simulated shock, 'No idea.'

But Ruth was really talking to Clorinda, 'He is a bit old not to be married?'

'Was but his wife kicked him out last year when it turned out he was a regular in Blythswood Square. He's been hanging around here ever since. I was worried he was after Mum for a bit. I think she thinks David is quite attractive. Described him as having something of Flashman about him. Dad doesn't see it though.'

'Like I said, creep.'

'Every time I meet him I feel like I need a bath.'

'How did you know he's not married?' asked Ben.

Ruth waved her left hand in front of his face, 'No ring, dumdum.'

Ben was thinking what ring? How would that tell you anything?

'Will Chris be going?' Angus asked.

'What one of Dad's golf trips with free beer thrown in. What do you think?'

Ben noticed that Angus had a faraway look. Somehow he felt on the same wavelength as his friend. He mouthed the words as Angus spoke them.

'We are going to go right?'

'Forecast is still good,' Ben responded.

Campbelltown wasn't really that far from Helensburgh as the crow flew. Unfortunately the hire company was all out of crows which meant that the journey became a four hour slog over mountain passes, through switchbacks and roads that were determined to go as close to the sea as possible. Ben's hand squeaked as he wiped the condensation about on the window. It was difficult to tell if was wetter outside the bus than in it. He gave up trying to see out since the cloud ceiling appeared to be more of a floor. Any attempts to cheer up Ruth and Clorinda were met with a grey chill that outdid anything the Atlantic could offer.

But by the time they go to the big old house in Machrihanesh the wind had torn the unremitting cloud into identifiable strips with promising patches of blue in between. The house, an old manse, was huge, Ruth and Clorinda ran off to pick rooms while Angus and Ben helped unload the provisions from the back of their bus.

The second bus pulled up behind them with two more of Mr Ferguson's friends. This one had less food, drink and sleeping bags but more people, all St Mungo's apparently. Ben was going to have to pay attention next time round to remember their names. First impressions made him think he probably wouldn't make the effort though. They too piled into the house laughing, obviously used to leaving the servants to sort that kind of thing out. Finally Angus and Ben had everything in, including the last slab of McEwen's Export into the kitchen. Several times the St Mungo's group had swept through but it had not occurred to any of them to help. Ben pulled two cans from the pack and passed one to Angus while he struck a match off the shell roughcast covered wall, lit two cigarettes passing one the other way. The pair stood at the kitchen door looking out to the sea.

'I get the irresistible urge to tug my forelock with that lot around.'

'Centuries of selective breeding. It's the English accents,' Angus flicked his cigarette so hard the burning head span off and he had to relight it. When he came back to the door it was still smouldering on the concrete path that wound round the house. The smoke rose up almost die straight.

'But they're Scots. Most of them.'

'Is English a posh Scots accent?'

'Hello lads. You alright?'

Ben jumped, 'Fine Mr Ferguson. Looks like it's going to be all right this afternoon.'

Peter pulled two more cans and handed them over getting another one for himself, 'Thanks for your help getting the stuff in. The kids are talking about taking one of the buses into Campbelltown. If you fancy going you better keep an eye on the others.'

'Need to find out what the girls are planning to do. Do you know?'

That made Mr Ferguson laugh, 'Never, never in a million years. Will you give us a hand with the barbeque tonight? There is always a steady supply of beer for those who also serve and it will save you buying any in town?'

'Aye,' said Ben, 'we're your men.'

Two of the St Mungo's burst into the kitchen. They were laughing so hard Ben thought they must have split a joint already. A girl with long jet black hair and grey eyes, Chlamydia Ben thought but wasn't sure.

'Come on, David's already in the van and Clorinda said we can't go without you two,' she added. They ran back out without checking to see if Angus and Ben were coming. Obviously the anonymity ran both ways. Mr Ferguson looked like he was going to say something but then snapped his mouth shut. Starting their second cans, the two said goodbye to Mr Ferguson and made their way to the white and rust coloured British Leyland.

The trip into Campbelltown itself convinced them that they weren't missing anything. There was some kind of music festival on. A Mod, which Ben had seen on STV before but this was something smaller, some kind of a practice run. Lots of Gaelic songs and Highland dancing, bit teuchter for Bens' tastes. By the time they returned to the manse, Mr Ferguson and David appeared to have knitted thick Arran jumpers and set up the barbecue down by the beach under the clearing sky. A tape deck and a couple of guitars followed.

Angus and Ben settled themselves behind the barbecue. One of Mr Ferguson's friends, returned from sorting out the green fees for the following day, had clearly done large scale open air cooking before.

'Right lads. You should find this simple enough. Six buckets, three marinated chicken, three marinated beef, keep one of each open at a time. All you have to do is keep the meat coming and I'll make sure that you never go thirsty.'

Ruth and Clorinda started off splitting the bread rolls but at some point they got bored and drifted off to join the dancing that had started on the beach. In the beginning Ben had seen the gas burners as a good defence from the St Mungo's group, but the girls going made him feel that the defence had turned into a trap. A group of young people from the Mod appeared and negotiated a deal with David for access to the barbeque. What must have been most of the off-licence stock of Campbelltown swelled their own beer stack and the calls for food came faster than ever. The girls were good looking but the lads all looked quite handy, all that sheep wrestling no doubt. And they were clearly on alert. One of them stopped beside Ben.

'Nice night. Where are you from?'

'Helensburgh.' The boy looked blank.

'Near Glasgow,' he used to say near Loch Lomond but other than jokes about 'Taking the high road' it had never helped, 'What about you?'

'I'm a Rhuoch, Isle of Lewis. But these folk are from all over the Western Isles. All the way down to the Uists. Mostly, we're down here for the Mod. You know. Need to practise in front of a live crowd. Good experience.'

The words came out in bursts so fast that Ben had to replay each statement on slow in his head. In front of them three of the choir had apparently decided to finish a bottle of trawler rum in a drinking game that involved a straw.

'Going at it pretty hard?'

'Oh we don't get out much. We have to make the most of it,' he smiled sadly, nodded at Angus and stepped towards a group of girls who were looking like they weren't so sure about making the most anything.

'Where they from?' asked Angus.

Ben shrugged, 'North. Friendly though.'

When at last the queue died down Ben started looking for Ruth. She and Clorinda were dancing with two of the St Mungo's boys. They were concentrating so hard on looking cool, the two lads didn't see Angus and Ben coming up behind them. Ben briefly thought about engaging in acts of random violence but decided it would spoil the ambience rather. Instead he began to copy Farquar or whatever his name was. It was Simple Minds playing so it was pretty easy to guess the next move. Pulling his jacket sleeves up to his elbows Angus settled behind Torquil and camped it up so badly that Ben had to stop looking. It was only on the final spin, one arm tight, the other high, that the pair realised that they had been set up. With hurt looks at the Ruth and Clorinda they slunk back off to the cooling barbecue and the remaining chicken.

The four danced, still laughing and then walked along the beach, shoes off, feeling the sand shift under their feet. Oyster catchers lamented being pushed along the shore. Inshore a lark made the most of the last bit of sunshine, hanging invisible somewhere above the dunes. The sky was a perfect blue now and the breakers, wild grey and white when the Helensburgh folk had arrived, were only an inch high, lapping translucently on the white sand. Angus wrote 'Clorinda' in copperplate in the sand with a piece of plastic pipe. The way the light caught it, the ten foot letters looking stunning, dark against the silver shell sand. He started drawing her a heart. Ben and Ruth built a wall to stop the tide washing it away too quickly.

'Thank you so much!' was all that Clorinda could manage in a choked voice that would have done an Oscar winner proud. They walked back, a little more distance between the two couples. Ben had given his tweed jacket to Ruth against the breeze that had sprung up and held her close as they walked. Some way short of the party they stopped, leaving Clorinda and Angus to stroll on. Ruth and Ben sank into the shelter of a sand dune and the long marram grass. It was still warm there, the heat of the sun had been stored up and now slowly released as evening fell. They kissed in the half dark of an Argyll summers night. Ruth rolled Ben over. She ran her hands through her short blue black hair, kissed his top lip and whispered.

'You can have a sandy arse this time.'

The tapes had stopped at some point and for a long time the only noise was from the snipe, its unearthly whirring somewhere above. Ruth had fallen asleep, still on top of him. His legs were freezing but there was no way he was going risk moving. In the silence the strangest noise started. Ben really couldn't make sense of it at first. It was as if it was so unlike anything that he had heard before that his brain couldn't do anything more than register that there was a noise, a huge noise that overwhelmed his senses, a sad noise, a song, a beautiful song, a song with a dozen parts for a dozen voices in a language he didn't understand. Ruth stopped snoring and lifted her head. A small patch of drool connected her cheek and his chest.

'What the hell is that?'

'That mob from the islands. But I am guessing.'

The pair dressed and walked along the edge of the dunes towards the party. The sky was brighter by the second. In the new light Ben could see Clorinda and Angus walking back towards them with a bottle of whisky.

'Cheers,' Clorinda said and passed the opened bottle over to Ben with a wink. She seemed to have only buttoned her shirt with one button at the top, leaving her modesty at the mercy of the way the fabric folded around her. Angus seemed cool about it. Ben thought he should be too. That was a button that shouldn't be pressed, or indeed thought about. On the horizon a vertical red pillar rose up from the sea. The fiery shaft twisted and boiled and was gone. Ben had to look twice.

'Does it always do that?' he asked, 'don't remember it doing that.'

'Jacobs ladder,' said Ruth quietly. She took a big mouthful of whisky and handed it back to Clorinda. Ben crashed the fags. He'd started the night with sixty but they were almost gone. A finger breadth of the sun appeared making the sea suddenly dark against the pink blue sky and the singing faded away. Eight Gannets in an off centred 'V' dashed low across the waves in front of them. As the choral song faded away the seventh wave crashed hit the shore with a soft rolling roar.

'Why do they call it Love?'

Chapter Eight

Angus and Ben sat on the wall of Tiny's house looking at Angus's car. Angus's dad's car rather. This wasn't something they would normally do. Both thought the lime green Chrysler Alpine one of the worst cars in the world. However it could carry four people in relative comfort, it kept the rain off and so consistently won over Ben's moped, no matter how heavily Ben claimed the latter was modified. It was really good of Angus's dad to lend his son his car. There were of course strict conditions mostly focused around not changing the shape Chrysler had intended. The pair were looking at Angus's dad's pride and joy very carefully.

'I don't think he'll notice the scrape, do you?' stated Ben. 'A wee bit of mud on it, he'll never see it. Probably.'

Angus had stopped looking at the car and was now looking at the smouldering ash wasteland that was his future, 'He is going to kill me.'

'We'll take the tyre to Kwick-Fit. They'll fix it. I'll split the cost with you. It'll be fine,' Ben pushed himself off the wall and rolled the deflated tyre to the back of the car. It had gone square on one side so it rolled and stopped, rolled and stopped. Ben heaved it into the boot, slammed the hatchback down and watched Angus still sitting on the wall with his head in his hands.

'After the blow out I was sure we were going through the bridge,' Angus continued to block out the world. He drew a huge breath and let it out shuddering. Ben wondered when was the last time he had seen Angus cry, part of him wishing he could do something, part wishing he was somewhere else.

'It was a great piece of driving. Main thing is we are still alive. I better go in and see how the girls are doing.'

He rested his hand on Angus shoulder for a moment. In the distance he could see a suited couple working their way down the street door by door. Mormons, Jehovah's Witness? Ben suspected there a difference but wasn't sure what it was. Either way it was time to be away from here. He walked into the narrow dark hall of Tiny's house. It was carpeted in something deep and brown. A black nail and metallic orange string geometric picture dominated the space, seeming to leave too little room to get by. To his right he could see Ruth and Clorinda sitting bolt upright on the square tan couch, their knees together with mugs of tea held defensively on their laps. Tiny was curled up in the far chair staring at them like a cat at two hamsters, waiting for some sign of movement. Then he would...

'Everything all right?' Ben asked. Tiny snapped into a sitting position, his eyes flicking from the girls to Ben. There was a silent plea from Ruth that Ben couldn't quite get.

'That's the tyre swapped. I'm just getting a cup of tea for Angus then we will go,' he paused. That wasn't what Ruth had wanted to hear.

'Angus could really do with a cup of tea,' he added weakly. It was two steps to the kitchen, he lit a cigarette and then put it in the ashtray while he put the kettle on. Tiny came in, sliding himself up onto the fake teak work surface beside the cooker. He used to do it all the time when he was a kid but really he was too big to fit anymore.

'Ben. Good to see you,' he picked up the lit cigarette and drew on it, 'Very good to see you. Been a while.'

Ben looked at the fag in Tiny's hand and then lit another one for himself.

'Been a strange day. Lots of people coming to see me. I haven't seen anyone for a long time and then today I saw Angus, earlier. And then these two girls walked into the living room and sat themselves down with a cup of tea. Just came right in and sat themselves down right in my living room. Without a word. And they are it man. You should see them. They are absolutely stunning. A pair of stunners just walk into your living room and sit down with a cup of tea. Does that not strike you as weird Ben? Would you go and talk to them and see what they want? Maybe they would like to go for a drink. Would you like to go for a drink? And we could invite them out for a drink with us? They're not wearing a lot Ben, you can see everything. I mean imagination is not required. They might be easy, if you know what I mean. Some girls are like that. Although I don't seem to meet any. Maybe we could just stay here and see what happens.' Tiny rubbed his eye with the palm of his hand. The kettle had boiled unnoticed and Ben put it on again.

'Tiny.'

Tiny looked like a child as he stared back at Ben, his eyes as out of proportion as a Japanese Manga character. It was this look that had kept him out of borstal all these years. 'Tiny, you really don't recognise them do you?'

Tiny was unsure how to respond so said nothing, though his legs began to swing.

'Those girls are Ruth and Clorinda. Clorinda is going out with Angus. Ruth is my girlfriend.'

'Of course they are. Sorry, sorry Ben. Of course. No offence meant. I just got a wee bit distracted seeing them out of context,' he looked away towards the hall.

Ben finished off the drinks and put the teabags in the sink. Tiny looked back and smiled nervously. 'No offence, they just surprised me. Aye, surprised. Where's Angus then?'

At that point Angus walked in to the hall, waved at Ruth and Clorinda and stepped into the kitchen. He signalled with his oily hands at Tiny, 'mind if I wash up?'

Tiny shrank back under the overhead units and shook his head, 'You carry on Angus. I was just saying to Ben here what a weird day it is. All sorts of people turning up.'

Angus went to the sink, squirting Fairy Liquid on his hands.

'I think you're right Ben. Car doesn't look as bad as I thought.'

'Trouble with your car then Angus?'

Angus and Ben exchanged looks, Tiny seemed oblivious.

'You should have stuck to bikes man. The chicks are always interested in a man with a bike. I'm telling you man, I've got two girls in the house right now because I've got a bike. What's up with your car?'

Angus dried his hands and took a sip from the mug Ben handed him. He drew breath to answer his brow furrowed when the doorbell rang.

Tiny shot up and caught his back on the edge of the wall units.

'Fuck's sake!' he collapsed briefly, an arm trying to reach his damaged back. He straightened looking at both Angus and Ben. 'Fuck that hurt. Did you do that?'

'No Tiny,' Angus said quietly. 'There is somebody at the door. Someone rang the doorbell.'

'There are too many people here already. Fuck.' He stepped out of the kitchen, arm still ineffectually flapping around the growing red stain on his t-shirt.

Angus put down his mug, 'I really think we had better go.'

'You okay to drive?' Ben asked

'Oh I think I've just realised how fine I am.'

'I'll go get the girls,' Ben stubbed out his cigarette and went toward the living room but stopped in the hall. He could see the two Witnesses on the path, sunlight streaming behind them they looked more like FBI agents.

The man was asking, 'Is your mum or dad in?'

Tiny filled the doorway, 'No I'm on my own.'

The woman glanced at Angus and Ben.

'My name is Phil, this is Marianne.'

The woman smiled warmly. 'Hello.' Marianne said brightly. 'Do you have someone in your life? Someone to guide you in your way forward, someone to protect you in the challenges of this world?'

'Protect?' Tiny's head went to one side. 'Protect? Do I need protection? You want to know if I'm protected?'

The man took a step back into the daylight, he glanced nervously at Marianne. This wasn't following the usual script. They were used to disinterest in all its various forms but here was something different.

'We have been sent to bring the Word to you,' said Phil.

'You have been sent? Which word? What the hell does that mean? There are lots of words. Thousands of them. Which word would it be. Is it a trigger word? Something that's going to get me to kill myself again? That won't work you know. I'm too strong for you and your word.'

Tiny's voice was getting louder. Ben looked into the sitting room.

'Time to go,' Ben said to Ruth and Clorinda. Problem was there was only one way out.

'Who sent you? Although I can guess.'

Phil looked really puzzled now. Marianne laid a hand on his arm, she looked frightened.

'God sent us,' she said, her voice wavered as she tried to sound calm.

'You think Rhino is a god?' Tiny was shouting now. Both Witnesses looked back at the road wondering how it had come to look so far away. The man laughed nervously at the bizarre accusation looking around for the hidden cameras.

'We don't know Rhino,' managed Phil.

Detached Ben watched Tiny's thin arm snap forward, there was a loud crunching noise as the man's nose split. He staggered back dazed, his arms circling slowly for balance. Tiny stepped into the gap hitting Phil's face again and again. The woman began to scream as her companion fell to the concrete, Phil's face a bloody mess. Tiny dropped one knee onto the man's chest, there was a rotten cracking noise as something gave way.

Marianne hit him with the bible in her hand. Everyone, including Tiny, seemed to expect smoke to rise from the point of impact. Tiny twisted round snarling, he drew back one bloody fist and sank it deep into her stomach. Marianne reeled back against the white board fence. It collapsed with her as she went down. Tiny stepped off the man, kicking him in the groin as hard as he could. Phil groaned, rolling up onto all fours, throwing up a mixture of blood and vomit. Another kick followed.

Ben's rugby tackle took Tiny past the wreckage of the fence and out onto the road. Ben was aware of the ferocious blows from Tiny but didn't really feel them as he fought through the flailing arms trying to get a grip of something solid. Something that would stop the punches, the hate, the anger. Suddenly the hitting stopped and Ben was aware of someone screaming, the high scream of a girl. He looked round for the source.

The man was still on his hands and knees a waterfall of red slime slowly cascaded from his face. The woman was on her side gasping for breath like a just landed herring. There was a ragged slash where one of the nails from the broken fence had torn through her hand as she had scrabbled away from Tiny.

'Ease up Ben I think you've broken his arm.' He could hear Angus' voice but not see him. Ben realised his right eye had closed up from a blow. He looked down at Tiny, face down on the white stoned tarmac. Tiny's left arm folded back almost to his neck as he howled with pain.

'You can let go now.' But Ben couldn't, he wanted to, but couldn't. If he let go Tiny would start hitting him again. Ben blinked with his one good eye trying to see Angus, get some reassurance. He started to release the twisted limb. The screaming subsided and Ben could hear now the sounds of sobbing from the garden, and Ruth and Clorinda back in the house, on the phone getting an ambulance.

Tiny rolled over, still pinned by Ben. His face was scarlet with blood but Ben couldn't see a wound. Ben's own blood dripped from somewhere above Ben's eye onto Tiny's T-shirt. Suddenly angry again Ben punched him on the shoulder.

'What the fuck was that for?' Tiny asked, aggrieved. Ben raised his fist again. 'They were trying to kill me man!' Tiny's voice was small, barely audible, but full of self-righteousness. Ben sat back. He couldn't breathe, hawked and spat blood and snot onto the road. Tiny continued his defence, 'They are ruining my life, they made Alison hate me, they've taken my friends, they drove me out of school.'

Ben leant forward, his weight on his left arm, and pointed his finger an inch away from Tiny's angelic, wounded face.

'The only person who has fucked your life up Tiny is you. Not your parents, not the teachers and certainly not Alison. Just you.' He heard a siren wail somewhere in the distance. He had to turn the top half of his body to see Ruth. She was trying to separate the woman and the fence without causing any more damage. She managed a reassuring smile as she propped Marianne up.

'They said the police would have to come too.'

Ben nodded and stood up, stepping back from Tiny who tried to get up.

'Stay there, you've done enough damage,' Ben half shouted. The sirens were getting louder.

The Incapable was a sprawling pub down by the loch side. Its main attraction was that it was out of the centre of town which meant it didn't attract that many visits from the Police. This in turn meant that the staff took a more relaxed attitude over the age of their clientele than anywhere else in a ten-mile radius. It was the place where Ben felt that he had grown up. There was a disco hall at the back where he had briefly tried dancing, the table football where they had scored for Scotland against a visiting team of Norwegian sailors and the various dark corners where he had gone for a grope, a slash or thrown up as circumstances dictated.

Being Wednesday it was a quiet night. Now that he was eighteen, Ben was experimenting with social drinking. It certainly had a novelty factor, although Ben felt that since they could now imbibe alcohol legally, the whole thing had lost a lot of its appeal. But he had discovered drinking socially also a lot easier on the pocket.

Angus was already in the Bar. It was the first time they had met since last Saturday at Tiny's. Angus had already ordered Ben a pint of Tennents.

'How you doing Angus?'

Angus carried on drinking from his pint but pointed at the other on the bar.

'That's uncommonly kind of you. Cheers,' Ben finished the pint and put the empty glass down. 'I needed that. First one I've had this week. How did your Dad take the news on the car?'

'Surprisingly well,' Angus chuckled as much to himself. 'I'm never to drive it again and I have to pay for the panel work and a new wheel and tyre but yeah, I'm not dead.'

'Heard anything about Tiny?' asked Ben.

'He's fucked man,' stated Angus.

'I think we knew that,' confirmed Ben.

'My mum does the admin in the Police office, Aye?'

'Aye.'

'Well Tiny has been explaining to the trick cyclists about how ever since Tiny has been going out with Alison that Rhino wants to break them up. He wants her, loves her, needs her. But every time he tries to put things right some outside force makes him blow it.'

'Rhino?'

'Is the right answer. Nothing mundane you understand. Rhino has been using his mind control technique to make him, Tiny, behave badly towards Alison. But since Alison really loves Tiny, true love triumphs and Rhino's evil plan is foiled. They are all set to get back together as they should be. Rhino in desperation uses the mind control on Tiny so that he kills himself.'

'I would have said he was doing a pretty good job of that all by himself,' Ben had finished his second pint and he hadn't noticed. This social drinking was trickier than it looked. 'My round then.'

'Remember we are deep in the Psyche of Tiny Gilchrist here. So Rhino is trying to force Tiny to commit suicide in a variety of ways. When that failed Tiny confronted Rhino with the fact that he, Tiny, knew the truth of his foul acts. Rhino was too frightened to continue.'

'Killing a chicken and throwing it repeatedly against my door would certainly have persuaded me to lay off any psychic experiments I happened to be doing.'

'All this is bubbling away in what's left of Tiny's mind. A cruel twist of fate means that the day we turn up with a dead car is the precise point at which a Jehovah's Witness knocks on the door. An evangelist ready to spread the Good Word and ask what is the purpose of your life. Tiny, already freaked out by us tramping all over his house, answers the door, sees the dudes in suits and sunglasses, and realises that Rhino has cast aside the subtleties of witchcraft and hired assassins to kill Tiny outright and seize the prize, Tiny's true love, for his dark purposes.'

'Shite. And he's explaining all this to the Police? What did they make of it?'

'They patted him on the head said it would be all better soon and carted him off to a padded cell in Lochgilphead,' Angus finished looking concerned.

Ben let out his breath, 'That's not funny, really. At all.'

'Certainly wasn't for the poor sod that believed he was about to save someone from their sinful ways.'

The last six words acquired an echoing quality as Alison and Rhino walked into the bar.

'What sinful ways?' Rhino put his arm around Alison and steered her towards the bar. He wrinkled his nose at the large number of empty glasses on the table, 'I thought we were going to take it easy.'

'What sinful ways?' Alison asked the question again. She clearly picking up the flashing neon 'guilty' signs flashing above the boys heads. 'If there is anybody being sinful round here I want to know about it.'

Rhino burst out laughing, it took years off him.

Alison turned round and winked at Angus and Ben, 'I'll drink to that.'

Ben was still chuckling at Alison and looking at her in a new light. His hand went subconsciously up to his right eye, it only hurt now when he smiled. He thought of Tiny and what the future held for him.

'When do you start at the Art school?' he asked Alison.

'I have been thinking about this. I'm going to take a year out. Chalk the streets, take the chance to see a bit of life before I get trapped in front of an easel.'

'You going too Rhino?' Rhino shook his head and managed to convey the idea that whatever his future held in store for him right then he didn't want to talk about it.

'Angus?'

'Piano maker. I've been accepted as an apprentice by a firm over in Edinburgh. What about you Ben?'

'Glasgow Uni have seen the golden opportunity they would be missing and let me in. Much to my surprise I'll be a student at Glasgow after all. I still can't really believe that that's school over and done with.' He raised his eyebrows looking into middle distance.

Alison looked around the bar, 'What about Ruth?'

'She might be going to Edinburgh to do Maths. Ruth, Clorinda, him,' he nodded at Angus, 'and me were going for a walk up the hill tomorrow but Ruth has to help her mum with something.'

'I can't make it either Ben. I'm on a very short leash till I get the bills sorted. And you offered to pay half I believe?' asked Angus.

'I did, didn't I?' said Ben. 'I'll see if my Aunt needs a hand at the shop and that should generate some cash. Shame I was looking forward to a swim in Craig's pool.'

Avoiding the boggiest parts Ben and Clorinda came off the hill too far to their left. They laughed as they hopped from clump to clump. He used every opportunity to hold her as they went. But he was so intent on his companion that they came out at the back of the reservoir and the old skating pond.

'Did you come up here when it froze in the winter?' Clorinda asked.

'We did. Even managed a bit of curling when no one else was on it. Didn't have proper stones mind. Just some rocks from the edge. It was good fun that,' Ben's voice trailed off as they walked and he thought about fun. The fun they had just had. And would they be having that fun again. Thinking about fun must have been written all over his face even though Clorinda seemed to be looking ahead.

She dropped his hand, 'It was good cool swimming today. In the pool.'

'Yes.'

'It was a shame that Ruth and Angus couldn't be there. Wasn't it.' Clorinda had made a statement, not a question.

'Oh aye, a shame. They missed themselves.'

They broke through a thin line of young Silver Birch and out on the road that would become the main street through the town. As soon as they hit the tarmac the temperature seemed to rise but at least they had lost most of the cloud of flies that had followed them hopefully down the hill. As they cleared the bottom of the reservoir, they passed a sign in royal blue marking the town boundary. It had been carefully repainted. Ben read it out.

'Welcome to Utopia'. Do you think whoever did that knew that it was the Greek for 'Nowhere.'? Or do you think he was just being ironic about our idyllic home?' Clorinda looked at him blankly.

'I'm hot. Have you got any water?'

Ben shook his head and missed Ruth. He was thinking you got a good view of the Sugar Boat from here. A small freighter, with a name Ben could never quite remember had got stuck on a sandbank in the middle of the Clyde. For some reason she had not been salvaged and lay on her side slowly working her way down the Clyde. An odd half ship marking the midway point in the flat plain of the firth. Chris had talked about taking them out for a tour in his dads boat. That might be more likely now that he and Clorinda might be...

And then he saw her, Ruth, trudging up the hill with four fully loaded Wm Low shopping bags. She was just about to turn left into Kennedy Drive. She stopped at the junction and looked at them. He waved. She looked. Clorinda and Ben finished their bouncy walk down the street towards Ruth. Ben dropped his gaze to make sure that he and Clorinda weren't still holding hands. When he looked back up he could see Ruth's face fixed in horror. The bags forgotten, resting on the hot black tarmac, sagging slowly on to their sides.

'We decided to go up the hill anyway,' said Ben.

'So I see.'

'Had a nice swim and just came back. How about you?'

'My Dad's left home. My little sister has locked herself in the toilet since last night. My Mum is in the garden burning his clothes. There was no food so I went shopping and now you, her, this.'

Ruth gathered the bags back up. One cucumber refused to go back in. Ruth threw the vegetable across the road narrowly missing a chocolate brown Saab and its surprised occupants. 'Bugger off.'

She turned and walked away along Kennedy drive. Ben watched Ruth go, unable to follow her, unable to help. Clorinda said something and then disappeared out of sight after Ruth.

Rocket Surgery

Interlude- Deep and Crisp and Even December 1987

After years of winter just meaning the rain got colder, snow had made a surprise return to Scotland. As usual it had teased at midwinter and shown a callous disregard of the hopes of millions of young Scots by skipping Christmas completely. But now, as New Year approached, the weather had turned Glasgow into a substitute Moscow. Ben met Angus off the train from Edinburgh and they walked through the city that had become a Bond film set, to catch the train back home.

'You look older Angus.'

'Thank you very much Ben. Good to see you have lost none of your charm. You are looking pretty shagged yourself.'

They walked down Buchanan Street, or rather slid, as the day had stayed so cold that the snow had refused to melt and so was just being pushed around from pile to pile leaving a thick film on the roads and pavements.

'Shagged is one thing I haven't been. I've been off woman since Ruth.'

'That's three years man! Seriously no women since then?' asked Angus.

'It's not been that hard.' They both smiled. 'Erectile dysfunction is no laughing matter,' Ben continued. 'No it's just that I fucked up everyone's lives so badly that day. You know?'

'I know but I've got over it.' Angus shrugged. 'I think she had already lost interest in me by that point anyway.' And they walked briskly to get to the relative warmth of the station and a train to Helensburgh. 'Is that why the low profile? Like three years of seriously low profile.' Angus asked as they stepped on board the train. The seats were covered in a strange brown striped material that seemed to be the extent of the refurbishment of the train. But at least the seat didn't sink all the way down to the heater or smell of warmed piss. Angus passed Ben a Regal Dinky and they lit up now that they were out of the cold.

'Yeah sort of. Lot of guilt stuff flying around and I thought it would be easier if I was elsewhere.' Angus drew on his cigarette and looked out on the already darkening sky as they pulled out of the Queen Street station, snow whirled by the window out of an already dimming scene. They sat in relative silence as the train rocked its way through junctions. After five minutes Ben picked up where he had left off.

'There have been a couple of moments where I could've, should've, would've. But I don't know, couldn't, shouldn't, wouldn't.'

'Fair enough man.' Ben suspected Angus could out chill Chris these days. Ben wanted to ask Angus if Ruth had been a similarly tormented soul but really couldn't face the answer, which in all likelihood would be a 'no'.

'How is Glasgow University?'

'It is doing very well.'

Angus smiled weakly, 'And you?'

'Oh I'm fine. Angus. I have managed to get a couple of exemptions, so as long as I keep my drinking under control we should be good for a piece of paper.'

'And what then?'

'Doing the milk round at the moment. That's where companies come round looking to recruit the best and the brightest...'

'And you.'

'...to come and work for them. They seem to be mostly English though.'

'You have to go where the work is.'

'Yes. There is a company based near Windsor that made me an offer.'

'So you will have the Queen as a neighbour. What kind of a job?'

'Customer Co-ordinator,' Ben said with an air of mystery.

'Which is?'

'No idea but it's £6k, a company house and there is an option to get on their management training programme.'

'Brilliant.'

'The only worry is they seem to advertise in the Herald every month.'

'Is that a bad thing?' Asked Angus.

'It either means they are expanding, which is cool. Or they lose staff as fast as they get them. Which would be bad.'

In the absence of any offer otherwise, Angus passed over another Regal.

'Thanks Man. Hopefully I can borrow some money before we go out tonight.'

'I hope so too,' Angus said with feeling.

'How about you?' Ben finally remembered to ask. 'How did it go with the piano tuning thing?'

'Fantastic. It turns out there is a worldwide shortage of piano tuners.'

'Who knew?'

'Indeed. And it also turns out I have perfect pitch so now I am an excellent piano tuner with a declining amount of competition.'

'That is indeed excellent.' Ben was struggling to think of an original positive word.

'So I have been earning money for the last year and a bit. As long as I make it clear I'm still not qualified then the school are very happy for me to build up a business.'

Ben broke into a smile, 'That really is excellent Angus. I'm happy it's worked out for you.' He watched a gloomy Clyde slide past, looking for the outline of the Sugar Boat somewhere beyond the condensation fogged windows. It had been a while since he had call for so many positive words, he could see he was going to have to remind himself of a few more before the evening.

The Incapable was packed; Helensburgh's adventurers returning from across the land with flaming brands and tales of triumph and the world beyond. Ben returned to his corner of the seating carrying three pints, one for him, one for Angus.

'And the third is for?' Angus asked.

'Sorry I was bit distracted. Stuart greeted me like a long lost friend,' Ben looked back into the throng but he saw Rhino and Alison instead. He put down the drinks.

'Pint there for you Angus. Great to see you both. What are you drinking Alison?'

Alison went to kiss Ben while he tried to shake her hand, 'Good to see you Ben. Cider please.'

He noticed Angus managed a Hollywood air kiss without conscious effort and Ben slunk back to the bar cursing his own social inadequacy. As he settled into the long wait at the bar, he found himself looking as more people packed in to the bar, watching the mix of hugs, kisses and slaps going on. When did all this social interaction start? And how did he miss it? Through all of this movement and bonhomie, Ben noticed a still point at the far end of the bar. A gaunt version of Tiny was there shredding the label off a bottle of the King of Beers while he met his own dark stare in the mirrors behind the optics. Ben looked back at the woman behind the bar.

'A pint of cider,' Ben said quietly amongst the shouting, pointing rather than speak up and risk discovery. While he waited Ben found the pressure growing not to glance right. Would Tiny see him and come over? In his mind's eye, Tiny was now standing inches away staring at the side of face, waiting for him to turn and recognise him. Show Tiny some kind of recognition of the friend he once was. Ben couldn't do it and stared at himself in the mirror behind the optics hoping Tiny was still doing the same.

Back at the table they were deep in conversation. Even with all the noise they looked conspiratorial but Ben put that down to paranoia. He slid the cider over to Alison. She was looking from between Angus and Ben a question formed on her lips but unable to depart.

'What?' asked Ben.

'Is it true you haven't been seeing anyone since Ruth?'

Ben tried to give Angus a Paddington stare but since Angus's shoulders were going up and down so hard he was either going to laugh or explode it wasn't having any effect. Rhino was just smirking. Alison reached across and patted his arm, 'that's sweet.'

'Stupid,' said Rhino. 'What's the point of going to Uni for three years if you are not going to take advantage of all that...' Only at that point did Rhino's brain engage that Alison was sitting next to him. '...nice young ladies.'

'I'm not saying I couldn't have done. Just that I haven't,' Ben tried to think up something witty to show that he wasn't bothered but he couldn't get past 'Fuck off the lot of you.' Which fell short of the repartee that he felt was required. 'Anyway I know all about the piano man here. What have you two been up to?'

Alison took a long sook from her pint of cider leaving Rhino to pick up the slack.

'I have joined the Ministry of Defence Police.'

'Mod plod. Excellent,' Ben cursed his shrinking vocabulary. 'Doesn't that mean you get a gun?'

'It does. I have received firearm training. But it's more than that. I was down in England for four months getting my basic training sorted. And then it's six weeks teaching us which end of a gun to point at the bad guys.'

'That's slightly scary Rhino.'

'Actually it's fine. They train you so hard that it really is fine. They get you ready for anything.'

'And now he is guarding the Peace Camp at Faslane,' commented Alison. Rhino wrinkled his nose which took Ben straight back to his school days. 'The Police keep moving tinkers up to the camp and then all the CND folk complain that the gypos are stealing everything. Rhino has to go in and sort all of them out.'

'It is good work. Got me fit,' Rhino winked at Alison in a suggestive manner.

'And what about you Alison?' asked Ben wanting to move on quickly.

'I'm still drawing but to get some money in I'm working as a care nurse up at the Home at the top of Sinclair Street?'

'Enjoying it?' Ben asked.

'No. It's washing old dears, helping them to the loo and it can be quite horrible. But the care part is lovely. So I have started a couple of SVQs that should get me where I want to go. Less changing nappies, more interesting things like getting them on a better diet, looking at using exercise to get up here,' Alison tapped the side of her head, 'working better. I want to get more involved in that if I can.'

'Great.'

'And it means we have been able to buy a wee flat on Clyde Street.'

'That seems amazingly grown up.'

'Ben,' Angus interrupted.

'What?' Ben asked. It was clear that Angus had changed his mind about whatever he was going to say.

'Nice to see you out. It's been too long,' Angus looked round the table. 'Same again?' All of them nodded.

'So,' Ben was focused on Alison. 'Have you seen Ruth? At all?'

'We kind of lost touch after school. But no, not for over a year. She was going out with a solicitor. Nice bloke, old. Nearly thirty I think. But he turned out to be married. Ruth wasn't very happy and broke it off. He arrived on her doorstep in Leith saying that he had left his wife, and his job and that he was ready to move in with her.'

'Blimey.'

'She closed the door on him and left him sitting on the step with all his bags around him crying.'

Angus was back with a tray.

'Have you not seen Ruth?' Alison asked Angus. He looked at Ben and then back at Alison.

'Eh no. Edinburgh is a big place.'

Alison gave Angus a big false smile, 'Thanks Angus. I wouldn't have thought that was possible. You big city folk.'

After that the evening picked up pace as various folk from various years joined them, caught up on the news and drifted away again. Clorinda wandered passed in a killer red dress that had Angus looking wistful for a moment. She talked briefly of her new life in Stirling, starting out with on a fast-track management program with a bank. It was clear that although they had made it as bit parts for her life so far they would not be getting a call from casting for her second film. Ben hated to think how he had looked as she paused on her triumphal tour round the bar before moving on and out of their lives for a final time.

Rhino had a stream of stories about the interaction of the LGB and Traveling communities up by the cornerstone of Britain's Nuclear Deterrent which had Ben was laughing so hard he couldn't see for tears.

'So anyway, there we all are with the full gear on, guns, torches, helicopter on its way. And this lezzer is balanced on the top of the wire fence holding onto the MacDonald's Balloon saying 'I only...'

'Nice to see you all enjoying yourselves.'

Tiny stood at the end of the table not only impervious to the good cheer around him but seemingly illuminated by a different, less effective, light source. Angus recovered first.

'Tiny, didn't know you were here. Please, come and join us,' Angus shuffled round to make room.

'Bit late for that,' Tiny looked round each of the group with his sunken eyes. Ben was expecting resentment or bile or anger but there was nothing in those flat eyes. 'Happy New Year when it comes.'

Tiny turned his collar up and walked through the crowd and out the door.

'I didn't know he was here,' Angus said, in a way that Ben would swear was genuine.

'I did,' Ben admitted

'Yup.'

'Me too.'

'What do you say to a man who has lost everything?' Rhino asked. They sat for a moment sharing in the gloom that Tiny had left them. Ben let out a breath.

'So how did she get off the fence?' Angus asked.

ROCKET SURGERY

The Tomorrow People

Chapter Nine June 1988

As Ben walks it is difficult to remember that he had been full of life, enthusiasm when he'd first come to England. Even the name of the company says it all - 'Tomorrow'. How much more full of promise could it be?

The Tomorrow office had started out as an open plan apart from the office across the stairs which didn't count. The MD, Hermione, sat at her desk, the same size and shape as the rest of us. As promised it was a new beginning. A new attitude to corporate life where the boss would sit with and understand the frustrations of the telesales person. Everyone was to be equal, apart from the MD, Hermione. She didn't have to be equal as she would provide 'Vision'. Everyone was trained to help in sales, stores, customer service and accounts. Everyone worked for the good of the Team. The Thermometer, the Monday Morning Meeting, was the focal point of that Team. Every employee in the company would be there to express themselves. How they felt angry when somebody said this. Or delighted when Steve helped with that. Or even how good it was that Helen had got back with her ex. We all share the experience of being part of a Team, reworking the essence of office.

However the Office Manager, once there was one, felt that she needed an office as she had to have lots of motivational chats with people. In order to make sure they were motivated. That was Joan. But that was okay since that was really no more than a formal acknowledgement of the role she was already fulfilling. Joan wanted everyone to be motivated, and focused. Focused on their personnel success and motivated enough to succeed. A rewarding place to be really.

Joan needed light to keep herself in tiptop motivational gear so they built her office up against some of the windows. Then the Marketing Manager, Clare, needed an office as very often she would be in hostile negotiations with the suppliers. Or, worse still, in deep conversation with the product marketers over in Flagstaff. This tended to be mainly about why the hell our product was still in Arizona rather than with our customer. Or why the stock that had been the stock we thought we had ordered was in fact the stock that had been sold to some dude in Minnesota and the replacement stock would be twelve weeks and twice the price. In those conversations, harsh language was often required. So to keep Telesales motivated another office was built beside the first.

Finally Hermione, obviously conscious that there was only one potential office space left and that the Finance Director was circling the spot, looking wistfully at the chance of getting out of accounts, sealed the fate of the last free windows in the office. And with it the last of the oxygen supply. Ben remembered looking up at the skylights, cunningly designed to let the sun in, but sealed so they didn't let the heat out. For a while the office baked and complained that it would be much better if they could open the skylights and let some air in. Eventually they painted them white instead, the last opaque glimpse of sky gone.

It was a cool place to be, just not in a physical sense. Slough wasn't cool. It was hot. Actually it was so hot Ben questioned wither Scotland really ever got hot in an English sense. There seemed to be an entirely different heat scale in this part of the UK. He also learned that when it was hot the office was not the place to be.

Business attire had started as smart casual. Smart casual had been shed as the temperature rose. Davie used to come in a 2000AD 'Beware Illegal Mutant' T-shirt and shorts. It wasn't pretty and Ben hadn't been able to eat chicken drumsticks since. The phones kept ringing though, the future was calling them.

Hermione had spotted two trends and created a winning strategy. One; being the late Eighties the labour pool was full of overqualified and very cheap labour from Scotland and Ireland who couldn't find work at home. Two; property prices in the south-east were only going one way. To capitalise on these two simple certainties Hermione built Tomorrow up by hiring a continuous stream of graduates from the Celtic fringe, intelligent and eager to work for peanuts, and housed them in a cul-de-sac that Tomorrow had bought and furnished as a job lot. The profits rolled in. Since the houses in 'Brookside' were heavily subsidised, the salary became, effectively, beer money. Joan later had the idea of encouraging some of the Field Sales, who failed to have Vision, to go look elsewhere and this left some spare cars that became house-cars. This encouragement meant that Tomorrow could pay the staff even less since they now had a car as well as a house provided. Every few months another set of fresh-faced Paddy's and Jocks would sit through the four-week course on how to become a Tomorrow person before being launched out into the Team.

The fact that all the houses were kitted out exactly the same - both in terms of furnishings and occupants - increased the sense of dislocation amongst the staff. This unexpected side effect made it all the easier to imprint the Tomorrow Vision on them, and people were often found working six or even seven days a week in order to keep up with the workload. It was all a bit chaotic but still exciting. After Saturday night's dislocation session, Ben's head was a bit chaotic too.

'Hello I'm Ben,' he was sitting at the table with a copy of the Independent, a bowl of Alpen and a fag he had stubbed out half way through.

'Davie,' said the man on the other side of the table. Who was reading an old Economist and applying Marmite to a large stack of toast. The toast and Alpen were consumed in silence. 'Interesting choice of paper,' commented Davie.

'I'm not sure I like it. I just the need to read something and this seemed to be the least likely way of offending anyone.'

'You keen not to offend anyone then?' asked Davie as he tossed a king size Regal across the table.

'Always happy to cause offence but I want to know that I am doing it. Thank you.'

As they both lit up a woman walked through the kitchen and put the kettle on. She turned and leant on the kitchen unit with her arms folded. She was wearing a t-shirt which was long enough to be decent as long as you knew all the people in the room well. The three looked at each other. It was Ben that broke the silence.

'I think this is 27 and therefore I'm in my house. But since I have seen neither of you in my house before, I'm less sure about that than I was.'

'I think this is 26,' said Davie. 'The odd houses are orientated the other way. You can tell from where the fridge is.'

The woman smiled, 'This is 26. I'm Siobhan, one of the new management trainees. I arrived here last night.'

The accent was strong. Irish but Ben then didn't know enough to pin it down further than that. Ben and Davie waved their hellos. 'I thought all the houses, odd and even, were non-smoking?'

Ben winced through the smoke in his eye, 'Not so far. At least 27 isn't. I don't feel I can speak for 26. Is that a problem?' he asked Davie. Both Davie and Siobhan shook their heads in time though Siobhan's hair followed later.

'Fine, just a little early for me. Anyone else want a cup of tea?' Nice Irish, not the scary, shouty Irish you saw on the telly bombing each other. Ben groped for a better description, Southern Irish.

'No thank you. But at least I now know that I am in the wrong house,' he looked at the paper which said Friday, 'but I'm really holding out for Sunday morning.'

'Yes it is,' Davie said. 'Good night last night then?'

'I have no idea. Look I better go back to my own bed and start again. Fancy the pub tonight? Siobhan ? If it's your first day tomorrow at Tomorrow then it would be a good chance to get to know some folk?' He left the question there.

By the time they had walked out to the Dumb Bell, they seemed to have gathered most of 26, 27, 29 as well as some of the older hands who had scraped enough together to live somewhere else. 28 had said they were revising for the training tomorrow and didn't want to come out and play. Nobody ever invited 30, ever. The pub itself seemed a little overwhelmed by the Celtic tide and hung on to the bar muttering 'Sweaty Socks coming down here to steal their jobs, and our women.'

'I think you will find we seem to have brought our own,' Davie waved at the assorted beauties around him.

'Actually,' Siobhan interrupted, 'I think you'll find we brought ourselves.'

Sweaty Socks and Bog Trotters were all too much for the locals and they withdrew into the darker corners to play dominoes. There was a pub quiz machine which provided the focus for the evening. With an average of slightly more than one degree per person, the machine soon had its back against the wall financially as well as physically.

Ben was on his third or possibly his fourth beer and lost the concentration required for the academic mugging.

'When you think about it. We haven't made that much progress from our ancestors.'

He had ended up talking to Davie and a girl that was mostly a ball of white hair and very large glasses.

'How do you mean?' The girl's accent was English which threw Ben a bit after most of the conversations he had had today. But still, he was in England so he should make allowances. And she did appear to be attractive. Actually she seemed to be friendly which was probably distorting his critical faculties.

'All of us here. Scots and Irish. Our grandparents or whatever would be living in tied cottages. Trapped. Can't save because the salary is lower due to the accommodation.'

'You're right Bob,' Davie said. 'I've been down here for nearly a year now. It's hard to save for a house. Impossible. And if I leave this job then I lose my house as well. I would be back home planting spuds.'

Ben leaned on the girl before realising what he was doing and pulled away, 'Sorry. I was just thinking; our ancestors-' Ben pointed between Davie and himself, 'had their lives based around potatoes. Whereas we.' He did the finger waggling thing again. 'Working for an electronics company. Our lives are based on chips.'

'Don't give up the day job Bob,' Davie clapped him on the shoulder and moved off through the crowd. The English girl laughed though. Ben wondered if it was too late in the conversation to ask her name.

Chapter Ten

There was an exciting buzz in the Tomorrow building. Ben had really been marking time till the Fast Integrated circuit and Semiconductor Training was about to start. In order to get everyone in tip-top training condition, they were flying in some of the best product marketeers in the world to get everyone up to speed. Then there was a detailed training programme on sales. Tomorrow had developed a magic script that would make any Electronics Buyer putty in your hands. And it would all be theirs. Cue evil laugh.

First though, it was a state of the art computer system specially developed for Tomorrow and the UK was going to be the first place where it rolled out. The training room was filled to capacity; well beyond capacity actually as new and old employees waited excitedly for this premier system to be unveiled. Ben noticed that Davie, Steve and the other established company people were at the front, leaving the new folk to try and arrange themselves as best they could behind. A powerfully built black girl and another with mousey brown hair were talking to Davie and glancing darkly over to Ben.

'Good morning everyone.'

Joan, who had been helping out with some of the basic training, was standing at the front beaming at everyone with a wave of love. She looked like she wanted to hug everyone in the room in a friendly, almost maternal, way. Clare who was head of the UK Product Marketing Team was standing behind her looking less cuddly and more embarrassed.

'Good Morning.'

'Settle down please everyone,' Joan said with a motherly twinkle. 'I know that Hermione, (that's our MD),' she said for explanation to the back of the room, 'was planning to be with us today to say a few words to us all but unfortunately she hasn't been able to get back from Arizona as planned. She will be on the plane tonight with the rest of the Fast Integrated Circuit and Semiconductor Training team. So you will have to make do with me.' A wave of appreciative noise washed through the room.

'So the new IT system will form the core of the new operation. The new way of working that will allow us to outgrow the industry. Nancy will you take over?'

A small lady with a sharp bob suddenly became the focus of everyone's attention just as she was struggling with a monster 17' monitor. Several of the blokes at the front lurched forward and then stopped, unsure whether helping was allowed in a liberated egalitarian world. Hamstrung by correctness the entire room watched the lady with a television representing fifty percent of her bodyweight stagger into position. Ben became conscious of just how close they all were to each other, physically as well as part of the Vision.

This particular IT Manager didn't look very happy, like she hadn't quite seen the Vision clearly yet. She switched the monitor on, and Ben could see little orange characters start to gather in various parts of the screen. She kept looking from the screen to the large crowd and back again.

'This isn't really big enough,' she said.

'No,' agreed someone from the crowd helpfully.

'We could try and hook it up with one of the portable projectors.'

Portable was a loose description, applied to the company projector in the same way as it could be applied to a 150mm Howitzer. Aware that the chances of it working, and being the right way round before everyone had lost the will to live were slim, Joan said very firmly, 'That will be fine. Nancy.'

The IT Manager met Joan's gaze for a moment before straightening up and addressing the mob,

'Right, attention please! What we will cover today is the creation of a new customer account. This is very simple and has been designed to capture the information on your Tomorrow customer cards.'

There were general groans.

'Which you have all filled in, eh Davie?' Joan tried to skewer the Internal Account Manager with a malevolent stare. The groans faded away.

'So, first you select 'Create New Account' from the menu, and that will drop you into a series of structured questions. Can I have a Name?' she read out for those more than twenty four inches away.

'Helen,' said the small mousey haired woman who was, presumably, Helen.

'No! Name of the customer.'

The IT Manager looked out a sea of dimly-lit but blank faces.

'I'll put in Test for this one.' The machine beeped unhappily. 'Ah, so, you won't see this page. The coding isn't quite right, so, because we already have a Test account, then it's dropped out here.' Her fingers flashed across the keyboard, appearing to type in a hundred commands in a few seconds. There was a pause and the machine beeped again.

'So, we'll just pretend that what you see now is the address field, which you fill in as on your cards. Don't forget the phone number. And we have added a space for a Fax number if they have one yet.'

She turned back to the terminal and typed again at a nosebleed-inducing speed, 'Put your contact in this field.'

It beeped again.

'Ah, I put in my boyfriend's name, but I forgot it has to be less than twenty characters. He's Polish. Anyway, you put the name in here, and then the time each week that you have agreed to call him.'

The collective 'Huh?' from the room impressed Ben with both its inarticulacy and universality. Joan tried her third death look of the morning at the hapless IT lady and stood up, facing the room, 'I haven't had a chance to tell you about that yet. Sorry,' she made an odd bobbing motion while she laughed in a self-deprecating way. 'been very busy. Anyway, I thought it would be a good idea if we put a reminder to call your favourite customers in the machine. That way you wouldn't have to remember because it would remember for you. All part of helping you perform better you see.'

'So,' said Nancy looking at the back of Joan's head with an interesting expression, 'we put that information in there. Only it won't look like this. The layout will be better, for some reason this still has the last software revision on it. Anyway. After that, all you need to do is raise a quote by putting in part number, quantity and price.'

There was another beep, more plaintive this time it seemed.

'Ah yes, it will also check the stock automatically. It will show the UK stock here and the US stock here. Escape out of that, and type the information in here. Then get the pricing from this table here. The part number search doesn't work yet, so you will have to look through the list again. Escape out of that, and there you have your quote,' Nancy pointed at two parts of the warmly-glowing screen. From this distance she could have been pointing at the results of the 2:15 from Doncaster on Teletext.

She typed furiously again.

'Okay, the link seems to be down at the moment. But when it is up, it will auto-populate all of this. And then, and this will make it all worthwhile,' she promised, trying hard to keep her audience with her, 'you select this option and you convert the whole quote into an order without having to retype it.'

This time there was a murmur of approval round the room.

'That bit is good,' Ben found himself saying to Siobhan who was looking more sceptical than Ben would have believed possible during your first month at work. She nodded in a reluctant way. Out front, Nancy soaked up the surprise favourable reaction, and then went a step too far and pressed what must have been the order option. With a loud 'pink', the distant screen went dark. Nancy stood with her finger on the Return key, obviously looking for the 'I'm really sorry, I didn't mean to press that last button' button.

Joan was back on her feet.

'Thank you, Nancy. Very impressive, marvellous and will save us a lot of work,' she looked at her watch with exaggerated care. 'Right, twenty-minute break, and then if we can have the new people back in here, then Clare can start her training.'

Everyone shuffled out of the room and Ben found himself walking into the girl with brown hair before he could get to his quad. She didn't look friendly.

'These new quads kill the sound remarkably well,' she said.

'You managed to make that sound really threatening.'

'It's meant to. I understand you took an interest in Debbie last night?' she asked. Ben looked blank, which he was good at. 'Lots of hair, big glasses.'

'Oh yes. And you are?'

'Her friend, Helen. She's been through a lot and is vulnerable at the moment. I just wouldn't want her to get hurt by some newbie out for an easy conquest.'

'That really wasn't the plan. I don't think I touched her.'

'Well she said it was full body contact.'

'I bumped into her once.'

'Thought you hadn't touched her?' Helen's eyebrow rose to a level of scepticism that Siobhan's whole face couldn't match.

'I'm not going to convince you but I have no interest in Debbie.'

'Keep it that way. Newbie,' Helen walked back to her own desk frowning as she went. Ben sat down rather heavily at his desk. He counted days out on his desk-pad calendar. Never had the end of his probationary period looked so far away. He leaned back in his chair and rubbed his face. Not a good start.

'What's up stranger?'

Ben looked through his fingers at a well-groomed young man. Black hair combed away from a tanned face and clothes that Ben didn't even know you could buy outside of a film set.

'I appear to have made an enemy of Helen.'

The man smiled and sat on the desk. He shook his head but still smiling said, 'I wouldn't have done that...what's your name?'

'Ben. And you are Steve,' he held out his hand which the man shook.

'Yes. Don't worry. Probably not life threatening unless it was to doubt Our Glorious Leader. What did you do?' he asked.

'I am accused of trying to snog someone called Debbie.'

Steve held his hands out each side of his head, 'Lots of hair Debbie?' he asked.

Ben nodded.

'Did you kiss her on the lips?' Steve asked very seriously.

'I don't think so.'

'Then it might not be too late to save you,' Steve smiled again and looked like he was going to pat Ben on the head. 'Debbie lives with Catherine and is Helen's best friend. She used to work here. Left about six months ago after breaking up with her boyfriend in stores. We never found Grant's body so you should be careful.'

The following Monday they were issued with Customer Folders where you wrote all the details in pre-printed fields on the outside and kept all your bits of paper inside and no one mentioned the IT system again. The MD did come back but the Product Marketers had had to stay in Flagstaff due to renewed focus being required there. Clare and Catherine picked up the slack with a huge stack of acetate slides that showed you more than you would want to know about Logic Gates, EPROM and RS232 Connectors. A lot of people washed through the company, most left including Siobhan but some stayed. Ben really started to enjoy himself.

Chapter Eleven

'We were Tomorrow people. We were the best.' Even in the heat of a Slough summer he had great technique. He would take the call, hunched under one shoulder as he wrote out the number on a scrap of paper. In the absence of a functioning computer system, run to one of the two microfiche viewers. A fiche was a micro-dot style sheet of information best viewed through a projector microscope. It was amazing how long the 'gone fiching' joke ran. These little spy documents were shipped out from the States every two weeks. If you were unlucky you would end up with information a month old. It made quoting stock less of an art form - more divine inspiration. Find the right sheet out of thirty and the right line out of three hundred. Write down what you had gleaned on what free space was left on your bit of paper. Dash back to the phone lying on the desk and stab uselessly at a solar powered calculator trying to work out what price to quote. Ben always managed to get the order though. At one point somebody in the Thermometer had suggested runners for the best telesales so that they could be even more focused. But it was felt, especially by the potential runners, that that wouldn't be very motivational.

Living in Brookside was still a bit wild but it did mean there was always a social life just a step away. Sometimes not even that. Living with all the people that you worked with, pushed them out into Slough where at least they could meet people that they did work with but didn't live with. This was viewed at the time as a step forward. Alcohol did play a big part in this wider social circle and there were few places better for Alcohol and circling socially than Sneaky Pete's.

Ben had fallen onto the floor of Sneaky Pete's once. Well, technically, the table they had been dancing on had collapsed; others glided away like surfers, but Ben had gone down like a poorly-tossed caber. The carpet he hit had soaked up years of beer and alcopops, judging by the smell, both before and after consumption. This potentially lethal glue, combined with the large amount of Pernod and black he had already imbibed himself, meant that he had no option but to stay where he fell. It had been Debbie that had peeled him off sometime later, although in the darkness and confusion she had stood on him first.

A good night, that. It had started a lot earlier than usual. About two in the afternoon, in fact. The whole company had decided to go bowling. Team building. There was some attempt to roll balls down the aisle, hit the pins at the end, that kind of thing. There was Accounts, irritating everyone by working out all of the scores in their heads and being serious about knocking down the pins. There was the traditional sliding halfway down the track after the ball. There was the forgetting to let go, resulting in the ball crashing to the floor and a stern talking to from the staff. Mostly, though, there was drink. Hermione had really picked up on the cultural model of 'We work hard but we play hard,' and it was practically compulsory at Tomorrow but compulsion wasn't part of the Vision. People thought it really was a valid business model. Maybe it was. It was certainly a lot of fun.

By the time it was five o'clock, the balls were going in any direction. The last of the scores were being totted up before anyone started talking about law suits. Ben couldn't work out why team building always seemed to involve competition. He was working on his own score: 'I think you're wrong, Steve. I think it was six Buds, then I switched to Pernod and black, and I have had' - he paused to count the glasses - 'Six, seven including the one that she took away.'

Steve shook his head and emptied his Bud, 'I've matched you drink for drink, and this is my eighth Bud.'

Frowning, he reached for a spare bottle, not sure what this meant for the sums. Ben felt a cool arm round his shoulders. Catherine grinned at both of them, 'Fancy Sneaky Pete's? Helen, Joan and the gang are up for it. You coming?'

Ben took in the mention of Joan, but then looked around at the group. Few of those not already slumped in corners looked like they would pass muster, even at Slough's least desirable nightspot, and he said so.

Catherine said, 'It'll be fine. They are always desperate to let girls in. No one in their right minds goes to Sneaky Pete's. And there will be eleven of us and they can't afford to turn away that much business this early. Besides, it's a normal bar till seven,' she shrugged, 'Once you're in, you're in.'

Steve emptied the latest bottle and put it down slightly too hard on the glass table, 'I'm in!'

Ben returned Catherine's smile, 'I'm always on for a party. Seen Davie?'

'Oh, he's going,' Catherine looked across the room. Davie had been circling Helen all afternoon. In a nonchalant, casual kind of a way, a friendly, passing for a chat kind of a way. Just never in a close enough to have that deep conversation followed by the desperately-yearned-for kiss, kind of a way, 'Helen asked him.'

'Ooooh,' Steve and Ben hammed it up like schoolgirls while picking up their jackets. 'Tonight could be his lucky night,' Steve managed to scoop another half-bottle of something off a table on the way out.

Ben was laughing as he followed him out, 'There is no way you're going to catch me up, my boy.'

The Tomorrow people burst noisily out from the Super Bowl onto the late afternoon high street. Ben had only hazy memories of that walk. Tight, in both senses of the word, the Tomorrow party splashed into a bustling street full of shoppers trying to get their film into Boots before it shut. It made for a very uncomfortable mixture. The youths of Slough looked on confused. Surely it was their job to be loud and offensive? It hadn't occurred to them how effective singing 'New York, New York' and 'My Way' with volume and swagger was as a means of intimidating those around them. The youths shuffled, uneasy at the sight of other people, older people, doing their job so effectively. Demarcation, Ben thought, being a child of the Seventies; but it would take ten of the bush-dwellers to spell it and even, he thought, they would probably come up with a type of brown sugar.

Ben hadn't done anything as trippy as that walk since Chris had driven them back from Glasgow. Lucky there were no dead chickens at the end of this, just the night club Sneaky Pete's, which always looked slightly uneasy in sunlight. This is possibly why it became a night club. It was shut, the coherence of the group wavered. A few of the stragglers saw their opportunity to duck out. Joan quickly corralled the slow-witted into the Pig and Whistle to wait, and have the odd beer or three. Ben much to his surprise found himself next to Debbie.

'Where did you pop up from?' asked Ben, only fairly sure she hadn't been at the bowling.

'Why? You been avoiding me?' Debbie asked back. She was grinning in a fragile way and Ben couldn't resist looking around to see if Helen was near enough to stab him with a mixer straw through the back of the neck.

'No no, just busy.'

Her smile relaxed but only a bit, 'Buy me a drink then.'

Ben did.

By half past five the first bouncer of the evening was out, and the group shambled out of the bar. Ben's conversation with Debbie had gone well, he thought, maybe a bit over-earnest, tempered by the thought that Helen might ritually slaughter him in the middle of the pub. But now he'd lost her, Debbie that is, and somehow had ended up with Steve and Davie as they approached Sneaky Pete's. Ben hated nightclubs. He had never really got the hang of them. The thing that he really didn't understand, though, was that no matter how indifferent he was about the idea of a nightclub, the closer he got the more desperate to get in he found himself. The mysterious force drew them towards the magical tunnel and its guardian troll. As is traditional, the troll didn't look very happy. But women know how to handle trolls. Helen looked back through the group: 'No! Split the boys up!' she hissed. 'Too conspicuous like that!' Davie was shuffled forward, Ben back.

'How many of you?' asked the Troll. Ben suspected this was not so much an opening remark but more of a plea for help.

Joan engaged the man with her biggest, warmest smile, 'Fourteen. Mostly girls, and we're here for a quick drink before we go home.'

'Know we'll have to throw you out at seven? We've got a very strict dress code.'

'Yeah. No problem. We'll be long gone by then.'

Joan and the first wave of the party rushed up the stairs.

'I haven't got a dress,' Davie's voice cut nicely across the afternoon traffic. He had his arm around Helen in a way that indicated he really wasn't aware of what his body was doing; Helen seemed quite aware, and comfortable. Steve started to laugh. Ben rolled his eyes: Davie had been tricked into speaking English by the border guard; for him, the escape was over. Ben hoped he didn't drag the rest of them down with him. Ben wondered if mixing metaphors was an inevitable consequence of mixing drinks.

Davie carried on digging, 'No, really I haven't. The kilt's completely different.'

The bouncer's brow furrowed. He wasn't too sure what had been said, but it sounded foreign; possibly even Jock, and therefore a likely source of trouble.

'You can't come in like that. We don't let football strips in at any time,' the bouncer straightened up, comfortable now on the firm ground of a definite rule. Confused, Davie tried to focus on the one article of clothing he was proud of: the red and white hooped shirt proudly bearing the crest of the Orkney Rugby Football Club.

He protested, 'It's a rugby shirt.'

The bouncer was a rock: 'Don't care. You can't come in a football strip. It always starts fights.'

Davie held up his hands, 'Oh aye,' Davie, high on life, tapped the side of his nose, 'You'll have a lot of lads in from Shetland tonight. Understood. Not a problem, my good man.'

The bouncer took a step forward, sure that he was being mocked, just not exactly how. Davie unhooked himself from Helen and stepped out of the queue, 'Could get messy; a bit excitable, Shetlanders. Go on in, folks. Have a nice time. I will see you Monday.'

Steve was bent double with laughter. The bouncer, now in his stride, rounded on him, 'You're not coming in neither.'

Steve paused, visually checking his outfit: loose white cotton shirt, chinos, good tan, great hair, and the epitome of good taste, 'Why?' he asked, looking genuinely puzzled.

'You are not getting into my nightclub with those,' he pointed down at Steve's feet. Where there should have been a pair of brown Armani loafers, two-tone red and blue leather shoes did their best to reflect the smogged Slough sun.

It was Davie's turn to hoot.

'Bowling shoes! Top man. I'll come back with you, since this twat clearly has no taste,' Davie's accent had left the bouncer way behind, otherwise an offer of pain would surely have followed.

Ben, Catherine and Helen were the only ones left yet to go in. Helen said to Davie, 'I'll come with you too,' and looked like she meant it. Davie looked back, and Ben wondered if he was just now registering how things had been going with Helen tonight. Davie's eyes seemed to fill with tears; he smiled and said, 'Don't be daft. See you Monday. Come on Steve. You should keep those, they suit you. Could set a new trend.'

Ben watched the two weave back into the crowd. Helen didn't move to follow.

'You coming in or not?' asked the bouncer who had been joined by his twin. From the new arrival's winning smile, Ben suspected that they had been dealing with the happy troll all along.

'Shall we, ladies?' All three gave a final look back, but the two dapper men about town were already out of sight, and they climbed the stairs. Debbie was waiting at the top of the stair well.

'Dives shouldn't be upstairs, surely,' Ben said to her and she laughed. It was bad luck for Steve and Davie but Ben couldn't suppress a grin. It should be a good night. He could see the rest of the Tomorrow people across the dark dance floor; the music was already pounding. He got to the top of the stairs and stopped: not that he wanted to, he just suddenly had to concentrate on lifting his feet. He shouted into the dim light, 'The floor is unbelievably sticky. Anyone falls on this and they're dead.'

Chapter Twelve

They hadn't gone back to Brookside, they had gone somewhere else. That had been a mistake. The party had carried on with lots of Tomorrow people and lots of people who weren't Tomorrow people. After a while a few of them settled in a room with a large telly and something dodgy from Channel Four. Ben sank into the old couch. It was very old and he sank quite a bit. The three other occupants of the room were focused on the telly leaving him free to look around as he slowly settled all the way to the floor.

'This a Red triangle film?' Ben asked the room.

'I think they stopped doing that years ago,' Debbie said, curled up at the other end of the couch. Ben's impression in the flickering light from the television was of a mass of white blonde hair held in place, in part at least, by a pair of huge seventies glasses. White fluffy shirt and black leggings completed the ensemble. The scarlet lipstick was the only thing that attempted any colour but even that was washed out by the blue glow from the TV.

Catherine's brother John laughed his way through the room. John, huge guy, made his sister looked like she just had a tan. John's main focus was to have a good time and get laid and he was always happy to help others in similar pursuits.

'Do you want a joint?' John asked. Ben cast his mind back to happy afternoons sitting up on the grass bank with Tiny, Rhino and Angus.

'That would be good. How much do I owe you?'

John looked a little hurt, 'Nothing for a friend.'

Ben still didn't take what looked like a white cigar.

'Honestly.'

'Cool. Thank you,' said Ben who took the monster joint and lit it. 'Cool' he repeated. The thick smoke curled round his face filling his nose and mouth. Ben rather fancied he could feel it working its way through his ears as well. Ben blew out slowly trying to remember the last time he had had a joint. It certainly wasn't like this stuff. Whatever resin had made it as far as Helensburgh had been cut so many times it had the narcotic power of tea. Finally Ben understood the meaning of the phrase 'good shit'.

'Straight off the boat,' John flashed a brilliant smile as Ben's transparent thoughts stumbled across his forehead. Ben went to hand the joint back. John held up his hand, 'Enjoy.' He laughed and moved away.

'Cool,' repeated Ben taking another draw. He watched the whirling fans on the electric fire trying to replicate flames. But it was too regular, you could work out the pattern in seconds. With the joint triggering associations, Ben remembered the fires on the hill with Tiny, Rhino and Angus. Flames leaping into the night sky, sometimes green as the copper in the paint burned. Badly cooked sausages and being chilled to the bones in the morning. But the fire. The fire was nothing like this.

'You all right Ben?' It was Debbie, he remembered, a friend of Helen. Some part of his brain that was still doing a good job added that last part in. She was lovely, very lovely. Helen wasn't lovely, well she was but only lovely in the same way that a tiger was lovely. A loveliness that also contained bone-breaking teeth and tearing claws. Debbie didn't look dangerous. But she did look interested which Ben had always found attractive in a woman. He could feel the normal personal space requirement between him and Debbie had vanished. You could just fall into the space. He was conscious that he hadn't said anything in response to her question but had just been smiling back at the fire.

'Me and this fire have seen a lot of things together you know. The stars. The improvised explosives. The sausages.'

Debbie looked at the bad plastic fake wood effect complete with spinning convection fans. Ben took the opportunity to look at her, a lovely face, what you could see of it anyway between the glasses and the Persil white hair. Garfield, she was really into Garfield. When she saw that cat her face lit up and she looked like an angel.

'I really have to go. I have had way too much of this,' Ben said quietly, she looked back from the fire and smiled, brushing hair that had fallen around her face.

Ben took a long draw of the joint and then offered to her while he held onto the thick smoke. She took a puff but coughed up more than she inhaled, 'a little strong for me.'

Ben took it back and tried to focus on it, 'and me. So you here with Helen?'

Debbie lit a B&H and shook her head. She let the smoke ease out of her mouth in a way that made Ben think of Helen Mirren.

'She and Davie left a while ago. I think they said there was a party up in town they were invited to.'

Ben looked back at the fire. There was a vague sense of sadness at not seeing Helen or was it not seeing Davie. But he had his old friend, the fire and his new friend Debbie. 'Cool,' he said smiling at them both. A friend. He could have a new friend, and he wouldn't want to do anything because Helen would...

'Is he all right?'

Ben could hear the voice from far far above him. Just fine Ben thought. I don't seem to be able to move any of my limbs but fine. Debbie had been stroking his forehead earlier and that had been mighty. He must have oozed off the couch as he was lying on the carpet in front of the fire. His head to one side but he couldn't move. Couldn't speak he discovered. Someone had cut all means of communications out from of Ben's brain to the rest of the world. He should really panic but he didn't have the energy. Those Fourth Years had finally had their revenge.

It was dark, cold, hard, a taxi? Someone was reassuring someone else that he wasn't going to sick. Was he? Dark again, warm, lovely and warm, with a really heavy never ending duvet pressing down on him. There was somebody in here with him. Lovely and warm and in bed but not home, then. Huge eyes staring at him, unblinking. He reached out and stroked its fur. Someone pressed up close, the feeling of skin on skin. He was rolled on to his back and he felt the weight of the other holding him down from head to toe, mouth on mouth, hips on hips. They started to roll over again but hit a wall. Someone laughed, Ben didn't think it was him and distracted, it all went dark.

Ben struggled for a moment in that classic 'where am I' moment. This moment though appeared to show no signs of coming to an end. It was warm and dark and soft. He could hear a radio somewhere in the distance. He separated out the soft into two or three huge fluffy pillows under his head and some monster tog duvet above him. That would explain the warmth too. His desire for air overcame the dread of light and he pushed back a corner of the duvet for some oxygen. Garfield stared disapprovingly across the pillows. Fur, good, not mad then.

The voices were clearer though, laughing, not radio but two girls talking, one excitedly. He rolled over to the wall and the window above the bed pulling aside the dark blue curtains. Ben cried out in pain at the mass of light that resolved itself into a jumble of sky, houses, anaemic municipal trees doing their best despite being snapped off where the support pole ended. He fell back onto the bed, bouncing three or four times like a car whose shock absorbers have gone.

'I'm in a fluffy bouncy hell of my own,' he put his hand to his pounding head, 'and I'm fucked.' The word triggered something. Small snippets of the night before started their own flash advertising campaign. 'Not good.' One of the messages from his own frightened subconscious got through. Debbie in the light of the digital clock riding him for all he was worth. It kindly pointed out that his tongue had been hanging out while she did so. That can't have been a good look.

He went back to the window again trying to make sense of what he saw. The window was propped open by an inch. Should he just jump now? A trifle melodramatic. His clothes had clearly been thrown against the far wall last night. Move fast, grab them, out the front door, dreadful mistake, terribly sorry.

Footsteps on the stairs. Ben sat frozen, pulling the covers under his chin for protection. Rational thought beyond his battered mind, he stared as the door was slowly pushed open by a tangled mass of white hair and smoked glasses. Debbie looked surprisingly cute in a giant white towelling dressing gown with a Garfield complete with towel and toothbrush on the right hand side. She held a tray of tea and toast in her hands, stepping hesitantly into her own room.

'You're still there!' the statement was as much question as exclamation. 'I was wondering if I'd dreamt it.' She put the tray down on the bed and sat beside it blocking all hope of escape. She beamed at him in such a way that Ben felt like a new kitten, fresh from the box.

'I can't believe I've got you,' Ben nodded, he felt pretty much the same way. 'This is the best thing that's ever happened to me, the best.'

Ben struggled with that one. Debbie pushed some of the hair out of her face so that Ben could see the trepidation, the fear of rejection.

'Oh I know you're not meant to say things like that, you're supposed to be cool. But I can't help it, I'm just so excited,' her shoulders went up in a girlie shrug and then she leant forward and kissed Ben, open mouthed for a second, then pushed herself back upright off his chest.

The primitive Ben, obviously still functioning just as well as it has been last night without him, noted that her gown had come undone and suggested that perhaps they could enjoy the tea a bit longer. However the shrapnel that formed what was left of sentient Ben, was overwhelmed by the stupidity of what had happened. Debbie beamed at him, Ben braced as he thought she was going to squeal with delight again.

'Look. Thanks for the tea and, like, everything,' Ben waved his arms around ineffectually. He watched in horror as the happiness evaporated in Debbie. She started to collapse, no longer capable of bearing the weight of her dressing gown. He took her tea off her before she dropped the cup.

'It was a brilliant night,' he reached out and cradled her cheek in his hand. Her eyes closed. 'You are lovely.' She looked up through moist eyes. Ben looked for somewhere to put the rescued cup, nothing solid within reach. He struggled to get his right leg to the floor. It hurt but he shifted his weight anyway to kiss her, 'Lovely.'

He let out a small gasp of pain and looked down at his foot where a plastic brush had dug in deep enough to bleed. Ben pulled the brush free and kissed her again. This was Ruth all over again. This was what he had been trying to avoid for years.

'I need to go; I have to get some things sorted. But I'll see you tonight.'

Debbie nodded, looking hopeful now. Ben had sounded like he meant it. Even Ben thought that he sounded like he meant it. He quickly pulled on his clothes and stumped down the stairs. Catherine stood in the hall, leaning against the door frame. She had a Mona Lisa smile and her dark eyes gave away nothing. Her finger however pointed at the far end of the hall.

'The way out,' she said quietly.

'Thanks,' Ben found he had to drop his eyes and bumble through the house to the back door. The garden took four long strides from Ben to cover. Out past the gate and onto the street. He kept rolling through the waves of nausea trying to get out of sight of the house. Dizzy he walked into a lamp post and held onto it, his stomach bunching for a leap, as everything swam. He threw up into the rose bush, only after looking around to see if anyone had seen him. Catherine quietly closed the door to the kitchen.

'That went well.'

CHAPTER THIRTEEN

Ben had gone straight home and sat staring out the window for the rest of the day trying to work out what had happened. The next day work beckoned, which wasn't as relaxing as he had hoped. There had been enough people that had seen him at various points in the evening that they had pieced together a fairly good idea of what had occurred. Since he was struggling with large bits of it himself he found the process useful in parts, up until the part where Debbie had been spotted trying to stuff Ben into a taxi like an un-cooperative bean bag.

'I'm really sorry I missed it,' Steve smiled at Ben and Davie.

'I'm glad my social difficulties to have provided some diversion.'

'What did happen after you were poured out the taxi at the other end?' asked Steve.

'I am too much of a gentleman to discuss that.'

'It can't have been too much,' Catherine had snuck into the kitchen quietly and had been making a cup of tea. Ben almost leapt away from her but she sat against the kitchen units and smiled over the top of her cup. 'The ragdoll I saw would have struggled to raise a smile.'

'You were there?' Steve asked Catherine.

'I was, I didn't want to get involved but Debbie needed help to prop him up between the giant Garfield and the enormous Odie.' Ben felt the blood drain from him. 'Ben fitted in perfectly. Luckily he still had his clothes on at that point.'

'And?' Steve was determined not to let this go.

'And nothing. Debbie was so happy to have added to her toy collection, Ben here started drooling which kind of went with the 'Odie's new pal' look and I didn't feel the need to hang about.'

Ben looked for a sliver of sympathy in their mocking smiles but comfort there was none. In his mind's eye Ben could see now the legion of stuffed animals bouncing off the bed as Debbie made the most of his one working part.

'Lucky escape for you though Ben,' Catherine continued, 'if you had taken advantage of Debbie, Helen would have your balls dried, hollowed out and made into a pair of maracas.' Catherine left the kitchen still smiling.

'That reminds me,' said Steve, switching attention to Davie, 'I hear you two headed off for parties elsewhere. How did that go?'

'Really well, I was glad I circled back.' Davie said, 'Me and Helen. On our own at last. A party, the man of her dreams.'

'Which wasn't you?' Steve asked.

'Huge fellow,' Davie held both arms out trying to invoke the Terminator but in reality closer to a strong domestic cleaner. 'Just huge,' he looked distraught.

'You two should have come with me. Two nights in Brighton. Absolutely fabulous,' Steve offered. Neither Davie or Ben seemed too keen.

Ben spent the next two days in Stores. Arthur was the most non-judgemental person Ben had ever met. It was either that or the simple fact of him being downstairs meant that he was impervious to all the malarkey going in the offices above.

'I don't really care why you are here Ben,' Arthur was shorter than Ben but much wider and still managed to put a comforting arm round Ben's shoulders as he steered him to the prep area. 'Always glad of the help.'

'It's all right Arthur I haven't killed anyone,' Arthur looked very seriously at him for a moment and Ben found himself wondering how many times Arthur had had that conversation with someone who had.

'I know Ben. I just want you to concentrate on this for a while. Most folk find it quite therapeutic,' Arthur smiled reassuringly at his use of the word. 'Let me show you around.' The stores were quite small but the idea had been that most of the stock would be held on the other side of the Atlantic, ready at a couple of hours' notice as the Twentieth Century drew to a close. 'You see,' he waved his arm across the gleaming stores, 'all of these,' Arthur pointed to neat rows of boxes, each holding hundreds of small cardboard sheets, 'these stock cards match what is held in stock in the US. I get a fax every morning that tells me what has been sold. It means I can manage the stock that's physically here and held over there for us.'

He looked at the cards like they were his children.

'When Hermione said that I finally had the chance to organise stores the way I wanted I thought she was kidding. But she wasn't. After watching all those mistakes, all those missed opportunities I get to build a system that's as good as I hoped it could be.'

They paused for a moment and smiled at each other.

'She is quite something,' chimed in Ben.

'Certainly is. She is why I am here. Right let's get you strapped in?'

Ben was jolted out of his happy reverie, 'Eh?'

'Anti-static straps. They go round your shoe,' Arthur passed over some nylon and steel webbing. 'Stop you blowing the product? Have you not done store training?' Arthur asked.

'Well you know. I was meant to but there was an empty sales desk and a target to hit and I never got the chance after that.'

'Well. The good news for you is that there are some new folk starting today. Company Orientation with Hermione today and then I have them for three days on part numbers and store management. I think Clare was meant to be doing her introduction to Product Marketing but that will be delayed till next week. You come back down with them tomorrow morning. That will work out really well, you know all the about the product so you can help them while you are all helping me.'

Arthur held his hand out to recover the straps, 'tomorrow then?'

'Okay.'

Ben wandered back upstairs. The Thermometer Room door was open so Hermione must have finished the first part of her induction. Joan was standing outside of the toilets waiting to take them round to meet the teams. She picked them off one by one as they came out.

'And this is Ben,' Joan waved cheerfully at him. Eyes as bright as a button. 'I was wondering where you had got to. Phil, Ben. Nula, Shaun and somebody you might know.' That meant the third person was Scottish, Joan worked on the principle that all Scottish people knew each other and was surprised when they didn't. The new BBC weather maps had only confirmed what she had previously suspected, that Scotland was a very very small place tucked on the top of a very large England.

'This is Ruth McCarthy. She is from your home town Ben.'

Ben looked at the toilet door and Ruth standing in it. She looked older, her hair had grown, her eyes were just the same as the last time he saw her, disappointed. Behind her he could see the Clyde and the sugar boat on its side in the sun and Clorinda standing too close beside him with her bra hanging out of his pocket and neither of them had said anything for far too long. Joan looked from one to the other, brightly, expectantly.

'Ruth,' was the only word Ben could manage.

'You two must know each other then,' Joan stated

'We didn't know each other at all. As it turned out,' Ruth said flatly.

'Different schools,' agreed Ben, 'and we were a lot younger then.'

Ben stumbled back to his sales desk and sat down. He picked up some customer cards and shuffled them and then put them back in their hanging files. He ripped off the top of his desk jotter and started transferring any useful numbers from the old one to the new one. Every time he heard the Thermometer room door open he found himself looking up to see if he could see Ruth and locked eyes with Helen instead.

'I can't believe you tried to sleep with her,' she hissed. Ben looked completely blank for a moment till he realised she was talking about Debbie, not Clorinda. 'She was getting herself together and since the weekend she sits her room and cries.'

'I didn't try…'

'I don't believe that for a second Ben. You just couldn't help yourself could you. Some girl offers herself up and you just can't say no.'

'I couldn't…'

'That's what I thought,' interrupted Helen, 'I am surprised you are shameless enough to admit it though. Bloody men!' She stomped off to the toilet, her heels leaving little bullet holes in the carpet. Ben tore the desk pad up and threw it in the shred box. And then realised he hadn't transferred any of the numbers off it. He rested his head on the desk.

CHAPTER FOURTEEN

Ben had got into his stride competing with Davie and Steve for the top slot in Sales. Who was going to be the top Tomorrow person this month? Ben had worked his way into contention pretty quickly and after that it was a three way fight every month. Internal competition was good for motivation, but so was the money: having been in at the beginning they were now on a straight 3% of what they sold. Later arrivals weren't on such good terms, as economic realities had bitten into Hermione's ideals. But the stress of staying on top was getting to them.

Hermione was out, seeing a customer, and that was always cue for things to get a little strained in the office. Joan cruised past Ben who had been avoiding Ruth, and Davie who was trying to do the opposite with Helen by hanging around her desk, and said,

'Shouldn't you to be on the phones?' Davie clicked his heels together and said, probably too early for her to be out of earshot,

'Ja, mein oberfuhrer.' He looked at Joan's disappearing figure: 'When we started this company we weren't going to have middle managers, I'm sure.'

Helen glanced over at the empty MD's office and said loyally, 'you know there was a good reason. Hermione just had too broad a reporting structure. She had to bring in some changes. She was very clear at the time that it didn't in any way reduce our position in the company and that her door was always open.'

Once there was a door thought Ben.

'The whole company relies on us to be self-motivated and professional. Joan being Office Manager doesn't change that.'

'It'll be Team Leaders next,' Davie smirked

'Hermione wouldn't do that,' Helen snapped.

Ben left them to it and made it back to his desk before Joan rushed past again, back toward her office this time with Ruth in tow, glowering at all her self-motivated and professional staff. Since Helen had kindly told Ruth about Debbie, Ben usually found it was frostier in the office than outside. Steve came back from the toilets, laughing quietly to himself. The office was cold, but Steve's considerable forehead was beaded with sweat. When he sat down, the lights picked up the veins throbbing on his temples. Steve clapped his hands together and, pulling the next quote from the top of the file, picked up the phone, still chuckling, ready to win another order and put himself back ahead. Ben glanced over to Davie who had been watching too. Davie put his forefinger in his mouth and pulled it out sharply. The 'pop' dropped into the office, hushed as an angel passed.

The sound drew Joan out of her lair, but just then someone who was passing the open door of Hermione's office glimpsed the outside world and said,

'Hey guys, it's snowing!' As one, everyone rushed towards the offices, with their precious windows, to catch a glimpse of this once-in-a-decade event in Slough. Joan, having drawn in enough breath to bellow the whole motivated team back to their desks, changed her mind in that instant and instead said, 'I'll go and see if I can get some mince pies, shall I?' leaving a stunned office silent but for the fax machines eternally emitting the R2D2 chorus.

Later, Ben wandered up to the meeting room beyond the stairs. It was deemed too far from the sales floor to be used as a proper office. Anybody marooned out here would have found themselves politically dead within a week. It was reserved now for private tears of frustration and reviews involving shouting along strictly motivational lines. It could also be very tranquil, away from the whistle and hustle of the main office. Steve was sitting there on his own. He'd pulled one of the chairs up against the window and was watching the flakes fall, entranced as a five-year-old.

'It's getting thick out there,' said Ben. Steve smiled but kept looking out the window: 'You never know, the dragon lady may not make it back.'

'I can hear an engine.'

'That's Davie. He's doing doughnuts in the car park across the road.'

Ben pulled up a chair beside Steve and sat staring out too. For five minutes they sat in the half-light of the snow watching a red Manta circle round the car parks pay machines. Apparently happy with a job well done Davie slithered back into the Tomorrow car park. Walking towards the office he looked up and saw his colleagues, threw a snowball at their window and disappeared inside.

Ben asked quietly, 'What's with Helen? She just about bit Davie's head off when he mentioned team leaders.'

'Well, Joan's not going to make her one, is she? And that would put another layer between her and her true love,' Steve said.

Ben, puzzled asked, 'Helen's not ambidextrous?'

Steve shook his head very slightly. He still looked very much the schoolboy hypnotised by the endless stream of giant flakes, 'No. I don't think so. I'm not sure Hermione is either. But Helen adores Hermione, that's clear. And more importantly, Joan is paranoid enough to think there might be something there, which could seriously undermine her new position. Anyone normal could see there's no threat from Helen, but Joan's probably ready to restructure the whole office to make sure nothing happened.' Steve made a sound of disgust: 'And then there is Ruth.'

Ben didn't move a facial muscle but Steve wasn't looking anyway. He continued.

'Joan seems so happy to have found a soulless mate. Everyone is so frigged up about their position in this company. You wouldn't think an organisation obsessed with equality could create a workforce so obsessed with status.'

'Yes it does seem odd,' agreed Ben.

'It's the blackball system. It just feeds paranoia.'

They sat side by side, still looking out the window. Ben found he was looking at Steve's face instead.

'Go on then, you can't leave it there. What blackball system?' he asked reluctantly.

'I thought you knew. Up till the end of your first year the company can just fire you without having to prove anything.'

'I've been through my probationary period,' Ben stated.

'Which is good. But you are not safe up till the end of your first year. After that, well they have to do all the verbal warnings, and written warnings and opportunities to improve and all of that. But before then, in your first year, they can just fire you. So at the end of every month the managers get together, look at the list of who's coming up to a year, and anybody who gets a blackball is out. No questions asked because it's much better to weed us all out then than to go through all that tedious due process stuff after the first year.'

'I didn't know.'

'Why do you think so many people have left? Siobhan, do you remember her. Said to Joan that she couldn't believe how bad the computing system was and that was it. Out.'

'And Hermione is all right with this? It just seems incredibly brutal.'

'It was her idea. Tomorrow is a company where the best will be very well rewarded. The unspoken flipside of that is that some people will not be the best.'

'You will be all right. You have Clare looking after you.'

'It doesn't work that way. All you need is one, black, ball.'

Steve's sentence slowed to a stop and they returned to looking out the window.

After a while Ben asked, 'Are you all right, Steve? The poppers in the bogs is a bit wild, no?'

'I'm fine. Amyl nitrate is harmless. It just makes it all a little more fun. Makes the day pass more easily. What's the harm in that? You've done poppers, haven't you?'

'Yeah, but not in the middle of the sales floor, man. You're sitting there with your foot on the brake and the accelerator at the same time. There has to be a cost.'

Steve's voice was still calm and neutral as he turned to look at Ben,

'How much did you have to drink last night, Ben? Or the night before? Or the night before that? You, me and Davie: we're the best here, and we're each frigging our lives up in our own way.' Steve paused, obviously thinking about what he had just said, 'Only I'm not. I'm fine. I'm in control.'

Ben looked back out at the snow. It had made Slough beautiful. No mean feat. A cherry red Mazda 323 saloon slid round the corner and came to a definite halt against the kerb, the left front wheel folded neatly under the car. Car and driver sat there, both deflated.

Ben got up: 'This is where your rough, tough Talbot Matra Rancho will come into its own. Can I get a lift home with you?'

Steve shrugged, 'The one day that you wouldn't have laughed at my car, and I walked in.'

CHAPTER FIFTEEN

'As the company has grown so quickly Hermione and I have been thinking...' Joan allowed herself a little giggle then at the idea of her being able to contribute to an idea that Hermione had had. The older team members laughed at this too, though for possibly different reasons. 'Have been thinking that we need to try and make sure that we keep strong the ideas, the values, that make Tomorrow such a special place to belong to.'

This made everyone sit up. A reshuffle was in the offing. Ben looked round the room at all his onetime colleagues and now competitors.

'At the same time we need to recognise that some specialisation is required. To this end I'm pleased to say that Catherine has joined Clare in Product Marketing.'

Ben felt a pang, to be away from the endless pressure of sales held its attraction. Those close enough passed on their congratulations without disturbing the room too much.

'As you know Hermione put me on a course with all the Founders to set our goals for the company. A Personnel Awareness and Development course that was just brilliant!' Joan threw her eyes heavenward to indicate the level of inspiration it had delivered. 'And we thought we should get a couple more on the course to try and get that positive energy out into the company. Two people to help me with positivity.' Ben realised that he was sitting forward just like everybody else in the room, even Steve and Davie who would have hated it, if they had realised.

'The role is to make sure that the Values that we have built up in Tomorrow are kept fresh and that they are continually fed back in to the company and the people that make the company what it is. The job title 'Value Trustee' reflects the importance of this role.' There was some rhubarb noises round the room.

'So I have picked one person.' 'Ruth' thought Ben. 'I chose someone who has been such a committed Tomorrow person since she joined the company, it's hard remember that it has only been a few months. Ruth,' she shrugged conspiratorially in Ruth's direction.

'And Hermione,' she paused for dramatic effect. 'Well she chose Ben which goes to show you can never second-guess her and what she is thinking and that's why she is so brilliant.'

She smiled sweetly at Ben.

'Bugger,' thought Ben. Steve and Davie looked like they were thinking that too.

Ben hadn't seen so much of them recently. With Ruth being in Brookside he had switched to the house in Maidenhead with a couple of the electronics engineers that no one else would share with. It meant he was only a moment's carelessness away from dysentery but he wasn't bumping into anyone. Which could have been sad but as he also hadn't resolved being used as Garfield's stunt double, isolation suited Ben fine.

Now though, Ben was trapped with Ruth for a week. So excited were the pair of them that when Davie came to pick them up in the Manta he had to keep up a cheerful monologue all the way to the venue. Ben suspected that even Davie couldn't be oblivious to the stony silence from the back seat and the staring into the middle distance from the front passenger. They pulled up outside the hall with a large sign that Davie felt the need to say out loud in case his two passengers had lost the ability to read as well as speak.

'New Life Programme- Build a better you. Is this run by Wayland Yutani then? If I had known I would have signed up myself.'

Davie wound the window down before he got out and pushed his seat forward so that Ben could climb out from the back. He got the two bags out of the boot and put them on the pavement.

'Joan was very clear you two shouldn't operate any heavy machinery after the course, so Helen will come and pick you up on Sunday night after you are all rebuilt and everything is spic and span.' he looked at Ben and Ruth and smiled. 'Well you two have fun. No problem at all giving you both a lift. I love being up this early. Not at all. My pleasure. Bye.'

Ben watched the red Opel drive away and then looked at Ruth. He could think of nothing to say that would make things better.

'Shall we go in?' Ruth asked.

'Yes. I'm quite looking forward to this.'

'I was,' Ruth picked up her bag and walked into reception. They dumped their bags in a cloakroom and made their way to a table looking for name badges. Instead a woman came out to greet them.

'You must be Ruth.' The voice was American, Ben immediately thought of Carl Sagan, only feminine. She gave Ruth a hug that was enveloping. Ben held his hand out but got hugged too. 'And you must be Ben. Welcome both of you. We all know here that when a company sends you on a course like this you will have a lot of doubts. I am here to take those doubts away. Have either of you been to a New Life Programme before?' Ben and Ruth both shook their heads. 'That's great. You guys are in for such a treat.'

She held both Ruth's hands in hers and looked deeply into her eyes, 'My name is Dawn. Dawn Sintani. You are going to have such a wonderful time.' She took them both arm in arm and led them into the hall where all the other wonderful people were.

There were a few warm-up exercises. Ben noticed that when Dawn was leading they seemed enhancing and real but when somebody else was corralling them in to being a tree he just felt silly. He found himself and Ruth sharing a couple of embarrassed glances. But then as he stretched into a wind battered Rowan on top of a hill, he thought of a wet bra hanging off him in the sun and wished it had been Ruth's.

Now that everyone was here, they had Dawn full time for the whole hall. She wanted everyone to concentrate on who you were. Not the work persona, or the home persona or even the persona that you told yourself you were. That was the one that was popular, made the right decisions and never procrastinated. Ben was that one all of the time. This first day was about the naked you. Not literally as it turned out, but Ben did think it was heading that way. They had split into groups and as the group started to discuss who they wanted to really be, people were collapsing in tears about their family life past and present. The group sat and waited for the next person to feel comfortable enough to speak. Ruth sat and looked at him through several of these and Ben had no idea what to say or how to read her impassive face. She coughed and they all looked at her expectantly. But it was Ben who spoke.

'I really don't know how to say this but I have made a real mess of things and I would appreciate your ideas on what I should do.' Ruth's face was frozen in position. 'I don't know where to start.' And, thought Ben, I don't know why I started.

'Well Ben. Sometimes that means that you are approaching the truth,' Dawn's voice felt like Irn Bru on a hungover mind.

'I had met this girl at a party. Actually I had met her before. And she was nice but I didn't fancy her. Really. But she was interested in me which was kind of fun. Anyway. We meet up at a party but I had way too much to smoke and blacked out. The next thing I know I wake up in her bed clearly the morning after the night before,' Ben mimed the moment of peering over the duvet.

'What did you do?' Dawn asked.

'I panicked. I hadn't planned to be there. I didn't mean to be there. But that's where I was. All my clothes on the other side of the room.' One of the guys smirked at that. 'But since then I have felt so guilty. I have felt really bad about it.'

'I don't see the problem,' the smirking guy said.

'I knew she was vulnerable. I had been warned and yet there I was taking advantage of the situation. Now she just sits in her room and cries and all the guys at work think I'm out of control. I've made that girl's life miserable.'

'You don't sound very happy about it either. You don't want a relationship with this woman?'

'No.'

'But you still slept with her?' asked one of the group sounding very unimpressed.

Dawn stepped in, 'Wait Melanie. Ben, did you say yes?' she asked.

'I don't understand the question?' said Ben.

'You said you blacked out. But this woman still had sex with you. Did you at any point say yes?'

'I have no idea,' Ben answered surprised at his own words. 'But does that matter? I clearly wanted to otherwise I wouldn't have been there. I wouldn't have been able to, you know, do it.'

'It's funny how the victim always blames themselves,' Dawn said.

Melanie snorted.

'Okay Melanie. If it the other way round and you had got so drunk you couldn't stand and some guy had sex with you while you were unconscious. How would you feel the next morning?'

It was Melanie's turn to look confused.

'But that's different,' Susan said and Ben agreed.

'Because?' asked Dawn.

'He's a man,' stated Melanie.

'Yes he is. And now we are starting the journey to work out what essentially being a man or a woman means.'

Day two was a lot more positive. It was about setting out your goals. What did you, the real you, want to achieve? Ben had gone into this thinking it would be easy but the group gave him a hard time over the large house in rural Oxfordshire, Renault 25 and clever and beautiful wife that had expressed concerns over Ben starting up his own company solely based around him having to hand his company car back. Ben was challenged to put aside the shallow and worldly badges of success. Where was his personal development? Where was the path in his soul taking him? Only by discourse with himself, or with the group if he could be that open, could this map be revealed and the deep progression begin. Ben sadly packed the clever and beautiful wife off in the Renault and walked down the long gravel path to the bus stop on the road while she phoned the AA. He took a last look back at the Manor and boarded the bus to Essentialism.

The third day was better; he really felt he was getting the hang of it now. In order to stay focused on what each inner person truly wanted to achieve, they each had to build their own totem. This involved a lot of cutting out pictures from a huge pile of trashy magazines and sticking them to a piece of four by four. Some of the more talented people, largely those men and woman with beards Ben noted, even started to carve their totem in the shapes of the Eagle of farsightedness, the Badger of determination and so on. At the end of the day each person on the course stood proudly beside their own physicalisation of the meaning of life and explained their Wishes, Hopes and Dreams to the collective. To Ben and Ruth, hardened veterans of the Thermometer, a WHD session was a walk in the park. Especially as they didn't have Hermione asking what they really wanted or, in Ben's case, have Joan asking why he hadn't done anything about it.

Day four started when it was still dark. They had all surrendered their timepieces at the start of the course but Ben was sure it was bloody early. He had woken with Ruth still curled up in a ball in his arms. There was no drool this time but Ben hadn't moved in order to make the moment last as long as possible.

'Good morning all!' came the chime of Dawn's voice. Ruth looked up at Ben and started.

'Morning?'

'Yes.'

'You okay?' asked Ruth. The temptation to kiss her was almost overwhelming. But this was not school. Ben wanted to get this right.

'I'm just a bit freaked out how much this course is changing my thinking,' he said, the thought coalescing about the same time as his sentence.

'Can you change your thinking?' asked Ruth. Ben thought of Rhino.

'Rhino always said he never recovered from the long term impact of Gormenghast.'

Ben felt Ruth laugh.

'We need to get back in touch with them. I hear Alison is expecting.'

'Blimey. That seems like, really grown up. Helensburgh feels very far away.'

'Okay people. We have a lot of ground to cover today,' Dawns voice had enough edge to get them moving. For the first time he saw that at least some of Joan's mannerisms were a pale reflection of Dawn's.

Ben felt the cold air rush in where Ruth had been and sighed. Day four blurred into a stream of master classes. The topic was the same: how they were going to achieve this wonderful life? What tools would they need to achieve what they had outlined?

The principle was very simple. Look at somebody successful. Both Ben and Ruth immediately wrote down Hermione and laughed. There is something about what they do that makes them successful. But it is not enough to copy what they do; you have to think the way they do. So Ben discovered he should take the real Ben as defined in days one to three, coral it up in a corner of his mind leaving the decks clear for the new and successful Ben. This Ben would be unlimited by all the worries and handicaps laid on him by his life experience up till this point. At least he would always have his Totem Pole as a handy reminder of who he was, or rather who he used to be.

Having learned the process in day four, day five, which ran on without sleep from day four, marked the transition into putting the new Hermione-Ben hybrid through its paces. Role-play was something that Tomorrow had encouraged. In fact Joan had the entire company doing this kind of thing every month in training. The Disinterested Buyer scenario 'I already have four good distributors why do I need you?' The Blinkered Procurement Manager. The 'Startled to meet a human' Engineer, and The Obviously Plain Evil Purchasing Director in black battle armour wreathed in shadow. Ben had taken them all on and won. Tomorrow tended not to focus on the 'Win-Win' model so much as the 'Crush your enemy, drive their cattle before you while you listen to the lamentation of their women' model. In this environment Ben had plenty of room to back off and still cruise to victory. Not that it was about winning.

On day six they were allowed a lie in. Ben remembered that morning. They had sat facing each other cross-legged. They talked about the old and the new. About their past lives and their future. About what they could do for Tomorrow now that they had all this potential at their fingertips. Finally the conversation turned to what had happened three days previously. It was Ruth that started.

'It is hard to try and split out all the excitement of being here.'

'Yes.'

'And us.'

'Yes,' his concentration was failing. They'd been talking all morning and Ben was dying for a fag.

'So you think we should leave it for a while and then see where we are?'

'Yes,' Ben's numbed brain replayed the last line. 'No.' This would be so much easier if he could just nip outside for five minutes. She smiled at the perplexed look playing across Ben's face.

'It is very confusing. We should wait.'

Ben didn't trust himself this time and just nodded and then shook his head.

'I think we could have something very special here' another nod. 'We should talk about it again next week end. Yes?'

'Yes,' more of a sigh of despair than a word.

'I will have a present for you then as well. I thought it was really nice that you still had the watch I gave you back home. But I thought you should have something to help you focus on the new you. And the new me.'

Ben raised an eyebrow.

'You will have to wait and see,' she kissed him on the nose and slid off the bed. He watched the outline of her jeans as she skipped out the dormitory.

'Does it get much better than this?' Ben thought. He lay back on his bed, hands behind his head. Ruth was just perfect. He had grown up enough to realise that now. He had the job, the money, a car. Not the Sapphire Blue Renault that he'd pasted on his Totem Pole but at least now he knew that was only a matter of time.

'Gotta wear shades,' he sang the tag line to himself. Ben snapped up to the vertical, 'gotta get a fag.'

That night was the closing ceremony. All of the people that had been on the course gathered in the main hall of the hotel. There must have been over a hundred there. First there were the testimonials. There had been six different courses running in the hotel that week. From elementary time management courses to the Paramilitary Fundamentalist improvement course that Ruth and Ben had just survived, there was a huge spectrum of development and potential. As the evening went on Ben and Ruth realised that they had covered in a week more than some had covered in a lifetime. But as the Master Ninja Black-belt students spoke they saw how far they could go. It was an incredible feeling. Ben kept looking at his fingers expecting to see sparks fly from them. He asked Ruth if she could call her champagne glass from the buffet table. She stretched out her hand first as though she could and then laughed, pulling his arm around her waist.

They started handing out little candles to everyone in the hall. The ceremony was running late, some of the drivers had started to arrive. Davie had turned up for the Tomorrow people. Joan's crash meant that no one was allowed to drive themselves back from these things. Too spaced out by what they had seen and done. Helen should have done this run but had refused to go anywhere near the place. The drivers were handed little candles so that they could share too. Ben shook Davie's hand. Ruth hugged him which left Davie looking at them both confused.

'Really glad you're here. I bet you can't wait till it's your turn,' Ben said. He missed Davie's response as the lights dimmed and there was lots of hushing until they were all standing in complete darkness and the silence was complete. Somewhere in the darkness a soft rhythmic voice began to speak.

'A long time ago people from around the world began to realise what the potential of a human being really was. These people were alone in that realisation. They were unique in their societies. In Egypt, in Babylon, Greece and Rome, in the Yucatan Peninsula, China and the jungles of Borneo. So similar were the ideas separated over space and time that people began to think that the source must come from one place. They were right. That place was called Atlantis.'

A flame appeared on stage lighting up the slim moon face of Dawn framed by her short black hair.

'You can probably do that after the Master Course. Light candles with the power of your thought.' mused Ben.

'But the real source was inside. Inside each one of us is the potential to reach that place. The light of Atlantis is where we can be without fear, without want. Where we can be all or as little as we choose to be.'

She paused for a moment as the hall filled with a tide of whispered yeses.

'Now if you could knew where that wonderful light was and had found how to get there wouldn't you want to share that light with others? Wouldn't you want everyone to be in touch with their Atlantean self?' Dawn lit the candle of the man next to her. The Leader continued to talk but Ben's mind was held by the picture of the light as the man turned to those around them and lit their candles, they to the person behind them. Within a minute the light had spilled off the stage and spread across the floor of the hall. Ruth lit Ben's candle and reached up to kiss him. He turned to light Davie's but he was already lit. Candle held in both hands tears streaming down his cheeks.

'You okay?' he whispered. Davie could only manage a nod. Ben turned back to Dawn, glorious in the reflection of all that released potential. Ben was sad that he had missed even a fraction of her speech.

'Go out and show others the light. Show them the wonder of Atlantis,' she bowed her head for what seemed a moment and an age then looked up smiling at everyone at once. 'Thank you.'

Far above the neon lights plinked into action and everyone cheered and clapped. The room was filled with the smell of snuffed candles. Ben wanted to do it all again.

'Right I better get you back,' Davie's voice was choked with emotion making Ben do a double take.

'Despite not being on the course you were really in touch with your feelings there Davie. I'm impressed,' Ruth said, she went to hold Davie's arm. He still had a few tears in his eyes and was grinning from ear to ear.

'Yeah. I didn't think you had it in you,' Ben agreed.

'I'm not quite the callous man I'm portrayed by some of the management you know. Come on, my car is out the back.'

He led the way, whistling a tune from an old Coke advert. Ben looked carefully around the hall, 'We should remember this forever.'

Ruth spun slowly on the spot with her candle still lit, 'We will. We were here. They have taught us the secret and now we can teach others. It's incredible.'

Arms entwined the pair wandered out of the hall.

Chapter Sixteen

Ben sat cross legged on the hull of the MV Captayannis. He had double checked the Sugar Boat's name when he had chosen it as his safe place. Today he was feeling good so the clouds were just peeking over the top of the Arrochar Hills to his left and Ben Bowie to his right. Gulls and Cormorants circled above waiting for him to bugger off back the office. Greenock to the south, Helensburgh to the north and Ardmore Point reaching out towards where he sat listening to the sound of the waves against the steel. He watched a cloud form above Ardmore and spin slowly on itself although Ben couldn't feel a breeze. A bell rung in the distance. Time to go. Reluctantly Ben stood up and walked across the steel hull. There was an opening with steps that led down back into the Thermometer room where he could see himself, Davie and Ruth lying on the floor.

'Ben.'

'Ruth.'

'That was a special week.'

'Yes it was.'

'I'm glad to have found you as a friend again.'

'Good. Yes. I.'

'We need to take this slowly. There is our past. Which is still there. There is working and being a Value Trustee. Which is tough.'

'Yes it is.'

'But I hope we can find a way to be us. Together. I know that will be difficult for you given what happened. But I would like to walk towards a relationship. When you think you are ready.'

'That would be good. I would like that. More than like that.'

'Okay then. Better get back to work. Don't forget to wake up Davie.'

Now that Ben was a Value Trustee and was developing his Atlantean skills, he found living with the engineers had lost its appeal. He had played Russian roulette with his health at least one time too many. He rented a room in the centre of Slough feeling quite grown up that he had finally left any association with the Brookside culture behind. And quite a deal poorer too. It was about the same time that Davie and Steve moved in together. Being Sales Guy Number One

Steve bought the house but needed Davie as tenant to come anywhere close to paying the mortgage.

However both Steve and Davie had decided to turn their backs on a cruel world and that their best defence was a tidal wave of alcohol, what could loosely be described as recreational drugs, and the new and exciting world of video games. Which were good as, unlike life, there was a replay button. When he could, Ben joined them. They let him play as long as he promised not to talk about work.

The three men sat on the sofas in the dark, their faces lit by the handheld game consoles on their laps. It wasn't deliberate. It was just that the sun had gone down and nobody had noticed. Ben realised his eyes had dried out. He hadn't blinked for five minutes as his eyes frantically searched the colour LCD screen looking for signs of his two foes. His body screamed at him to move something after hours of the same hunched pose.. In the game Steve's character popped out of one wall. The word 'Steve' strobed in sixty four colours above his head. That would be handy. Probably kill off the name badge industry but make discos a lot easier. Ben jet-packed towards the exit only two jumps away, The word 'Davie' lurched from behind a large mushroom and Ben died in a hail of toxic slime. Ben dropped the game console into his lap and rubbed his eyes.

'Bastards. It took the two of you though,' he pointed at his opponents but could barely see them in the fluorescent gloom. 'What the hell happened to the day?'

'At the end of the day-' Steve said, leaning over to put on the electric fire.

'It gets dark.' finished Davie. Ben laughed and used the light of the hopelessly unrealistic coal effect to find the light switch.

'When are you two getting married? Eyes,' Ben asked. The main living room light clicked on, the hundred watts fixing Steve and Davie in its sudden intensity. They swore. Davie, arm held feebly over his eyes appeared to be sitting on a green carpet rather than the brown that occurred in the rest of the room. He started to count green bottles.

'Twenty four,' he belched and scratched his stubble.

'Impressive bladder control,' Ben commented.

'I went at least once,' Davie shook his head slowly. He peered down at his own trousers. 'Hope I did.'

Ben stepped to the kitchen. Steve had already started to redecorate in here. Half the orange tiles had been painted over blue and white. He joined Ben in the kitchen and put the kettle on. His tight white T-shirt and immaculate jeans the very antithesis of the check-shirted beer monster next door.

'There was no way you were going to get me without you two teaming up. How are you and him getting on?' Ben couldn't resist asking.

'Earl Grey?'

'Coffee please.'

'Walter Mathue without the wit,' Steve filled the kettle, 'or the charm. Or the dress sense.'

'He's getting worse on that front. There was a time when he was quite trendy.'

'I think he's trying to make it clear that he's straight.'

Ben stuck his head back into the other room. From the noise Davie had either fallen asleep or had a Vietnamese pot-bellied pig rooting in his lap. A finished bottle of beer was firmly clenched in his hand.

'Absolutely no doubt about that matey boy. Only a woman would consider taking that project on. I heard you were dabbling the other way yourself.'

Steve laughed at that, 'Davie was trying to convince me that I was missing out.'

'And?'

'The fish thing really doesn't do anything for me.'

Ben pulled a face and decided to change the subject, 'You're doing a nice job in here.' He sipped the coffee. He hesitated halfway through lighting his cigarette, 'Do you mind?' Steve shook his head. 'Thank you,' he looked at the walls. 'Very nice.'

'Thank you,' Steve echoed the gratitude, 'and how is your love life going then Ben? You and the other Value Trustee seem very close.'

'Straight to the point Steve. Still think you're in with a chance?'

Steve pulled a face, 'You're a little old for my tastes but I'd make allowances for a friend.'

They both chuckled.

'I'm sure you would. No me and Ruth are good. She gave me this,' Ben pulled a small pewter snuff box and opened it up. Inside was what looked like a lead crystal. Glinting in the fluorescent lights.

'The rumour was a diamond ring.'

'No. It's crystal for absorbing negative energy. Any time I think bad thoughts. I open this up and put my bad thoughts into this.'

'Really?'

'Yeah. Look,' Ben held the crystal up to the light and showed Steve the smoky line through it. 'It seems to work. I feel better. It makes Ruth happy. And that makes me happy.' They drank in silence watching the snores from next door send ripples across the tops their drinks. 'That can't be healthy. What am I saying? Of course it isn't.'

The doorbell rang. It took Ben quite a while to register what was happening and peer at his watch. It was nearly 'Don't'.

'It's almost three. Who the hell's that?' asked Ben. Steve put his cup down and walked slowly down the hall to the door. He couldn't see anything through the peephole and said so. Ben came up close behind him, coffee still in hand. 'Maybe we should...'

Steve opened the door. About a foot below where both men were looking stood Clare. She looked odd in her civvies, a dark bomber jacket, jeans and trainers. Underneath the blond hair her eyes were twinkling like mad.

Steve took a step back, standing on Ben, 'Clare, want to come in?'

She was grinning from ear to ear, 'I was going to ask the opposite. Do you want to come out?' She swung something round on a strap.

'Gun!' thought Ben, Psychotic Marketing Manager cuts down talented salesmen in ritualistic double killing. No, camera. Big one too.

'I'm going to London.'

'To see the Queen?' asked Steve.

'Doubt she'll be up,' Clare had acquired the look of a munchkin staring up at Steve, sparkling for all she was worth. 'We could take a shot of her house,' she shook the camera again. 'They look amazing at night. Want to come?' She shook the bag again and showered the hall with pixie dust.

Steve, obviously under the fairy influence, beamed down at Clare, 'Why not. It would be cool.'

'Get your coat then.'

Steve looked back at Ben, coffee steam and smoke still wreathed around his head, 'Eh yeah. I'm in. It's either that or watch Davie try to refill the bottles so that he doesn't have to drag himself all the way to the toilet.' He grabbed his coat. Out on the road a black XR3i stood with its lights on and Prince playing quietly to itself. The roof was down.

'This really will be cool.' said Ben.

Clare wrinkled her nose at him, 'Eric has got a good heater and it is the only way to see the city. With the roof down it's like you're really there. Otherwise you might as well watch it on the telly.'

'Mmm. Be warm and comfortable,' complained Ben. Clare was already in the driving seat, the engine kicked into life.

'Ben, you always have the option of staying behind.' She pointed out.

Ben slid into the back seat, he pulled the collar up on his jacket. Steve hesitated just for a second before sitting next to Clare.

'And miss out on the fun? Drive on!' Ben shouted theatrically.

The short blast along the M4 was as cold as Ben had feared. Soon though Eric was purring under the plane trees. It was curious to see the Houses of Parliament from the river and St Paul's Cathedral or the Thames Television logo as Ben had thought of it up till now. He was sad to see that someone had removed the giant white kitten from the Post Office Tower. They stopped outside the new Lloyds building. It broadcast an eerie blue glow. Clare got quite excited as she ran about the empty roads trying to get it all in the lens. Ben and Steve wandered around a bit but stayed close to the car.

'Do you realise the first three floors are made entirely out of compressed Filofaxes?' Steve mused.

'Amazing what they can do now,' Ben answered, his voice filed with wonder.

'What is amazing is that there are still people working in there. Don't they have homes to go to?'

'What like us?' They drove further east.

Home. How long had Ben been down south? He gave up, too tired and comfortable to work out just how long. And he'd never managed to escape the pull of Slough. Well he'd been to Bracknell and Basingstoke but they were really just extensions of Slough. Pieces of the amoeba that had managed to take root and flourish in other parts of the country, as unattractive in every way. Did Slough reproduce asexually? As the skies began to flush pink, a strange blue

Disney castle tower appeared suddenly ahead, winking at its twin on the other side of the treacle Thames. Clare pulled the car over and killed the engine. She jumped out and began a curious dance with one eye through the lens. The Towers were her partner. Ben and Steve leaned on Eric's bonnet. Steve pulled out a quarter bottle of Tequila from his jacket. He took a swig and nudged Ben with it.

'Steve my man. Outstanding,' He passed the bottle back and lit up. 'When did they do this?' He waved his free hand at the London Bridge.

'Victorian isn't it?'

'The light thing.'

Clare had come back. She took a gulp from the bottle and took a photograph of Steve, 'I need to go down there to get some better shots. Do want to come with me?'

Ben shook his head, 'I'll stay here thanks.'

'Me too. Don't want to cramp your style.' Steve added.

'Bloody lazy more like,' she skipped off.

'You're in there you know Steve. And you could do a lot worse. She's worn well. Kept herself trim.'

'I've told you before Ben. I'm not interested.'

'Yeah but you're on the rebound. Dangerous times. It might be one of those Tomorrow moments where the inner you makes an inflexion life choice. Why are you holding out your hand?'

Steve looked at his watch, 'It is without doubt the weekend and you have just said the 'T' word.' Ben said the 'F' word and pulled a fiver out of his pocket and slapped it in Steve's hands. It occurred to Ben that despite starting to play computer games with Steve nearly twenty-four hours ago this was the longest conversation they had had.

'How are you anyway?'

Steve pushed back long departed hair from his forehead, 'I don't know Ben. I can't see me making target.'

'Nobody is. Davie is on a written warning for missing the first quarter. The year's going crap and I don't see it changing,' said Ben.

'Can you do that?'

Ben shrugged and passed back the bottle. He dug deep inside his jacket for a packet of B&H, his practised fingers taking the cellophane off without glancing down. He pointed the unlit cigarette at Steve, 'Put you on a warning? What we can do you for is telling your line manager to 'fuck off' and offering to slash her tyres if she tried the same stunt again.'

'Did he? I know he is under pressure but...'

Ben interrupted, 'Davie? Rather skin Thumper than damage a car. But that is what is on his record.' Steve stood up and began pacing in front of Eric. Ben continued, 'Difficult though. Davie's my friend but Joan thinks he's bad for the company. Not professional enough. Once she gets an idea in her head it's very difficult to change it. But she does have the interest of the company at heart.'

'Who has?' Clare had come back from another swig of the bottle and tried to snuggle into Steve's jacket. Steve looked down at her. 'Could actually see the pair of them working' thought Ben.

'Get your hands out of my trousers you trollop,' Steve wriggled away from Clare, 'I've told you the only one I'm interested in round here is that one over there.'

Clare kept stepping back inside Steve's arm. She squinted at Ben, 'Nah. Wasting your time there. He is shagging Ruth.' There was an explosion of tequila off Ben.

'Bollocks. Does all the office think that?' asked Ben.

Clare shrugged and answered the question Ben was thinking, 'Well if you aren't you should be. It's been obvious for ages. Nice girl.' Steve looked like he'd bitten into a lime. Clare defended her statement 'She is.'

'Might be but if you talk to her you might as well talk straight to Joan. Cut out the middleman. Everything goes straight back,' Steve began to pace again.

'I know Catherine is really glad not to be in sales. I don't know why everyone makes it so hard. The trick is to sell stuff for more than we buy it for. It is not brain surgery, it's just selling electronics.' Clare shook her head. That seemed to hit a cord with Steve.

'I really wish I wasn't. Sometimes it's brilliant. But right now it's a lift screaming down from the forty-second floor. The cables snapped and the earth is rushing up towards me. I need to be able to step off. You know like the roadrunner does and the lift hammers down into the ground beside him? But he is fine. He's okay. I need to be able to step off but I don't know how,' he faced out over the river. Clare stepped to his side and held his hand in both of hers. 'It's going to destroy us but none of us are allowed to leave. None of us get close to Hermione anymore. Joan's always there watching, listening. Nobody ever says what they think.'

Steve looked back at Ben. The sun had come up across the city, Steve's face was pale, 'Don't put any of that in your Personality Profile Matrix, Ben?'

Ben held up both hands, 'I always make allowances for a friend. You know that.'

Steve rubbed his eyes. He looked tired. Clare was watching him like a concerned puppy. Steve kissed her very lightly on the nose.

'I'm fine. You got all your shots?'

Clare nodded.

'Let's go home then.'

Slightly drunk in the back of Eric with roof down, the best of Cat Stevens blasting away Ben felt fine. He felt the heat from Steve's leg against his but decided not to move it. He felt disdain for the stressed masses as they clogged up the roads into the metropolis. He had seen the city; the white cat had gone. The sun rose.

They arrived back at the maisonette to find every window open. Hideous Gaelic rock music was blasting out at an uncomfortable volume. Concerned the flat had been turned over by Hebridean mafia, the three rushed up the stairs. The door was open. Davie, obviously showered but still in last night's clothes was hoovering the hall as he sang about the fearsome Highland Warrior striking terror into the hearts of his enemies. He looked very embarrassed.

'Thought I'd tidy up a bit.'

He dived into the living room and turned down the stereo. He reappeared. Steve stood in the hall looking in amazement at the kitchen, two bedrooms and the living room.

''s clean.'

'Bog as well. That was disgusting by the way. You need to do more than just wave a bottle of bleach at it every month you know.'

'Eh, yeah.'

'Hello Clare. You had a nice time? The breakfasts ready by the way. Thought I would do it properly. Black Pudding, two pounds of sausages, white pudding, the last of the Lorne sausage, toast, sliced haggis, tinned tomatoes and beans. All you need to tell me is how you like you eggs. Go on through to the living room and I'll bring you a cup of tea.'

Clare looked back at her car, 'I'd better go. Wouldn't want to deprive you.'

'There are loads Clare, go on through.'

Ben followed Clare and Steve into the living room. It looked huge now that all the pizza and beer boxes had gone. The net curtains were in the washing machine by the sounds of things making the room bright, airy, pleasant.

Ben wandered back and helped Davie with the tea, 'You all right?'

Davie winked at him, 'Once a year thing. Sometimes I get so bad that even I'm revolted. It'll keep Steve in a state of shock for a month anyway. What you been up to?'

'Clare, London for the first time, pictures of the city at night.'

'Glad I wasn't there?' Davie passed him two cups of tea.

'Why?' asked Ben. Davie put down his barbecue fork and talked as though to a five year old.

'Gambit loves Purdey. Purdey loves Steed. But Steed loves Steed.'

'Who's Steed?'

'That's the question. Fried or boiled? I can't do poached just goes all messy.'

Chapter Seventeen

'So in closing I think it is important to remind ourselves of where we were three years ago.' The whole company had crushed into the Thermometer room; it was filled with the smell of overheated office staff at the end of a long day and then packed very tightly together. The lighting was subdued. At the far end a man with the best suit and the best tan in Royal Berkshire held the hushed Tomorrow People enthralled with his measured West Coast tone.

'Three years ago Hermione came to us and impressed us with her vision of the opportunity that Europe represented for Tomorrow. Back home in Flagstaff, Hermione convinced us that Slough, England would be the right place to begin our penetration of Europe. Even then Hermione had a list of people that she wanted as part of her team; many of the people on that list are here tonight.'

Ben looked around the expectant faces trying to figure out which of them had been on that list. They could print a medal, when Tomorrow had made them all rich. I was there, one of Hermione's chosen. We had some crap years, the timing had been bad, a lot of the industry had been against us but we had made it. Ben could see it quite clearly.

'It was obviously that vision that attracted us.'

Ben realised he had missed a bit. 'The clarity of thinking to develop a long term, self-funding growth into the UK and beyond. You must be very proud working for her.' Ben found himself cheering with the rest of the company. Steve and Davie were clapping from the back but Ben suspected that, mentally, they were doing sea lion impressions. Ben, taller than most, could see Hermione, horribly embarrassed as she stood just out of the light.

'I have said enough. I think there is some food and drink organised?' The Executive Vice President of Global Business Development fired the question off into the relative dark. Several people attempted a 'yes' back but they sounding very English and surprised, the sheer ineptitude of the response broke the spell that The Executive Vice President of Global Business Development had woven. 'Good. Enjoy. Hopefully I'll get a chance to talk a few of you as the night proceeds. If I don't get the chance let me say now 'Good luck with Tomorrow' and thank you from all the guys in Flagstaff. You've made us proud.' Aaron Johnson, Executive Vice President of Global Business Development stepped out of the light as the room went wild.

Ben had hit his second can by the time Steve and Davie had extracted themselves from the Thermometer room and made it out to the end office. He passed a beer to each. Davie looked back into the room while pulling the ring back.

'Cheers big ears,' he said over the hiss of the Carling. 'You had a word with the great man?' The other two shook their heads.

Steve responded in a perfect copy of the easy West Coast accent, 'The only thing I want to say to you guys is 'what the hell did you guys do with December?' Just as Clare came into the office. Davie burst out laughing, unfortunately he had just taken a big swig of beer which frothed up out through his mouth and nose. Clare jumped behind Steve with a squeal as Davie collapsed coughing in the floor, the dark purple carpet soaking up the mixture of froth and drool.

'Oooh that hurt,' Davie slumped back against the wall and laughed at Ben who was smiling but clearly not getting the joke.

'Tell him Clare.'

'Tell him what? I'm not sure I should be in the same room as the rest of you. 'Career limiting' is the phrase that springs to mind. Although my career appears to be over anyway. I'm clearly not on the list to be talked to. Tell him what?' she asked again.

'Christmas is cancelled,' Davie looked closely at his can. Steve slid onto a desk and smiled like an angel.

'You bastard,' Clare said to Steve, without venom, 'I told you in the strictest confidence.'

'And I told Davie in the same–' Steve waved his hand around a moment trying to pull the words out of the air, 'in the same strictest confidence.'

Davie shrugged, 'And I haven't got anybody to tell.'

'You could tell me,' Ben stated. 'Tell me what?' Ben held out a cigarette to Clare who hesitated and then took it. 'Go on. Tell me.'

Steve moved closer to the window, 'You allowed to do that?'

'Special night. Manager here, so it must be okay,' Ben tossed a fag down to Davie. 'Bout time we had a smoking room. Tell me what?'

'Hermione won't be happy, smoking kills you know,' Steve looked at the cherub faces of Ben, Davie and especially Clare and decided to give up. 'Been a bad year,' Steve started.

'The worst downturn in the past fifteen years,' added Clare in a line that she had been perfecting all through that bad year. She pulled herself up on the desk and admired her pixie boots. It always struck Ben that, despite having smoked for years, she still looked like she was just holding a cigarette for somebody else. In contrast Davie and Ben made them look like natural extensions of their bodies.

Steve continued the story, 'So if you start the year and business is bad. Billings, stuff shipping out the door, are light what do you do?'

'Sell more?'

'Should be the right answer but no. You have failed to take into account these complicated days of post Monetarist Econometrics coupled with the rise of Global Markets. Not to forget the impact of Price Inelasticity and near perfect competition. The favoured method is to ship early from next month. Customer gets his product slightly early; you give those that complain slightly extended credit. Billings make target and everybody is happy with minimum effort.'

There was a pause as they all cheered in unison and opened the four cans with perfect timing.

'But,' cried a dramatic voice from the floor, 'what happens in the following month?'

'Ah the long term view. Obviously now things are tough because it's February and you are already a week down on this month's billings. But hey,' Steve was back to being a voiceover for Welcome to Flagstaff, Arizona, 'Business is tough, take a week out of March. Hell, take two. February is a short month and everything is bound to get better in the next quarter.'

'Of course it doesn't. Every month you convince yourself that it is going to get better and it never does. August was unbelievable. We had to take three weeks out of September.'

Ben was beginning to look pale, 'It didn't get better did it?' He was thinking through his own sales figures.

'Nope,' Clare shook her head, 'I think the technical term is 'Fubar'. It got to December and there was nothing left to steal.' She held her hands palm upwards, 'All gone. Nothing left. Nada, zip, zilch.'

'Christmas is cancelled,' said Davie, the voice from the floor again.

'Shite.'

'Quiet right Ben. That's where we are. There was no way to hide the fact from Flagstaff that we seemed to have misplaced a month.'

'You mean they hadn't realised up till then. They must have known.'

'Didn't have a clue. All they saw was a bunch of figures that looked great. Slough bucking the worldwide trend. Gee those Brits are doing swell. Hermione's vision was really delivering,' Steve's face was lit up with glee as he described the company crash.

'Shite,' Ben repeated.

Steve opened the window and a chill air rolled into the room. resumed facing back into the room, 'All things considered I'm surprised the Executive Vice President of Global Business Development was quite so positive tonight.' There was a general murmur of agreement with that.

'So I guess that we are in here, not being wheeled out for a word with the great man in this moment of crises.'

'And management deception,' added Davie.

'That's a phrase I would not want to hear bandied about,' Clare commented.

'Should not be taken as a good sign?' asked Ben.

Clare's smile warmed up the room, 'That's right Ben. Do you think I would be hiding in a dark office, smoking and drinking with you lot otherwise? It's been fun guys but I think the party is over.'

'Bugger,' said Davie. 'I was planning on this glorious future.' He pushed his way up the wall, 'Shall we see what's going on then?'

'Have another beer first,' Ben was now in no hurry to see what fate awaited him.

Some time later they filed back out, the party had thinned. Steve took a quick swig and pulled a face at the tin.

'It's a man's drink.' Said Davie.

That made Steve laugh, 'What are you doing drinking it then?' Steve asked.

Davie looked wounded, 'I'm a man.' He looked for support but Clare and Steve wandered off leaving Ben and Davie looking over the empty office. The evening had fizzled out. Aaron had gone. Accounts were clearing up. They were like that, very conscientious in a way that the rest of the company just wasn't. Garfield grinned at him from Marketing, hung by the neck with tinsel, their one contribution to Christmas cheer. Davie was singing something traditional.

Ben was still in a state of shock, 'I can't believe they lost December. We lost December.' He ran his free hand through his hair, 'Man that's bad, a whole month! Can you whistle Davie?'

'Piss off,' Davie went over and sat in Helen's chair hoisting his feet on the table, just for the thrill of it.

'When you going to ask her out?' Ben asked.

'When she doesn't have a boyfriend that could pull my arms off.'

Ben slumped in Ruth's chair, 'Good point, well made.'

'I am apparently really nice.' Davie said, he was tossing Helen's favourite Troll up into the air and catching it by the hair. 'Too nice. And she needs some sense of danger in a relationship. Only she used the word 'excitement'. But I have seen several of her boyfriends and I'm sticking with 'danger'.'

'What are you going to do now?'

'Have another one of these,' Davie waggled the can. 'Write something suggestive on Helen's pad and then go home. What about you?'

Ben frowned, 'No I mean now that we're out of Tomorrow. Does that make us Yesterday people?' Davie chuckled in a tired way and washed his face with his hands. He pointed up at the poster behind Hermione's desk. A map of the world lay at the feet of the Tomorrow logo and Lone Star Semiconductors, overlapping as much as 'Corporate Consistency' would allow. At some point someone, probably Davie, had written 'Building better worlds' underneath.

'I would like to work for them. Good company, look after their staff, offices in all the interesting places in the world. Timing's not right though. What about you?'

'I have no idea,' and Ben hadn't.

He still hadn't the next day. He sat at his desk, binning all the bits of paper that had drifted his way and started tidying up his customer files so that whoever inherited the cardboard folders would have a reasonable chance to figure out what had happened in each account. People started to appear quietly. Helen, Catherine and Ruth. Davie, Steve and Clare. By nine o'clock it was clear that there were a lot of empty desks. What had slowed Ben down from realising how many, was that there was a few of the reps slouching around looking worse for wear and making the place look busy as well as untidy. Joan came in looking grey and went straight into Clare's office. When the pair came out they announced that the company should meet in the Thermometer Room. Arthur came out of stores but his lads stayed behind.

Ben had done a quick head count as the door was closed by Clare and the group clustered in uncertainty at the front.

Joan sat on the desk at the front, swinging her legs, 'As you will have realised last year didn't go very well. What that has meant is that Flagstaff–' Joan paused and looked carefully round the room, 'we, have had to look very carefully at our business plan for the year ahead. Clearly we are over resourced for the business level that we have achieved. Hermione has seen this as an opportunity to rethink what she really wants out of life, as have quite a few others in the company.'

That may have been the point where Helen fainted. They didn't find her till the end when the lights went up.

'Those of you here are safe. It's us here, the people in this room that have to make Tomorrow what we know it can be,' there were tears in her eyes. 'It's going to be hard and we are going to have to pull together. Arthur is now our only man in stores.'

The bull necked man shrugged his massive shoulders, 'Like I said last night. Done it before and I can do it again. And I know that you lot in sales are going to go and do the business. And you'll help me when you can. Apart from Davie.'

That startled a laugh out of a few. Joan looked at Arthur like she could kiss him. She opened her mouth but the words that came out were smooth and American.

'What Arthur says is right,' Aaron stepped out of the shadows. Ben swore along with a few others who hadn't noticed him. 'It's important to understand that Tomorrow is committed to Europe. It has to succeed. Other companies are already coming into the UK. They are buying companies, using them as a springboard for business. Hermione didn't want to do it that way. She didn't want to try and unpick someone else's mistakes. She wanted to start with a clean sheet. A handpicked crew and start building the business from the first floor up. It was the hard way to do it. She called it the Rocket Science of Electronics but you guys have done it. You have that first stage built. Now you have to have the guts to carry on and keep on building.'

Joan dabbed at her eyes with a hankie. Her expression as she watched Aaron was a study of neutrality, 'That's right. So we have a lot to sort out. Areas. Callout plans. Targets…'

'One of the things I'm hoping to,' Aaron slowed for a moment trying to pick his word, 'add to the operation here is some of the tactics that we have found to be successful across the US and even Canada.'

'As far away as that?' Ben could hear Davie whispering to Catherine in the row in front.

Ruth had her hand held up, 'Does this mean that Aaron will be replacing Hermione as MD?' The surviving management looked blank and then to Aaron, clearly the only man in the room who had the answer to that question.

'Hell no. Hermione was a one off and irreplaceable. I think she had a profile like nobody else within the Tomorrow Organisation and in the wider Electronics Industry. I'm here to help your management build bridges with Tomorrow in other parts of the world. There is a lot of expertise, a lot of momentum out there ready to help you. Once those bridges are built, once you're integrated into the wider Tomorrow culture, my job here will be done. I'd just like to say that I am really excited to be here and working with you guys and I am sure you will see this as the opportunity that it so obviously is.' Aaron smiled a warm and encouraging smile at them all before focusing on Joan and then stepped back into the shadow.

Joan's legs were now perfectly still, 'We have a lot to sort out and you must have a lot of questions. Lights please Clare. So is there anything that anybody would like to raise now?'

'Sort out?' thought Ben to himself, 'Half the sodding company has gone!' He couldn't form any words or thoughts beyond that sentence in a loop.

Davie already had his hand up. Joan looked slightly amazed, 'Yes Davie?'

He was looking slightly panicky at Helen slumped against him, 'Since the Hannah in accounts also seems to be rethinking what she really wants out of life, who is doing our first aid now?'

Chapter Eighteen

Business was picking up. Well it had to. It had been very clear from the beginning that Aaron Johnson, Senior Vice President of Global Business Development was taking personal responsibility for Tomorrow's performance. It was also absolutely crystal to everyone that anything that Aaron took personnel responsibility for, always delivered. So given these absolutes the Electronic Component Market in the UK had no choice but to buck up its ideas. Since everyone was now doing the job of at least two and often three people in the company, stress levels, previously thought of as 'intolerable' and 'inhuman', were now looked back on fondly. Ben and Ruth were under even more pressure as Value Trustees to try and keep moral up and make sure that everyone was contributing positively. It also meant a lot more contact with Aaron, which was exciting. In lots of ways.

'We are going to learn so much from him,' Ruth said enthusiastically.

'Every time I meet Aaron I wonder if this is the time he is going to fire me,' Ben said in the same tone. The pair sat in a side office, one without any windows. They were trying to put the stack of acetate slides into some sort of order by the light of the overhead projector. The slides though were living up to their name and refusing to stay put. Just as everything from 'Engaging with your core' to 'Identify three things that you are proud of' slithered on to the floor, Aaron strode in.

'Ruth, Ben.'

'Hello Aaron, we were just putting together the presentation that you wanted to see about the development programme.'

'Of course...'

'What we have done at the office is pick key performance indicators and create Personality Profile Matrices. This involves looking at what Hermione considered as key and then building a matrix mould that a person needs for a particular job. And where that person currently is in developing those skills required. We then asses how they are doing in a set of training development interactive sessions and they are awarded marks. However we found that people found the marks hard to relate to so we tend to summarise as stars. For example,' she pulled up Helens chart and slid it on to the overhead projector.

'Looks kind of like a MacDonald's trainee,' Aaron said with a smile.

'That's where Helen should be working,' Joan said as she walked in the room and closed the door behind her.

Ruth looked surprised but picked up where she had left off, 'We then have a series of performance indicators which Ben would like to talk about.' No he wouldn't he thought but Ruth had gone for it and so could he.

He pulled a couple of slides from the pool on the floor, talking as he did so, 'Yes.' He took a drink of water, 'These are less about the people's skills and more about their work ethic. How close do they align their own interests and that of the company? Do they volunteer for extra training or put in extra hours. Voluntary Additional Attendance for example is a really good indicator of the state of mind of a person.'

'How about spelling?' Joan's question tripped him up completely.

'I'm sorry, Joan?'

'So you should be. Attendance: a-n-c-e, not e-n-c-e.'

Ben puffed out his cheeks, thrown completely by the comment.

'It's okay Ben,' Aaron said, 'I get the idea. Look, the information you guys put together last year was great. It was better than great. These PPM's were the one concrete set of measurements that allowed me to evaluate everyone's contribution in the company. Without that it would have been random which people had to go. With your data I at least I knew I was making the right choices. It was a good job.'

Ben felt cold at the thought that all the work he and Ruth had put together to get the company in the right direction had resulted in that direction being out of the company for at least half the staff.

'It wasn't just Ruth and Ben,' Joan said, clearly feeling that she was missing out on all the praise.

'I understand that Joan. But sales, external sales, are a mess. A lot of them haven't done sales before. They don't have industry experience. They don't have gravitas. I understand what Hermione was trying to do. Clean sheet and all that but we haven't got time. I need this kind of clarity,' Aaron pointed at Ruth and Ben, 'out in the sales force.' Joan was nodding agreement as if she was sitting on the dashboard of a Land Rover going over a rutted field.

'That's why I need you out there Joan.' The nodding stopped. 'I need you to motivate the field sales in the same way you have the office. You retain overall responsibility for the office but your primary focus is getting the field sales into shape.'

'Right. Well I think I can do that but what about supporting Ruth and Ben?'

'I have thought about that. I've interviewed a great girl. Called Jana. She has been a great Team Leader at Staines Capacitors and Transistors. She has great experience. Knows internal sales and the team leader role inside out.'

'But we don't have Team Leaders, we are Value Trustees,' Ben said while thinking this really was a time to stop the words coming out, but they danced out there anyway.

'I know that and you have already demonstrated why Hermione put such great faith in you guys and the role. Which is why this will work. Joan goes to put some needed order into field sales. Jana can come in here and help strengthen you guys with some practical sales experience. And she is very keen to learn all about this,' Aaron pointed at the silvery lake that had finally stopped spreading under Ben's chair.

'When does she start?' asked Ruth.

'Next week. She was on four weeks' notice but I just hadn't found the time to tell you guys. But I'm sure that will be fine,' Aaron looked at them all beaming a certainty that Dawn Shintany would have been proud of.

'Absolutely Aaron,' Ruth confirmed in her best Atlantean positive response to a difficult situation. 'We will make sure we have a training programme ready to go for her.'

'Not too long though. I want to make sure that she is out there selling. You too Joan,' Aaron left the room clearly happy at a job well done. Joan sat for a moment staring down at her nine-part file.

'Well,' she gave them both a pained look. 'I better go round up Field Sales and tell them what's going to happen.' Joan stomped out of the room. Ruth and Ben sat in the quiet whirr of the OHP fan.

'Blimey.' Unfortunately he was distracted from saying anything more profound by wondering if this would a good time to ask Ruth out, properly.

'That's a lot to take in Ben.'

'Yes,' Ben said. And then thought 'but with Joan out on the road this is going to be a whole lot more fun with just Ruth and me.' He picked all of the slides off the carpet and started beating them back into the folder.

'We need to think about what essentials we cover with Jana.'

'Would you like a cup of tea?' asked Ben who then practically skipped out the room towards the kitchen. The good news had clearly not travelled that far yet.

'We should have proper ten minute breaks away from the screens. Not sneaking round hoping that Joan doesn't catch us away from our desks,' Davie said as Ben entered. Davie was trying to cram in a quick cigarette waiting for the kettle to boil. Catherine looked disapprovingly at the smoke and shrugged, staying non-committal. Davie glanced at Ben, stubbed out the hardly started cigarette and left the kitchen.

'I'll be glad once he's off on holiday,' Ben said.

'His last day today. He has a full fortnight back up north,' Catherine said in a Yorkshire accent as it was the furthest north that she could think of.

'Let's hope he gets himself sorted out.'

Joan appeared and smiled thinly at the pair of them. Catherine smiled back but in a way that could have benefited from a lot of Atlantean training. She fished out her raspberry tea bag and added milk to the coffee for Helen and finished off making Davie's abandoned drink.

Scooping up the three cups she left Ben to wonder where Joan was going to go. All out, appeared to be the answer.

Joan called him into Hermione's office, 'Ben. Good news. The customer Better Meters have decided to pull forward their order. Means an extra month's billings we didn't expect.'

'And the bad news is?'

'That they want it shipping Monday. I have taken Helen off whatever she was wasting her time with. She can pull forward the lines. You and Catherine can go into stores and pick the stock as Helen sorts the paperwork.'

Ben thought of the quotes he needed to get out today, 'Really pushed at the moment. What about Davie?'

Joan shook her head, 'He is enough trouble already. This is his last day before he goes on holiday and he has done nothing that I've asked him. If I am going to have to sort field sales out I can't carry wasters like him anymore.'

'Steve told me that those two were out on the piss in Windsor, went to get some more money from a 'hole in the wall' and it ate Davie's card. Steve said he laughed so much he wet himself. Davie was so convinced that he must have put the wrong number in that he put all three cards in the machine one after the other. Debit card, cheque card and credit card. He can't do a thing. He's written to the bank saying he is sorry and to cut a deal on paying back what he owes but they hold all the cards,' Ben laughed at his own joke.

'Davie and Steve are self-destructing so fast,' Joan said with feeling and then focused a smile at Ben. 'You need to stay clear or you will get caught in the shrapnel. Right I've told Arthur what's happening so you better get down and start clearing some space for the shipment. When he is away we'll find out what is really going on in his area.' Ben twigged that Joan's thoughts had returned to Davie. 'Catherine and Helen are covering for him I'm sure. I don't know why you hang out with him.'

'Don't see so much of him after he moved in with Steve.'

'Good,' She lit up her Silk Cut which Ben always felt was a complete waste of time. If you're going to smoke you might as well do it properly. 'Once I'm out on the road you will have to drive all this you know. Off you go then.'

Chapter Nineteen

Ben left the kitchen and walked to the front of the building and down the stairs. Here on the ground floor was Tomorrow's stores. Initially they had been little more than a cupboard. Hermione's plan had been to rely on having that big slick machine from Arizona attached to the operation. Tomorrow was that good that we would only need a single week's stock on site and the rest would flow through. A year of trying to make sure that we shipped the right box to the right customer at the right time meant that that the stock was now standing at around three months' worth and rising.

This was fine. Arthur could cope, he had always planned a big warehouse and had the system set up for expansion. The building couldn't though. The office that Tomorrow had rented was set against an earth bank. The ground floor stopped less than a third along from the top floor, leaving no room for that expansion. Arthur's solution had been simple and effective.

Ben walked through the first part of the stores. This was the part that they showed customers when they came up to the site. Bright indirect lighting gleamed off racks holding special antistatic trays, Smiling extras drafted in from other parts of the office dressed in blue jackets and antistatic straps, stood on carbon matting by the latest counting machines and checking orders with snazzy orange monochrome monitors. He grabbed a smock and a wrist strap before stepping on through a passageway between two rows of product and a door marked 'cupboard'.

Now Ben was in the part no one saw. Here the lighting was bare neon. The product was stacked in the boxes it had come in, often piled up where they had overflowed a particular bin location on a poorly cast cement floor. Ben gathered up a picking sheet from the top of the pile. It was marked 'Better Meters' but he thought he had better check. The neon flickered out for a second and something scuttled in the dark damp air.

'Dallas, talk to me Dallas.'

There was some swearing ahead to indicate a possible location. As Ben walked forward he could see the neat foundation of the building reach down to what presumably had been ground level. Now the rough concrete of the original piles had been exposed as they had dug out the stores around foundations. He had to crouch slightly since the contractors, presumably nervous about the digging had only excavated to Arthur height and no more. Later, after a few incidents of narcolepsy, the management realised that there was no oxygen in the new part of the stores. In an attempt to avoid having to issue pickers with canaries, they had fitted a large network of clear polythene tubing about the stores and attached to a blower to shift the air about. This reduced the ceiling further. The blower had to be switched off when customers were doing a tour, in order to avoid raising suspicions of what was happening in the cupboard. Poor co-ordination about an impending BS5750 Part 2 inspection could leave Stores men trapped for an hour or more 'in the dungeon'. No fatalities yet as Arthur always cheerfully pointed out at the Thermometer Meetings.

Ben found Arthur right at the back. This tended to be the really slow-moving stuff.

'Allo Ben. Thanks for coming down. Really appreciate it. I said to Joan this morning that there was no way I was going to get it out on my own. Not and get the dailies out too.'

'Not a problem Arthur. I've got the top sheet, where do you want me to put the stuff that I pick?'

The Operations Manager pointed at a small-wheeled trolley lurking in the half-light where stores ran out and the Giant Ant burrow began, 'Bung what you have picked on that and I'll come back and take it forward every now and then. You can finish off this sheet too. I have marked up what I have found so far,' Arthur took a quick look round. 'I'll leave my radio here for you. Thanks again Ben.'

Ben shrugged, 'Like I said, no problem.'

Arthur shuffled out of sight leaving Ben alone with 'Our Tune'. Ben ran his finger down the list, found the part number and then began to work his way along the shelves looking for the product. The radio talked away to itself.

'But at that point Jack was diagnosed and realised that he only had three months to live. He knew he had to track down, let's call her, Tracy. She was the girl that had broken off their engagement after she had told him she was pregnant with the child he thought he could never have.'

'74LS140, 74LS224, 74LS240, 74LS245,' Ben whispered as he counted, 'bingo!' A large pile of what looked like brown cigarette cartons lurked in a bay marked 'Resistors and Capacitors.' He began pulling them out in packs of two thousand five hundred and carrying eight packs at a time back to the trolley. As he approached, the top one started to slide.

'Jack caught up with Tracy in a high security prison in Colombo.'

Ben swerved but too hard and the pack slide off the other way, 'Shit!'

'Tracy had been acting as a mule for a cocaine cartel and was being held in solitary confinement.'

Ben tried kicking the carton along the alley way towards the trolley.

'It took a few bribes and a month of pressure from the British Consulate before he finally got access.'

The carton burst spraying black chips across the concrete.

'Shit!' Ben threw the remaining boxes the last couple of feet onto the trolley.

'It was only then when he met Tracy she confirmed that Jack was the father of their son Zack. But Tracy, driven crazy by months of drugs, imprisonment and deprivation refused to tell Jack any more until he handed over the $20,000 she needed to buy her way out of jail.'

Ben knelt down to sweep up the product littered on the floor.

'Shit!' Some of the chips embedded themselves through his thin work trousers. He stood up and tugged each one out of his knee and carefully put the six chips, pins bent and bloody on a spare bit of racking. Ben did a passable David Attenborough impression as he pulled out the last one free.

'The soldier IC defends the disturbed nest, attacking anything that approaches. Slightly larger than a Cleg, they can pull down a disoriented picker and devour him in less than an hour,' Ben studied the chips at eye level. 'I am going to do something horrible to you.' He couldn't pull his trousers over his calf so he quickly unbuckled his belt and dropped them. Blood had run down his legs and reached his socks.

'By the time Jack had persuaded the Nuns that he was Zack's father and left Utah for England, he only had a month left to live.'

Ben stood up too quickly and felt dizzy enough to have to hold the frame beside him. He reached up and stabbed the polythene pipe with his Stanley knife to try and get some air. It hadn't been replaced since Hermione had left, cutbacks. 'Watch the pennies,' Aaron had said, 'be a tight spender but a wise investor. It's an attitudinal thing.' Ben suspected the word didn't exist. He had always meant to check it. The pipe had been slashed so many times as people picked product, that they might as well try and feed the life giving gas through a colander. No air was getting as far as Ben's corner. Was his lack of oxygen then an attitudinal thing? A flute faded back into Ben's hearing.

'Jack then realised that Tracy, on returning, had already embezzled the trust fund and left father and son penniless before being tragically crushed to death between the dockside and a Russian Whaler. Jack now consoles himself in these last weeks that at least he has his son, Zack and that he has had time to make some video recordings to explain how much he loves the boy and the mother, Tracy, the boy will now never know. This is their tune. It's the Buzzcocks and'

'Ever fallen in love with someone you shouldn't have fallen on love with,' finished Ben. 'Excellent!' He began playing air guitar and singing along but forgot he couldn't breath and had to hang off the shelves for a moment as the dizziness returned.

Something rustled in the next aisle. Catherine put her head round the corner, the beads of her dreadlocks working intricate arcs around her head. She took in the trousers round the ankles, bloody knees and the drunken support on the shelving. She turned her head to one side, a little half smile.

'Nice singing,' she strummed her matching invisible guitar, 'maybe you should think about a holiday Ben.' She laughed as she backed off towards life above ground. Ben struggled to pull his trousers back up again.

'I want to hear sunshine, see the birds singing. All six of them. I want to live. Please let me feel the rain on my face again!'

'You're safer down here. She's in a foul mood. Breathing fire at everyone,' said Catherine from the dark. Ben was about to say why but couldn't find the words.

Ben worked through the rest of the day with an increasing sense of panic. No matter how much products he shifted, measured and weighed, the list didn't seem to get that much shorter. It was well after nine when he thought he was safe to stop. He took a walk out to the car park to have a fag and clear his head. After Catherine's visit the only person he had seen was Arthur collecting product from the little trolley every now and then. Hadn't seen him for a couple of hours which could mean the stalking Alien had got him, or he might have said he was calling it a day at some point. Ben's head was too full of Joan's relishing of her new role to notice.

'She is going to kill everyone before she leaves,' Ben said matter-of-factly to the night air. Ben looked back at the office. From here you could only see the end office which was always empty. But the door was open and it was clear that the lights were still on in the main office. Ben went back through the stores shutting everything down. Finally he closed the cupboard door and climbed upstairs. It was nearly ten o'clock.

The main sales office was silent. A large blue and white desk fan scanned the room noisily for intruders. On each pass the moving air caught the strange orange grinning thing swinging on his sparkly string. His days numbered since Joan had suggested it was time they take Garfield down. There was a short sharp buzz over the sound of the fan. Ben lit a fag and walked slowly past the fan, switching it off. The short buzz returned coming from accounts. Ben shuffled forward, careful not to bang his knees and slid his head round the door.

Davie was sitting cross-legged in front of the company shredder. As the thin white spaghetti slowed another sheaf of papers was stuffed in the top from a small pile on his left. A large pile of empty folders and ring binders on his right.

'Davie. What the hell are you doing?'

The man shot off the floor faster than Ben had seen him move in years, 'Ben! Oh my heart was nearly out my chest. Shite. Quite hypnotic this machine, after an hour or two.'

'Hence my question. What the hell are you doing?'

'Got a spare fag Ben? I'm all out.'

Ben fished in his jacket pocket and pulled out his evening pack, 'It'll get you home.'

'Eh aye thank you.'

Ben raised an eyebrow.

'It's very simple. Really,' Davie resumed his position, stuffing paper in at the optimum rate, 'too much and it stalls. Takes ages to sort out. Easy way to lose a finger too.'

Ben walked round and sat on a desk so that he could see Davie's face.

'You see Joan has told me. Told everyone, that if my filing isn't up to date she'll fire me. Which she will. She even put Helen and Catherine on the 'Better Meters' contract to make sure they couldn't help me. Mad bitch.'

'But you've been on top of things for a while now. I know your PPM. Your file co-ordination subset stats are amongst the best in the Team.'

Davie took time out for a draw and to wave a still attached finger at Ben, 'That's right. I have been. I'm more on top of things now than I ever have been. Took a couple of hours tonight but by say half seven everything was sorted.

Ready for a hand over. The old dragon could go through all my trays, files, folders and it would be fine. Fine and dandy.'

'Good. So?'

'It was at half seven m'lud that I found these. Exhibits A through to X.'

'Which are?'

'All the files that Catherine and Helen found the last time I went on holiday. They knew back then that Joan meant to go through my desk. They knew she was going to get me out for something. So they went through it first. Never told anyone but the pair of them came in at half six in the morning and bundled everything that didn't look right, out of sight. Joan and your good selves in the forensic team found nothing.'

'Good to have friends.'

'Can't beat it. I got back. They gave me all the files and made me promise to sort it. Which I did, mean to. I just never got far enough ahead to sit down and sort this lot out too. I forgot about them till I found them on my final search tonight. I knew that all our good work would be thrown away. Joan would have what she needed.'

'You could have hidden them again.'

Davie looked up, bleary and quite mad, 'Nowhere is safe.'

'You could have filed them.'

'There is the best part of three months quotes and orders here. It would take days.'

'Simple. Put them in the bin.'

Davie laughed, 'By the time I had realised what had happened the cleaners had long gone. It would fill one bin, so that would mean that I would have to spread the files around. Each bin increasing the chance of being discovered. Too dangerous.'

'So you shredded them.'

Davie dropped the last three sheets of A4 into the tireless machine, 'Every single one. It took a lot longer than I thought. You have to take out the staples. Initially I just tore off the corners,' Davie waved some little white triangles from his pocket. 'But I was sure that if she saw them she would realise what I had done. Staples had to go in the bin on their own. Shredding was my one hope. This way there is no evidence. It is a clean start. I am sorted and up to date. I can go on holiday without fear of what pits will be dug while I'm away. I am a free man.'

'You could have just put them in the car and taken them home,' Ben suggested.

Davie let out a long sigh, sagging as he let the air out until his forehead rested against the cool steel of the now quiet shredder.

'Never occurred to me.'

Chapter Twenty

Aaron Johnson, Senior Vice President of Global Business Development was continuing his big recruitment drive. Tomorrow was getting bigger because bigger meant more successful and Aaron was a successful guy. But size wasn't everything, Aaron was focusing on getting in sales professionals from the industry.

'I need people who can go out and get me orders Tuesday!' he said at the Monday morning Thermometer, underlining that a key part of being successful was knowing what day it was. The main criteria Ben realised later that day, was that they also brought something a little more concrete than experience. It was quiet in the office, everyone had dragged themselves home for a brief respite. Ben should have gone home too but he sat trying to encapsulate what the essence of Tomorrow was on the first slide of his Power Point presentation. This new PC had a full 15' VGA CRT monitor and it fascinated him. It was like watching snooker on a colour television for the first time all over again. He couldn't quite get it to do what he wanted but it had to be better than watching his pile of slides slither on to the floor, again.

The door on a side office burst open and Aaron came out with two men in suits Ben didn't recognise. 'Ben!' He shouted across the office.

Ben smiled, Aaron never ever hesitated for a name, you had to give him that. Days and names, he had it covered.

'Aaron?' he pushed the mouse away and stood up.

'Ben this is Neville and Christopher.' Both men smiled and held out their hands which Ben shook. Neville was all blonde hair and a slightly frightened look. Christopher was a big confident man and met Ben's eyes with a friendly but steady gaze. Ben wondered if the dark hair was borrowed.

'They'll be joining the external sales team and I want to make sure that they are welcomed. Guys, Ben here is in charge of making sure that we all keep the faith.'

Christopher looked surprised, 'You have a company chaplain?'

The eye towards Ben winked but his face stayed perfectly in sympathy with the question. Aaron took the question at face value.

'No it's just that we can't afford to fly everyone over to Flagstaff right now with the market being the way it is so it's down to Ben here to make sure that we are up to speed with the latest corporate thinking back home.' Aaron and Christopher smiled at each other and it was only then that Ben noticed they had matching moustaches. Neville didn't have a moustache and was struggling as a result. He stumbled towards Ben,

'Aaron said I should give this to you.' Neville held out a huge stack of green computer printout that looked as steady as Ben's 'An Idiot's guide to making your Volunteer Points count!' 23 slide presentation. Ben gathered the wobbly heap into his arms and dumped it on his table.

Aaron slapped Neville on the back, 'That's right. Nev here has brought a complete list of every account that Staines Capacitors and Transistors have ever dealt with.'

Neville tried to push his hair out of his face, 'It shows their spend, the top ten products and the purchasing contacts.'

'It's brilliant!' said Aaron. 'It's exactly what I need to get this whole operation up to where it should be.' Ben looked at Christopher expectantly, there was something infectious about that smile.

The new rep tapped the side of his head, 'My list is up here, but just as useful.'

Aaron threw an arm around them both, steering them towards the exit, 'That's right Chris, just as useful. Ben could you drop that list off at my home. It's sensitive material and it wouldn't do for it to be seen lying around.'

Neville stopped at that point causing the trio to swerve, 'No!' Neville recovered a little. 'No, it's got my name on every page, it mustn't be seen.'

Aaron looked appraisingly at Neville, 'Don't worry Nev, Ben here is one of the most trusted people in the company. In fact it's in his job title. Ben, take it straight home, make sure no-one knows it even exists.'

'Will do, Aaron.'

Back on course, with Aaron shepherding them towards the door, they left, sucking all the noise out with them. Ben turned and pushed the giant stack of paper back into some sort of shape. Neville was right, his name was indeed printed on each page. It was even on the front in huge letters. 'Complete Customer Base Extract' it said. 'Authorisation Neville Fletcher'. He noticed that the 'N' was made up of lots of little 'n's.

'What's that?'

Ben jumped as Clare appeared beside him, 'Can't tell you, it's secret.'

'Bollocks,' she said and held out a fag as payment. They both lit up and blew smoke at the reappeared Garfield, his absence had been viewed as bad juju. Marketing were a superstitious lot.

'It's a complete customer list for Staines Capacitors and Transistors,' Clare laughed and flicked through the first couple of pages with her left hand. 'Jana didn't bring this, she's way too smart.'

'Neville, another one of Aarons new recruits has turned up with it.'

'Staines Capacitors and Transistors are not going to be very happy when they find out this rep did what he did before he left.'

'Which is why it's a secret.'

'And how long do you think it will take them to figure out what' - she looked down at the stack and read out - 'Neville Fletcher, has done?'

'How would they know?' Ben asked

'It's a named report. Whoever wrote the program wanted to be sure that anyone asking for a full listing had to put their name in as part of the request. It's why Neville's name takes up two thirds of the front page,' she stabbed the page as if reading out the words: 'The company knows what you have done. Somebody would have to be really stupid not to realise that the company knew exactly who commissioned this. Luckily, Aaron has found his man.'

'I think that was what Neville was worried about. They can't do anything about it, though, can they?'

'This isn't the Wild West, Ben. There are laws here, business laws. People go to jail for this kind of thing,' she looked askance at Ben and went back to leafing through it. 'And knowing that he can do this to his old employer, how can we trust Mr Fletcher? When he leaves here what is stopping him doing the same to us? Apart from the fact that it would need us to have a working IT system.' They were silent for a few minutes while Clare started looking through in earnest, 'Asked Ruth out yet?'

Ben shook his head, 'We are working on it.'

'Just ask her. If you work on it too hard you'll probably break it.'

'She said that she needed to separate out the impact of the course. Which has taken longer than I thought. But then the course was brilliant. I have never felt anything like it. You have been on the course haven't you?'

Clare sat on the desk beside the customer list and kept working her way through it, 'Hermione made all the founders go when we started the company,' she said flatly

'And wasn't it the most amazing thing you had ever seen? Ever experienced? The sense of power, the ability to help yourself to be all you can be, to help others. Wouldn't it be a wonderful world if everyone lived like an Atlantean.'

'It would. But it would also be a wonderful world if everyone loved their neighbour as themselves. Think of the power to change the world for good in that simple one liner. Or how about 'Every man according to his need. Every man according to his ability.' Both of those have the power to create a Utopia.'

Ben smiled at that, 'I used to live there.'

Clare ignored his attempt at distraction, 'The reason that they don't is because we, humans, corrupt that message for our own gain. The 'every man according to his need' created the Soviet Empire. 'Love thy neighbour', Torqemada and the Spanish Inquisition. The problem is not the theology or ideology but in humans capacity to corrupt its implementation.'

'But neither of those invalidates the original concepts.'

'No they don't,' Clare tossed over another John Player Special and lit up herself, using the action to pause before answering. 'The ideas are fine, brilliant even. All I'm trying to say is that there many powerful ideas out there. You happen to have come across Atlanteanism and it's got a strong clear message of good. 'Be all you can be' is a good message. But what about the tools they use? People are complex, built up over years. You start pulling bits out and throwing those bits away and you don't know what you'll start, or if you'll be able to stop,' Clare looked a lot older than she would have liked. 'Joan, when she was on the course,' she made eye contact with Ben, 'well it wasn't pretty. I have said it before, this isn't brain surgery, and I don't need this. I come here to work, to earn money, this is not my life.'

Something clicked in Ben's head, 'What was your first big idea Clare?'

She smiled in recognition of a good question, 'A long long time ago I fell in love with a Scientologist.'

'L Ron Hubbard?'

'Yes. Not him obviously but one of the members of the church. Although it's not really a church. Anyway, took me a long, long time to think my way back out of that one.'

'But it doesn't mean that the Atlanteans are wrong.'

'No it doesn't. It's not a question of wrong or right. All I'm asking is that you think when somebody tells you something, why are they telling you? What is their angle on what is probably a good fundamental truth?'

'Because they wanted to share something wonderful.'

Clare gave Ben a warm smile and he thought for a moment that she was going to pat him on the head, 'That'll be it. Bloody hell, look what Better Meters are spending with Staines! That useless cow of a rep said they were giving us the lion's share of the business.'

'That's the problem with the world. There's no trust,' Ben looked past Garfield to the clock on the wall. It was nearly nine. 'Where does Aaron live? I need to drop this round to his house.'

Clare got up, 'I'll get the address for you. And let me know when you want some help deprogramming. I always volunteer to pick up the new cultists from the course so I can make a start straight away, but they never let me.'

It was a part of Windsor Ben didn't know at all well. He had to stop several times with the AtoZ and the post-it note Clare had scribbled the address on. The overhead bulb on the Astra SRi always managed to make the car feel cold, spartan. Finally he found it, well almost. He had pulled off the road into a drive with a huge iron gate across it. Ben got out the car and walked forward flicking his doubt like red tracer through the railings but there was no way through for anything bigger.

Ben had assumed that the Senior Vice President of Global Business Development and current key player in Tomorrow UK would have something big, large gardens, couple of old trees, Jaguar XJS for the weekends. Beyond the gate was an estate made up of large houses with what looked like shared lawns and drives at the front and private gardens at the back. The effect was slightly disturbing, too open, lacking the usual picket fencing and hedges to space out each house. Although all of this sharing openness was behind a ten foot high brick wall with some rather spiky decorations on top of that.

Each house had a mock Victorian lamp by its front door which went nicely with the mock Tudor woodwork in the eaves and mock medieval lead diamond effect on the windows. The light picked out an iron plate with 14 on it. Ben could even see the illuminated doorbell beside the front door. This only left him with the puzzle of how he was going to ring it. He had forgotten his hundred foot pole.

'It's an intelligence test,' he said to himself. Paced up and done wondering if he could summon a Pizza delivery by willpower. It was on his fourth perimeter of the gates that he noticed the panel set into the brickwork of the wall. There were 21 buttons in three rows of seven, each of the name plates were blank. His finger hovered over 14. Was this how you triggered the automatic flamethrowers? Taking a deep breath he pressed the stud.

A thin disembodied voice floated in from somewhere, 'Hello?'

'Eh, hello Mrs Johnson?' Ben said to the wall. There was a pause.

'Yes.'

'I'm from Tomorrow. Mr Johnson asked me drop some papers for him?' There was a click, more silence. Ben stepped away from the speaker grill wondering if he had got the right house after all. A hum filled the air and the iron gates began to lurch inwards. He looked around wondering if the peasants would storm while the portcullis was down but when he checked there was just him and his car. They both went inside and drove across the fan of drives and pulled up in front of fourteen. He waited on the doorstep for a couple of minutes and then rang the doorbell.

A woman's face peered around the open door. Ben got an impression of short dark hair and big dark eyes. Children gathered beyond Mrs Johnson eager to see what something from beyond the walls looked like but too fearful to step out from behind their mum. Ben hefted the computer print out onto one knee.

'Mr Johnson asked me to drop this off with you? For him?'

She went to take it but the print out must have weighed as much as she did.

'Is it all right if I put it in the hall?' The door was pulled further open and the children melted back towards the stairs and the double doors into the living room. Lounge, Ben mentally corrected himself.

'Thank you that is very kind,' Mrs Johnson tried out a flash of a smile but looked concerned at the open door.

'No problem at all. Glad to help. Goodnight,' he waved at the large-eyed children as they clustered back around their mother, smiled at Mrs Johnson and backed out of the hall into the cool night air. He turned to look at his car and saw that the gates had closed themselves, 'How do I...'

'Just drive up, not too close and they will open themselves.'

'Okay cool. Night again,' he felt like adding 'it's not that bad out there you know.' But he decided against it. The door closed behind him, the lock turned and the bolts put back in place. Ben went back to the car looking around the estate. The lights showed through the drawn curtains. In the eve of each house an alarm box flashed its 'Not this house' light. For a moment Ben wondered if he was right. Was it so dangerous out there this was the only sensible way to live? He started the Astra and the yellow dashboard lit up like Jodrell Bank. He eased his way out through the gates, passed the burning tyres and temporary barricades and back into the apocalyptic world beyond.

Ben drove for a while without really thinking about where he was going. Not wanting to go back to Chalvey, he found himself heading for Staines. Easier in those days because he still had a car. He sat looking at the outside of Ruth's house but only for a moment. Ben knew that if he started thinking again it would all be over. He stood on the door step. A young woman answered. She looked familiar to Ben but he couldn't place her. She smiled in recognition but didn't do anything else.

'Hello. Is Ruth in?' It took Ben right back to asking Mrs McCarthy the same question. The woman stepped away from the door but didn't invite him in. She shouted up the stairs and walked through the hall into the kitchen at the back of the house. Ruth came cautiously down the heavily patterned turquoise and gold carpet, stooping slightly so that she could see who was at the door before coming all the way down.

'Hello Ben. This is a surprise.'

'It's been a funny day. Looks like...' Ben stopped himself, 'That's all Tomorrow stuff. Anyway I just wanted to see you.' Ruth was sitting on the third step now, knees up at her shoulders looking at him over the denim. It matched her eyes. 'Because...'

'Would you like to come in?'

'Yes please.'

'I'll get Vick to make us a cup of tea.'

Vick, of course, Ruth's little sister. She would only have been thirteen last time Ben saw her.

'I didn't recognise her.'

'It's been a while. She is down here looking for work. As long as it's not Tomorrow I am happy to help her.'

Vick came in with two mugs of tea, 'I'll go up to my room then. Just like old times. Oh no. That was you two going up to your room.' Vick gave an unconvincing sisterly smile and went back into the kitchen and then Ben could hear her climbing the stairs. Ben smiled awkwardly at Vick's comment about old times.

'I need to say I'm sorry Ruth.'

'For what?' Ruth had curled up on the couch while Ben sat on a wide sprawling thing that made sitting upright almost impossible. She wasn't going to make this easy and Ben couldn't blame her for it.

'For going up the Hill that day.'

'You can go up any hill anytime you like.'

'I'm sorry for going up the Hill with Clorinda.'

'Nothing wrong with that. We were all good friends.'

'Well,' Ben started. Here was the tricky bit. If he said that he hadn't actually shagged Clorinda that day it obviously ignored the fact that they wanted to and probably would have had they not been disturbed. He was guilty in thought if not in deed. Is that the same thing?

'I am really sorry that we did what we did that day.'

Ruth watched him. A Little Ben Travel clock ticked away five times a second in the silence.

'Clorinda always insisted you two didn't do anything.'

'And we didn't,' Ben said slightly too quickly, 'but we wanted to. Well, I wanted to. And we buggered off up the hill instead of helping Angus with his dad's car or you with…'

'My mum. I really needed you that day Ben. Now that Vick's left home…' Ruth lost focus for a while thinking about Mrs McCarthy. The clock hammered away again. What happened to those clocks you used to get on folks mantelpieces that ticked once per second like a grandfather clock?

'So I wanted to say I was sorry. I was sorry then and I'm more sorry now. And I understand that may not be enough.'

'No,' said Ruth. She held him in her brilliant blue eyes for a while. Ben thought that he should leave and tried to finish the hot tea. 'But it is a start,' she said with a small smile. 'Now that you have burnt yourself with that would you like something eat?'

Chapter Twenty One

Ben would have to say that Jana's training as a Value Trustee was light. She was sharp, took everything in and repeated it back in a way that conveyed complete understanding. But both Ben and Ruth quietly agreed that interest levels had fallen away pretty sharply. They were both hoping at that point that they would see a corresponding rise in Jana's interest in supporting her team and spreading a little of her sales skills across all the internal team. Sadly no. It was clear that having met her team, Jana was using the time to work out what, or who, would be a better thing to be interested in.

Curious thing about Jana, Ben would have to say she was immaculately presented rather than beautiful. Rumoured to be a black belt in Karate and certainly a keen attender of the gym, she was without doubt the fittest woman Ben had ever met fit. But, if she was interested, she could turn up her attractiveness like a wick. Seeing her do it drove the breath out of your lungs and any coherent thought out of your head. She had taken a shine at Neville once when he was going through a coherent phase and she mistook him for somebody important. Ben had been standing next to Neville when she had flicked the gas to full. Caught as collateral damage it was an image that had stuck with Ben ever since.

The buzzer for calls-waiting barked out again. Ben glanced up at the wonderful outline leaning on the door frame and dropped himself out of group hunt. Which he could do as one of the privileges of being a Value Trustee. But Jana clearly had too, some time ago. If they all dropped out then the phone group was less of a call hunt and more of a shoot fish in a barrel for those who were left. It was part of her brief to answer calls, so why Ben was helping out while she stood at the door chatting to Aaron?

Movement beyond Ben's cubicle caught his eye. Ben stood up. Christopher, one of the few sales guys Ben could name without prompting was circling around the office. He looked like he wanted to get in to see Aaron but Jana was still holding up the wall. He noticed that Ben was watching him and came over adjusting his tie. It was a huge seventies thing with Sylvester stretching for Tweety Pie in its cage.

Christopher looked down, 'Breaks the ice with the customers.'

'I think you'll find they are all 'clients' now.'

Christopher's eyes twinkled and pointed a gun like hand at Ben, 'How right you are Mr Williams. How right you are.' He smoothed his moustache and leant on the cubical wall hard enough to make it creak, 'So Value Trustee extraordinaire, what do you know?'

'The world is round and recreational drugs are likely to be dangerous if misused.'

Christopher smiled, 'I was thinking of matters closer to hand.' He tried to indicate directly behind him with his eyes.

'I thought you might be. I believe the office sweep is still open about whether they have or haven't yet. The incontrovertible truth has yet to be presented.'

'That they have done the deed? Played hide the sausage?' he drew breath for more allusions but Ben cut across him.

'I thought you were talking about finalising the redevelopment plan.'

'Of course dear boy. I must say that the prospect of Aaron's love child gives me a rather queasy feeling.'

Ben looked distant for a moment before speaking, 'It may entirely innocent. No really I mean it. Sometimes these things just aren't what people assume.'

'For example?' Christopher fished. Ben thought of all the time that people assumed he and Ruth were an item when they weren't. And then Debbie and then Clorinda and then that people thinking was not a good idea.

'Ah, none that I can think of. Still if she was determined to get you, it would be rather hard to say no,' said Ben.

Christopher was still smiling but it didn't reach his eyes this time when he spoke, 'Actually I wouldn't agree. I've got two lovely daughters, a wife that I am incredibly fortunate and that is undoubtedly the word, fortunate, to share my life with.' Christopher looked under his arm at the fantasy silhouette. 'When she looks at you there is only one calculation going through her mind. That is 'Is he more use to me than my current interest?' There is no thought of sharing there, romance, common interests, life, joy if that wasn't such an unfashionable concept.' He went back for another look. 'I'm sure it would be quite an adventure but you are only ever always seconds away from being yesterday's project.' He winked, clicked his fingers at Ben and stood up, drumming the edge of the partition. 'I did want a word with our Grand High Wizard but I have to go see some customers,' he emphasised the word carefully. He finished his tattoo and headed towards the way out, 'Be good Ben.'

'And you Christopher.'

He felt sad and annoyed when Christopher left although there was little reason to be. There was nothing different happening here. Jana was not doing her work. Aaron was wishing he could get into her pants so badly he could sustain no other thought or function. Ben paused at that point about what Christopher and he had talked about. Could he condemn The Senior Vice President of Global Business Development for doing what came naturally? Did Ben know what he would do if presented with a Jana on gas mark 9? He thought of Ruth and hoped he was wrong.

What had sparked this thinking off? Thinking, as Ben well knew, was a sure recipe for disaster. He sank back into his cubicle and the comfort of his chair but somehow the soothing solace of his Deluxe Executive Velour chair, with optional arms rang hollow.

'What have you got there?' Jana asked making Ben jump as he hadn't seen her stop the dance of the seven veils and leave Aaron's office.

'Most powerful document in the world,' Ben paused for dramatic effect. 'Better even than a Lone Star Leatherette Cowboy hat. But it is a secret and so as Value Trustee it is my sworn duty to tell no one until Aaron deems it the right time.'

'Tell me or I'll break your arm,' the perfectly made up face, framed by the brilliant white hair gave nothing away.

'It's an organisational chart.'

'A new organisational chart replacing the last new organisational chart that was implemented so well only by the Management Team only a few weeks ago?'

Ben looked around though he knew that there were pretty much out of earshot. Value Trustees had panel extensions fitted to their quads some time ago but even so they were clearly heading to interesting territory.

'Apparently the implementation of the last new organisational chart highlighted some gaps in the skills matrix of some of our field sales.'

'They are sacking Neville?' Jana guessed.

Ben handed over the sheet, 'No we're bringing him inside where he can broaden his experience.'

'Kept an eye on you mean. Bet the fucker keeps his car and...' she paused. 'Still three teams led by You, Me and Ruth,' she smiled. 'That's nice, that why you are showing me?'

'Looks like we have to hang together.'

'Or hang separately,' she pulled out one of the new wheelie chairs and sat beside him drawing on the sheet with her finger.

'So we have Ruth with Mu with most of the newbies and Helen. Me in Lemuria and I get Davie who is down as Business Development Manager?' she asked Ben who had to shrug.

'An extension of what he is already doing in the mid-tier accounts.'

'Mm but no Catherine! I thought Aaron said she wanted back into sales.'

'Interesting. I hadn't heard that. Franchise Manager,' Ben pointed at a small branch off the main organisational chart under Clare.

Jana traced the lines round, 'And I get Steve who appears not to have a new or interesting job title. I don't know him that well but he won't be happy with that will he?'

Ben shook his head, 'His relationship with the company has been on a long decline for a very long time. His Training half-life has collapsed and he has abandoned his self-development course completely. I even suggested that the company would pay for him to go on a full re-orientation and goal setting fortnight and he just laughed at me. You will really have your work cut out with him.'

'Joan as Field Sales Business Manager. But I think that's just a new name for being in charge of the reps. Oh.'

Ben found himself looking into steel grey eyes. Joan's transition to Field sales was complete, no office responsibility, at least on this chart.

'You showed me this because we have to work together? That means no bullshit. Deal?' Jana held out her manicured hand. Ben resisted the automatic reaction to look around again and shook her hand.

Ben walked along the street enjoying the oddity of having Staines to himself early on a Sunday morning. Apart from the dog walkers and a couple running and somebody who looked like they hadn't made it home last night and was now walking home in somebody else's shirt. So apart from them, he had the place to himself. First was the hole in the wall, that marvel of technology. He thought of Davie and Steve the night the banks had decided to crush them, feeling slightly relieved when the money slid out and he retrieved his card. The early morning light caught him as turned around and hurt his eyes and he thought of the

Halifax advert when they were still trying to persuade people that getting money from a machine was a cool and groovy thing to do.

Ben found himself singing the Bill Withers song as he collected a Sunday Times and crossed the road to the delicatessen on the far side. It was run by a Portuguese family always keen that he try something they had just made. However this morning he was focused enough to only order croissants and some presunto, which apparently was much nicer than Parma ham. Ben was still singing as he let himself back into Ruth's house though he had got stuck on a bit in the song.

'Lovely day, lovely day, lovely day…' Fresh coffee, croissants piled high on the tray, he headed upstairs half hoping that Ruth would still be asleep. When he pushed open the door she was tucked up in bed, peering over her glasses at him. The bed was spread with lots of pieces of paper in folders.

'Wonderful. I was wondering how much longer you were going to be,' she pushed the papers off the bed and flicked back the duvet. Back in the real world. Ben put the tray back down on the kitchen surface and smiled. His subconscious was always the optimist.

He stood at the bottom of the stairs and shouted,

'Ruth, breakfast is ready!'

'Wonderful. I was wondering how much longer you were going to be,' she came down the stairs arms full of folders and Ben noticed regretfully, fully dressed.

'And you appear to have all the companies Personality Profile Matrices.'

'Well, we need to catch up.'

Ben brought the tray back into the living room and thought about chasing crumbs under cover.

'Concentrate on the PPM's,' he said to himself.

'Mmm?' mumbled Ruth, 'I've started dividing them into piles. These are the Merit Rise Recommendations. These I wasn't sure about and…' she paused to look at the largest pile. 'These are the no hopers.'

Ben reached for his cup of coffee and for the last pile, 'No hopers is a bit harsh. The whole point of the training is that everybody should have a chance.'.

'That's the beauty of the PPM's. Have a look at the graph and their Quarterly Scores and it just jumps out.'

Ben leafed through the folder looking at each of the three score papers in detail and then back at the cover. The coffee had gone tepid by the time he had finished.

'Blimey. You are right, he just isn't trying at all. I liked Michael.'

'I did too but he is never going to make the grade in terms of sales. All we are doing is torturing him. He scored 27. Anything under 50 we would have to say is 'At risk'. Have a look at Davie's,' Ruth pulled the file for him and passed it over. Ruth had written '149' in red felt tip on the outside cover. Ben worked his way through the same process. At some point Ruth nipped into the kitchen bringing back fresh mugs of coffee. A cigarette would have gone down nicely but there was no way he was standing at the back door.

'Okay. I get it,' Ben looked at the clock sitting in the telly. The green LEDs showed 11:37. 'An hour each. Well this is going to take a while. Even with two of us it's going to take a fortnight of nothing else.' Ben thought of roping in Jana. Would that be a good idea? Even if it was a good idea would it be a good idea to introduce Jana into this picture of domestic near bliss?

'I just wanted to make sure you were happy with the scores. If you are, then the process is a whole lot faster.'

Ben picked up a stack of folders an entire teams future is in his hands, 'No hope, no, maybe, yes, no, maybe, yes, yes, yes.' Ben carried on skimming them into piles until they were all sorted. 'Good. That was easy. What are we going to do for the rest of the day?' Ben wiggled his eyebrows suggestively.

Ruth laughed and pointed at the no-hoper pile, 'according to that we are going to recommend to Aaron that we clear out half the company before year end,' she pointed out. 'So rather worryingly it looks like 50 is too high. We need to look at what we are doing in training. As well as give folk the heads up that they really need to improve their input in the PPM system or if we were applying the rules fully, they would be in a rather difficult position.'

'Well better that than an unexpected black ball?' said Ben, more to himself. Ruth looked puzzled.

'It is how they used to do it,' Ben sagged against the couch and glanced over at the croissant crumbs on the plate. This day started out with so much promise. He reached for the pile again. 'Okay let us see who the lowest ten percent are.'

The new organisation worked surprisingly well. There seemed to be a determination from Aaron and Joan that there could be no more changes, for the time being. This was driven in part at least by the 24% staff turnover every six months. Ben, Ruth and Jana as Value Trustees were working pretty much flat out on training new people, scaring the No-Hopes and even some experimentation in chopping jobs up a bit so that new people could be trained faster/replaced more easily.

The office was in a strange mood. It was different, it felt odd and Ben couldn't put his finger on it no matter which way he and Ruth stacked the Personality Profile Matrices. Ben felt that he had been running for a year, waiting for someone to start screaming at him that he had missed a bit and how could he have been so stupid as to not identify the accident that was undoubtedly waiting for them all. It reminded him of the scenes in Star Trek when somebody switched off the background noises tape to underline just how much trouble they were in.

It was Jana that answered his question for them, 'They are happy. I don't think that will show up in your PPMs will it.'

'You can mock,' Ben said. He stood up, still with his headset on so that nobody would be sure of he was on the phone or just chatting. He looked around at all of the quads, people on the phone, talking, typing, writing on customer files. One day IT would deliver a working customer records system but not yet. 'Do you think so?'

'Yes, happy. Not dancing in the aisles, I want to stand on a table and sing happy but yes. Nobody is shouting at them. You and me and Ruth are keeping things positive. Neville is busy circulating notes for all the meetings.'

'Well it gives him something to do.'

'Clare has taken her Free Athenian board down and Garfield finally released into the wild.'

'Yeah I've noticed that,' said Ben.

Jana brought her monitor back to life, 'We have figures again and they look good.'

Ben slowly panned around the room. Jana was right, people were smiling. Of the old team he never saw Davie these days, Helen looked okay and Steve, well Steve was locked away in that end office calling out like nobody should. Jana was going to have to do something about that before Aaron spotted it. If he ever saw anything in the office past Jana. Not that Ben was complaining. But anyway, thought Ben, that will be Tomorrow's problem.

'We should frame this moment. Savour it. Treasure it,' he said.

Jana stood up and stretched, measuring all that she saw with a practised eye, 'Have it shot, stuffed and mounted more like.'

Chapter Twenty Two

With the relentless pressure of staying out of the No-Hope pile, the teams themselves had become pretty competitive. Lemuria tended to get the exciting projects. Mu regarded themselves as those who get the job done. Atlantis though were struggling. Jana wasn't keen on the points system while at the same time Steve's increasingly wild behaviour made maintaining discipline tricky. Jana's position of 'You sell like Steve and you can behave like him,' was wearing a bit thin. Meanwhile Joan obviously felt that shouting at Field Sales was the best way forward.

Ben was sitting in Marketing. Davie was in there as well. He was working on some really interesting back-to-back deals now with Lone Star and was becoming a disturbing hybrid of sales, product marketing and buyer. They were discussing the next meeting with Lone Star. They all had their diaries out.

'I'm really sorry,' Ben said, 'I can't do the 9th.'

Davie looked grumpy for a moment, 'it's either that or the next day Lone Star can do is the 23rd. Do you really have to be there?'

Ben rubbed his forehead, 'You know the rules. If there is a supplier meeting then a VT has to be present. How about Ruth?'

'Tied up with training same as you.'

Catherine and Clare were pursing their lips.

'What about Joan?'

At that point the Thermometer door opened and Joan's words echoed across the office.

'I told you to come up with one idea each. Just one idea, none if you have made any effort!' Her voice was breaking. 'You're all fucking useless! I'm going out for a fag. When I come back you better have come up with something constructive!'

The whole of the company listened to the training room door slam followed by the one at the top of the stairs.

Ben let out a long breath.

'Maybe not. If Jana will take 'Talent for making the most of Tantalum Capacitors' then we're on?'

'Thank you,' Ben said.

'She really has lost it,' Clare commented and then she fixed Ben with a hard stare. 'Not to be repeated obviously. I don't need another interdepartmental war.'

Ben nodded. Clare continued talking but her mind had drifted off again, 'Yeah I know you wouldn't. Anyway. So how are things in Mu?' The tension in the room dropped away and everyone sat back.

'Good. We've been the first team to get the new cold call programme implemented.'

Clare looked blank.

'Do you remember some poor sod retyped all of Neville's list to boost his PPM score? Finally got around to doing something with it. So now every morning when you log on it gives you ten cold calls that you have to complete by the end of that day.'

The two Marketeers looked like they were chewing a wasp.

'And if they don't?' asked Clare.

'They get a demerit,' Ben said.

Clare turned to Davie, 'From what Catherine told me there is no way you would keep up with that. How come you haven't got kicked out the company then?'

'Putting aside the slur on my professionalism, I've done a deal with Jana. As long as I keep my figures well ahead of target then she gets one of the new folk to make my calls. I have my own worries.'

'Major Account review,' Ben said.

'No you've lost me,' Clare said.

'I'm sure I have seen you in that room?' asked Ben pointing to the arch connecting them to the main office. At that point they all jumped as Joan shouted, 'Right! What have you come up with.' The door slammed again and noise level dropped in the main office to complete silence as the internal sales strained to hear Joan being motivational.

'I try not to look too hard. Do you think I've got out of touch?' she asked Catherine.

Catherine shook her head, 'I wouldn't touch it if I were you.'

'The Major Account Review is when the reps come in and try and steal the Business Development Managers accounts,' Ben interrupted.

'Because?' asked Clare.

'They are worth more than the ones reps have,' Davie chipped in.

'Davie and Helen and the other BDMs build up accounts, have to hand them over and get the customers the reps don't want in compensation,' Ben explained.

'Usually the ones they took off us six months previously, never visited or did visit and fucked up completely and then hand back the tattered remains saying that we had hopelessly overstated the potential of the account.'

'Meantime you're trawling through general telesales accounts looking for anything interesting that you can add to your total.'

'Yes because Aaron won't reduce my target. I can hand over a £250k business and I'm still expected to make the budget at the end of the year. Doesn't matter that some muppet has trashed it in the meantime,' Davie was getting grumpy again.

Clare was shaking her head while Catherine just smiled, 'So you are all trying to steal business from each other. Sales is just one big happy family.'

'It's all right for you,' Ben said.

'And you,' she countered, 'VTs don't have budgets do they? If someone misses their personal budget they have to go see the Revenue Team- Aaron, me and Neville to explain why. What do you have to worry about?'

'If the team misses any of its goals- and I mean Quiet Time, Personal Development Goals, attendance at Thermometer, cold call rates, warm call rates, time keeping, voluntary hours worked, average toilet break rates,' Ben was ticking them off with his fingers, 'Clean Desk Policy. I have to explain why to Joan.' There was a Gnu moment as they all grunted in sympathy.

Then Davie's face spilt into a grin, 'Does that mean every time I read the newspaper in the bog Jana gets into trouble?'

Clare and Catherine groaned.

'Way too much information,' Clare looked serious again. Ben left them to it and went to find Ruth. He stopped off at his station and had a quick look at the Thermometer Screen which showed all three teams and their targets. Someone had zeroed all of the stats. Ben could guess who. Ruth was on the phone answering Atlantis. Ben joined in and helped clear the backlog. Finally the pair pulled off their headsets.

'What do you want?' she asked

'I could have just be being helpful but in this particular case-'

Ruth laughed.

'- in this particular case would you be willing to cover Adventures in the world of Tants while I support Davie in a meeting on the 9th?'

'You could have picked something interesting.'

'Like what?'

'Okay, relatively interesting.'

'Is that a yes?'

'It's a yes but you're going to have to do better than-' Ruth stopped in mid-sentence watching Jana backing out of Aaron's office with her hands behind her back and swinging an imaginary dress like Dorothy. At the sight of her, Atlantis scurried back to their desks. Jana looked like the cat that had got the cream and walked back slowly to her quads which took her past Mu.

'Hello Ruth. Hello Ben.'

'Jana you're looking pleased?' Jana rested her hip on the partition and folded her arms, pushing her chest up in a way that Ben found distracting. But they seemed to be pointed at Ruth. Ben was further distracted by the thought that Jana was making the point about who had got the biggest chest. That wasn't how it worked with girls was it?

'Yeah things are looking good,' she took on a conspiratorial tone and hunched a bit making it quite difficult for Ben to continue to look. 'Aaron has thought this Joan thing hasn't been working for some time. But he didn't want to say anything since we all know the importance of stability. However Aaron thinks that the innovative style of the internal teams are being hampered by a slightly negative air in field sales.' She pointed towards the desolate training room of despair.

Ruth managed a dead pan, 'Do you think?'

'So he's going to call a full management meeting for ideas on how we are going to solve that problem and get the latest update on the IT situation. Now Aaron thought it should be just a representative Middle Manager but I said it shouldn't just be me since we all are impacted by what's going on over there and you might have a good idea which would be missed otherwise. So luckily he has agreed that all the VTs will be included in the meeting. It's set for the 9th so make sure you are there and ready to contribute. If you want to have a chat beforehand about it I'll be happy to help,' Jana smiled her cheerleader smile waiting for the gratitude that would surely follow.

'Thank you,' Ben said. He got a flash of Jana's heartrending power as reward and she unwrapped herself from the divider and cruised on to Atlantis. Ruth's small scream of frustration was drowned by Joan bellowing:

'Get out there and prove you are not as useless as everyone thinks!' The external sales team stumbled out of the office and back to clutter up the desks looking as motivated as hell. Joan walked out and shook herself down of all the hate. When she was done she smiled at Ruth and Ben in a way that Ben would have to say looked sincere and indeed warming. As one Atlantean to another it was impressive to see the level of control that Joan could deploy. Also, Ben felt, slightly scary.

It was Catherine's birthday and she had invited her friends and Davie and Ben to a paintball day. Ben hadn't thought through who Catherine was friends with until he was standing looking at Debbie with a gun in her hand. He beat a hasty retreat out into the wooded glen of combat.

'I haven't seen Debbie since that bowling night at Sneaky Pete's',' said Ben who felt her appearance needed a comment.

'It's not Sneaky Pete's, that's in Edinburgh.'

'The night club in Slough?' Ben asked.

'Yes. I can't remember its name. I don't think I have ever been in there sober but it's not Sneaky Pete's. It would appear she has a new boyfriend,' Davie said helpfully.

'I noticed. He looked familiar.'

'Your doppelganger Ben. It was quite spooky having the two of you in the same hut. You would have to say though it's a neat solution to the problem of you not being interested.'

'Finding another version of me that is?'

'Yes. Albeit a slightly more nervous looking version. It seems to have made her happy. Although, and as an Islander I have to tread carefully here, it doesn't bode well for the west of Scotland gene pool if she can find another you that easily.'

'Poor sod looked quite surprised when he saw me.'

'Most people look quite surprised when they see you.'

'Bugger off Davie. I am armed you know.' But the Marshalls were very clear that team shooting would be punished by expulsion so Davie and Ben were forced to use their martial skills on the other team. As a result they were quickly pinned behind a bunker. Somewhere beyond the smoke grenades, the blue team were closing in.

'So, now that we are alone together. And facing almost certain death. What score do you have to stay out of No-Hopes and keep your job with the company?' Davie asked while reloading the paint pellets into the magazine.

'I think we are keen to try and avoid a specific figure. Any specific cut off figure would be arbitrary.'

'And increases the FUD factor?' asked Davie.

'FUD?'

'Fear, Uncertainty and Doubt,' Davie was smiling as he said it but only just.

'That really isn't the idea. If it helps I think we have raised the floor to 41 now'

'Very reassuring.' To break the tension Davie looked back out through the gaps in the logs, 'Okay, changing tack. It seems like a good time to ask are you and Ruth an item?'

'That's an interesting question. Do people think we are? Does it matter?'

'Answering a question with a question. It mattered ever since you two made relationships a subset part of the PPM. So who does your PPM? Who watches the watchers?' asked Davie.

'In our case it's Joan really,' Ben was suddenly wondering if Joan had PPMs on him and Ruth, it had not occurred to him before.

'Well there are those rumours too,' Davie was smiling broadly now, poking his head round the door and snapping off a few shots. Some balls thudded against the door frame.

'About me and Joan? Bloody hell.'

'You must have noticed the way she has the hots for you.' Ben shook his head in genuine disbelief. 'You watch out next time she hauls herself onto a desk and points those puppies in your direction.'

'I've never really noticed. Isn't that just the way she sits,' Ben frowned as he spoke.

'Only when it happens to be you at the other end of the table,' Davie said confidently. Ben couldn't think of a response. Emboldened, Davie stepped back out firing from the hip in true Rambo style, 'Hah got one! Oh y'bugger.'

Davie dived back in as a hail of paint splattered on the woodwork. Ben sat with his back against the log wall. 'I'm out, give me one of yours?'

'Sure,' Ben tossed over a tube of refills while he tried to make sense of what Davie was saying. 'I really want it to work with Ruth.' Davie shook the refills so that the first ball loaded and fired at a shadow through the panelling, someone shouted and fell away clutching their middle. Davie went back outside, picking his targets this time.

'As for Joan I haven't done anything wrong,' Ben said when Davie returned.

'No smoke,' commented Davie. Ben swivelled round to look at Davie for the first time in the conversation but his full-face mask gave nothing away. 'They've run out of smoke grenades. We can get them,' Davie stepped back into cover again. 'Your heart's not really in this is it?'

Ben struggled to his feet, 'Sorry, you're right. Wonder where the rest of the team are?'

Ready to catch the bad guys by surprise the pair burst out into the sunlight and were cut down by a hail of blue paint.

Lunch was pork carved off the spit in a bun and a mug of tea, it tasted fantastic, which Ben put down to a touch of that 'having faced death and lived' feeling. Sitting as far away from Debbie and Ben-two as possible, Ben had his shirt off and was counting the bruises from the last attack.

'I'm bleeding,' Ben whined.

Catherine was laughing at him, 'The pair of you looked like you were off for a walk in the park and the screams! I thought I'd shot a girl'

'It sodding hurt,' Davie confirmed, sounding more butch than Ben. Catherine got another roll and pig and came over for a closer look.

She pursed her lips as she ran her fingers over the lumps and bumps, 'If you think it's bad now, you wait until tomorrow.'

'There is an evil side to you Catherine that I don't think I've seen before.'

She really belly laughed then, 'You don't know the half of it.'

Catherine's brother John came over and showed them the shot he had taken through the wall. There was an appreciative 'ooo' from anyone who saw the bloody mark. Chris was as wide as Davie and as tall as Ben.

He was still laughing as he said, 'You wait till this afternoon man. Your ass belongs to me.'

The early winter sun had set as they left the battleground for a swift pint at the local. Clare had come out to meet them there and give Catherine her birthday present. She looked amazed and horrified as they all showed her their battle scars. Ben wasn't sure if his sides hurt more from laughing or the pellet wounds. John gave them something to smoke to ease the pain on the way home but even though Debbie and the clone had left he shook his head. Davie said he was driving. They thanked Catherine and hugged her.

'Brilliant day. Thanks very much Catherine, and happy birthday.'

She walked away towards the small coach they had hired to bring everyone out. The two men walked over to Davie's Manta. He drove out of the gravel car park with a hint of oversteer.

'Can't beat a rear wheel drive car. Davie?' Ben lit the pair of them cigarettes and passed one over. 'I need to ask you about Steve. Have you seen him at all?'

'You know that I moved out?' said Davie as he concentrated hard to try and see in the gathering gloom.

'I don't know the details.'

'We just weren't good for each other. I had been saving up for a deposit. Which I blew. Steve discovered he had some headroom on his mortgage, which he blew. After everything was spent the bank would give me £300 in cash every month if I turned up and signed for it. They take everything else to pay back what I owe.'

'That must be tough.'

'I needed to cut my outgoing so Catherine helped me get into a Housing Association near the Britwell. However that kind of left Steve short, just when he needed it most.'

'Ah.'

'So our last conversation didn't go so well.'

'Mine neither.'

'I think we all heard that. And the bit where he called you and Jana the Stasi.'

'Yup. I'm glad my old Atlantis teacher didn't see that one,' Ben was about to start talking about Steve's PPM's but realised that would only underline Steve's point. They drove in silence for the rest of the drive apart from where Ben felt he needed to point out poorly illuminated obstructions such as pedestrians and corners.

'So…' Davie asked, with a pause that indicated this, and not how things were going with Ruth, was the question he had been building up to all day, 'what's this upcoming company weekend thing all about?'

'It's a sharing, training, caring kind of a thing. There was a plan to have a management meeting off site and it sort of morphed into this. The idea is that the whole company gets together and has a think about what Tomorrow should look like.'

'The whole company being put up for the weekend instead of just the management! Where was this off-site meeting going to be, Acapulco?'

'It should be fun. Though Aaron insisted that it wasn't going to be Dawns' company that did the training.'

'That certainly makes it more attractive. Do you think Jana has it in for Joan then? Think she fancies a company car?'

'I don't think that's likely Davie. Joan has done an amazing job in difficult circumstances. And Aaron has been very clear on the no politics rule.'

'No. No. Just me thinking out loud,' Davie backpedalled, which is tricky when you are driving. They pulled into Ben's street. The cars were parked both sides with a half on half off arrangement that meant there wasn't really room for a car with intact wing mirrors to make it all the way down.

Davie stopped and pulled on the internal light so that he could see Ben's face, 'Been good to see you out of work.'

'Yes it has. Goodnight Davie. Thank you for the lift.'

'No problem Ben.'

Ben watched the Manta pull away into the Slough traffic and then walked back down the middle of the road to his digs.

Chapter Twenty Three

'This is an exciting time for Tomorrow. We want you to share in that sense of excitement. That's what this weekend is all about. Teamwork, bringing the company together and excitement. We want to develop the skills that we know exist in the company. In the people that make up the company. We hope to achieve that by working together, away from the constraints and expectations of the office or the road. My role now is to capture what we learn here and take the best back into what we do together as an extended family around the world,' Aaron, the President of Global Business Development, looked round at the rest of the top table. Joan, Clare, Arthur Neville, Jana and the biggest Accountant all beamed out at their respective teams. Seeing Jana up there was like a bucket of cold water on Ben and it was clearly having the same effect on Ruth.

'I would also like to take this opportunity,' Aaron continued, 'to thank you all for giving up your weekend. Jana has suggested that it counts as double Volunteer points for your PPM which I'm sure will go down really well. She also has done a great job in organising all of this so I hope you join me in thanking her.'

The company clapped and Jana soaked up the praise. Ben was just thinking how that would skew every single PPM. All that paperwork and yet the bottom 10% would still be, funnily enough, at the bottom.

'It is amazing.' Ruth spat, 'how far she has travelled on her back in such a short space of time?'

'That's jumping to conclusions. You don't know they actually have done anything,' Ben said who instantly regretted any reference to people who may or may not have slept together. 'But you are right. It's not very subtle.' There were similar comments buried under the adulation from around the rest of the floor. Aaron called for silence and pulled over the front page of the flip chart.

'What we have done is divide you into squads. These squads will have a variety of tasks over the next two days. Some mental, some physical and some just for fun! We've tried to make sure there are no right answers here. The aim is to ensure spontaneity.'

Christopher, arriving late, slid into the seat next to Ben with his legs outstretched and his arms folded over his expansive stomach, 'If I'd been him I would have put a few drinks down our necks first. Loosened us up a bit.'

'I'm parched,' Ben agreed.

'We have a theme for the teams as you will see and we have tried to make sure that each team has a cross section of the company. Have a look at the flip chart to find out which squad you're in. You can then collect your…' he paused as one of the reps stumbled forward into the light, '-when I have finished Peter.' There was a ragged cheer from the back as the rep realised he was in the wrong place mid-stroll and retreated back into the darkness.

'Where was I?'

Distracted Aaron glanced down at his notes but he was back on song when he spoke again, 'Collect your badges, get together and elect a co-ordinator. The Co-ordinator should then get the list of tasks for tomorrow and the squad can prioritise and assign roles,' Aaron paused again looking at his notes. 'No that's it. Now Peter, time for you find out about your squad.'

The noise level in the room rose with the lights but quickly subsided as the staff of Tomorrow scattered evenly between those heading for the bar; those wanting to find out more about the team they had been given and those who weren't looking forward to being brought together, had had enough excitement already and had gone off to find a phone and get contact with the outside world.

Ben, Ruth and Christopher were in prime position for the dash for beer but found themselves instead drawn without discussion to the lists. They could see now that the lights had come up that Aaron's chart was just the outlier of a forest of curious three legged trees, each with their one white leaf. They paused for a moment at one board, 'Sir Lancelot' written in purple across the top. Below it, carefully mixed up in order to suggest some random element were Aaron and Jana. Ruth offered to get the first round of drinks in while Ben re-read the other elements of Sir Lancelot and recognised a selection of some of the fitter people and the minor sycophants.

'This is going to be more interesting than I would have thought. Ben?' Christopher's question made Ben stop reading the other teams and come over. Under 'Sir Percival' he spotted his own name, Christopher as a representative of Field Sales, and Ruth. Christopher could barely talk he was grinning so hard.

'My eagle eye spots that young Brian from accounts is our Squad Leader,' he picked up all the badges holding up Brian's with the letters 'TL' against his name. 'I to so love spontaneity and empowerment.'

Ben ran his fingers down the rest of the team names, 'It's all the duds in the company. And of course, us.'

Christopher reached up and scrubbed out Sir Percival, 'We can hardly be the chaste, not with you in the team can we?' he said chuckling.

Instead of taking offence Ben smiled when he read what Christopher had written. He spent a moment looking round the rest of the flipcharts.

'Looks like some of the others weren't convinced by their names either. Shall we go and find the rest of the ex-Percival's and give them the good news.

Some Park staff had appeared and were clearing up. There was one tired looking middle manager in a suit going around collecting up the team sheets. His bright gold name badge with '*call me Kevin*' undermining his attempt to emulate a serious business look. The Tomorrow people took the hint and drifted towards the bar. Ben and Ruth sat slightly separate from the rest, being Value Trustees tended to have that affect but the reduction from three to two made that separation all the more noticeable. They had a few drinks and left. As they walked back through the pines Ben reached out and held Ruth's hand. For the first time since Utopia they kissed under the trees by the light of the 'You are here' sign.

Chapter Twenty Four

It was the next morning as Ben came round snuggled up with Ruth in a better bed than he had at home. Ruth had slid in under the crook of his arm. She was already awake but had been watching the geese wander from breakfast to breakfast.

'Let's not go in. Let's just stay here and then when nobody's looking, we just go home.' Ben said.

She snuggled in even tighter, 'That is a superb idea.'

Just as Ben's hand pulled her in across the sheet Christopher strode out of one of the bedrooms and passed their open door with only an undersized white hand towel to protect the innocent.

'Morning dear hearts. No more gymnastics please. It's not good for those of us with a more delicate disposition,' he stroked his moustache but had to keep the other hand on the towel in case it gave up its unequal struggle.

'Shouldn't you not be here?' asked Ben.

'Dreadful cock up with reservations. Many kindly people pointed out that there would in all likelihood be a spare bed here. Though it would appear that you were both so eager when you got back, you forgot to close any of the doors making my key superfluous.'

Ruth had sunk under the duvet and Christopher laughed, 'Jolly good. Breakfast briefing at 9 in what I suppose we should refer to as Camelot.' Christopher laughed again, over-loudly to Ben's ears, and strode on towards the shower rewarding his landlord with sight of a bottom smooth enough for any baby to be proud of.

They made it on time, never be late was the golden rule. Ben had gone down like a nine pin when he'd closed his eyes in the shower taking the screen, curtain and rail with him. Ruth had thought she was going to be sick in the bushes on the way there but, eyes watering and gait unsteady, they were there, on time. Thank you very much. They were both so pleased with themselves as they gathered their official Tomorrow breakfast of croissant and coffee that it took them a while to realise that all was not happy in the legendary castle.

Aaron appeared to be arguing with an even more haggard looking Kevin.

'You have made the t-shirts up wrong! The instructions were quite clear. After the teams had picked their names you were to make up 12 shirts with each of the names and they were to be ready for the teams to wear this morning.'

'Which is exactly what we were up half the night doing,' Kevin missed out the word 'bloody' but was clearly there. Ben made a mental note that that would be a useful skill to learn.

'But it's wrong.'

'We printed the shirts with the names that were on the top of the sheets!'

'There isn't a knight called Sir Robin.'

Christopher positively pranced into the fray and scooped up the offending items from the exhausted Kevin's arms, 'Yes there is dear boy. And we are he. As it were.' Christopher's black eyes twinkled furiously as he started handing out the t-shirts to Team Robin, 'These are rather good quality Aaron. Must have cost you a pretty packet.'

'Are you sure Robin is a knight of the round table?' Aaron didn't look convinced.

Ben on a temporary pastry rush chipped in, 'Oh yes, he was the knight that wasn't quite as brave as Sir Lancelot.' Aaron looked suspiciously at the pair of them, sure he was being mocked by the Europeans but unable to prove it.

He picked up the next disputed pile, 'I'm sure Lady Galadriel wasn't a knight.'

Catherine came up to take them off Aaron with a smile, 'The team names were all blokes. Seemed a bit sexist to me.' Aaron blanched. 'So Clare came up with Galadriel.'

'Shouldn't that be Guinevere?' Christopher wondered hesitantly.

Catherine shrugged, 'She was quite clear it was Galadriel and I wasn't going to argue with her.' Catherine walked back to her team and started distributing their apparel.

'Could have been worse Aaron,' Christopher said loudly as he handed Ruth and Ben their shirts, 'could have been Godiva.'

Aaron looked round the room looking slightly hurt. By the time he had recovered himself Kevin had gone, leaving the remaining team shirts neatly on the floor. Ruth held her t-shirt and stood looking outside at the forest for a moment. Ben looked at both her and her reflection and for the first time Ben saw her as she was now, not the girl he had been so careless with a lifetime ago. She collected a pile of breakfast pastries and sat back down beside Ben with perfect poise. Her biceps bunched as she placed the heavily laden tray.

She looked at his puppy dog face and laughed, 'You going to change your top now Ben?'

'Put you off your breakfast.'

She tossed two rolls onto his tray and tore the head off one of hers snarling at him. Christopher sat down opposite them both. He was already in his team shirt.

'Go on,' Ruth said, 'You know you want to.'

Ben shrugged and pulled the buttoned shirt over his head and then ripped open the thin film on the pack.

'Not bad,' Christopher said.

'Thank you darling,' Ben said, and thought of Steve. Ben had a call from Steve's hospital Friday afternoon. Voluntary admission but on his doctor's recommendation. Unlikely to be back at work for quite some time. Ruth had been quite upset. He had tried to tell Jana, Joan and Aaron but they all had other things on their minds.

Ben returned the smile and hauled on the t shirt. He smoothed it down, 'They're alright aren't they? Shouldn't we go find Brian?'

Christopher put down his cup with exaggerated care and let out a long sigh, 'This whole thing is so choreographed it's a wonder Messer's Webber and Rice don't make an appearance. Clearly we have been set to fail.' He folded his hands together in front of his face for a moment. 'Given the sterling qualities of our leader I think the success of the team is in our hands. We three must make a plan of action. Once we have done that then we can tell Brian where it is that he must lead us.'

The morning was to be divided into activities varying from the physical to the mental. In each of the events Sir Robin would be up against two other teams with the winner getting five points, the middle team getting three and the losers getting one. Ben noticed the pattern pretty quickly. Sir Lancelot would tend to get the physical teams in the cerebral challenges. Then inexplicably found themselves up against the bookworms when trying to get all team members over two eight foot walls and shark infested custard with one plank, a wheel barrow and 60 foot of rope.

Ben quickly explained to Brian that this was to their advantage. Sir Robin, with all the people who were apparently viewed as neither smart nor fit, was the wild card team. Success could be in their grasp with a bit of planning, teamwork and shameless cheating. Soon Brian's management skills were soon the envy of the rest of the company as his unexpectedly willing lieutenants snapped around his team like Dobermans at a burglars' rally. By judicious copying, nobbling and a fair bit of hard work, Sir Robin and Sir Lancelot were neck and neck by lunchtime.

Ben was commiserating with the Sir Galahads about the mini treasure hunt where the other teams had been lucky to find only five of the six real locations on the map within the allotted span. He spotted Ruth gliding back to sit beside Christopher in conspiratorial fashion. Oblivious Brian sat at the head of the table basking in the reflected glow of his team's success.

Ben wandered back and stopped off, kneeling beside his successful leader, 'Doing great Brian.' He then spoke low enough that no one else could hear, 'Treasure hunt next. Word is the Lake clue is a red herring and teams that have gone after that clue didn't have time to get round the rest.'

'Right,' Brian said looking thoughtful.

Ben suspected that must be how Pooh looked when doing his especially hard thinking, 'How about we split up, and cover both these areas. We should have better chance of finding all the answers.'

The bear of great strength nodded, 'Hmm, but aren't we meant to do them in sequence, one clue leading to the other?'

'It'll be fine,' he straightened and walked down the table to Ruth and Christopher, tossing the heavily annotated clue map onto the table.

'Excellent Mr Williams. And Miss McCarthy here has some rather interesting ideas on our second from last puzzle,' he delicately picked up the map. 'I'll just go find a photocopier.' As he got up the balance of the whole bench shifted.

Ben looked to Ruth who was reworking a sheet of paper, 'That nice chap Kevin showed me this. I think he was trying to impress me.' The sheet she was smoothing out was covered in blocks of squares arranged three by three. Some had many numbers some had almost none.

Ben shook his head, 'Nope.'

'It's a number puzzle.'

Ben still looked blank.

'Each of the blocks have to filled in with the numbers 1 to 9 without repetition or omission and they all have to add up to that number there when you add up across the box, in any direction,' her pencil flicked across the boxes throwing numbers down in each of the blocks. Within a couple of minutes she had all but two filled in. She turned the paper round and looked at Ben through narrowed eyes. 'See?'

Ben had to shake his head, 'No,' he added up a few lines. 'They all add up so I can see that you have done it but how you did it I have no idea.'

'Not just a dumb blonde,' behind her long black lashes, her eyes were steel hard.

'Never thought you were. And I don't know how to break this to you but you are not blonde,' Ben sat back, both hands up in surrender.

'I could see it written across Kevin's face. 'I'll show this to the girl since she'll think I'm so smart and since she won't understand what she is looking at, no harm done.' Git. And it's not just men. Jana and Joan both don't take me seriously. Shit,' She had finished the last three blocks, marked as 'bonus' and threw the pencil across the table. Ben wanted to tell her they should have gone this morning. But then she might ask to go.

'I need some more water,' Ruth walked off towards the central food hall while Neville came the other way. He was smiling like a man trying not to.

'Hello Neville, you look different?' Ben said, a little unnerved. Neville looked both ways theatrically but Ben noticed that the hair stayed perfectly in place.

'I have just had a meeting with Aaron,' the smile grew into a grin but he stopped forcing Ben to ask.

'And it was obviously good news?'

'Yes it was,' confirmed Neville. Ben thought he was going to make him ask again so waited this time. 'Okay. Aaron hinted that after this little charade is over he is going to announce me as the new Sales Director in charge of Field Sales.'

'Wow. Hinted?'

'Well he wasn't going to be drawn, the whole point of this...' Neville waived his arm around at the forest and the teams scuttling backwards and forwards, 'is that the company needs more central control. A bit more procedure.'

'And you're the guy to do it.'

'That's what Aaron thinks. Anyway not a word. But I guess we will be working a lot closer in future,' Neville clapped him on the shoulder. 'It will be fun. I need to go win the games. I think we are up against you for Football this afternoon?'

'There are a few more puzzles first. Then football. Then, of course, the rocket building finale. It's a nice piece of symbolism. Aaron referred to Hermione's original plan as the Rocket Science of Electronics. A chance to do something really different, groundbreaking. And here he is bringing the whole company together to build rockets.'

Neville looked at Ben brightly but without comprehension, 'I'll be back for the football then.'

Ben watched Neville heading back towards the main compound. Christopher came past the other way eating something involving pecans and a lot of caramel with a pastry fork. He stopped and stared at Neville's back for a moment before reaching Ben.

'That's very strange you know Mr Williams,' Christopher smoothed his moustache. 'Our Sales Client Liaison Officer Whatever-he-is just smiled at me. And do you know I can't remember the last time he did that. What did you say to him?'

Ben looked at the pastry fork gleaming in the sunlight, 'My natural charm?' he offered.

Christopher looked unconvinced and said so, 'And Miss McCarthy?' he asked

'That didn't go so well. I need to go find her. You want to get the team into gear?' Ben jogged off after Ruth but paused as he reached the trees. He really needed some Irn Bru. He wondered if Ruth had had the same idea and headed towards the mini-supermarket. He could hear Christopher herding the cats,

'Right Brian, the rest of you. Treasure hunt next and this is how we are going to win it.'

Chapter Twenty Five

All the teams were now gathered in the main covered area. It had a vaguely Hawaiian / African hut theme, designed and built by people who had apparently taken their cues from Magnum and Daktari. Ruth told Ben that according to her notes that the Sir Robins were still first equal with Sir Lancelots. Jana and Aaron had not counted on a motivated wild card bunch of losers led by a man with unrecognised and surprising leadership ability. There was a lot of jeering from the Sir Robins now. Blood was up, adrenaline coursing through the veins. They were ready to win and said so quite loudly.

Kevin had to shout to get himself heard, 'Please listen. Your last task is split into two halves. In the first half you are the design team for a rocket. You will find your specific roles on the tables in front of you. You will also see a list of people that you can communicate with. That is one person up stream of you and one person down.'

Ben looked quickly up the length of the table. The gang of three that had driven Sir Robin to the brink of success were neatly isolated from each other and Brian who had been given the role of final assembly. The names had been changed, scribbled over the typed listings. Ben looked across at Aaron and Jana who were standing together laughing. How had they found time to do it in between all the games? Jana was scary.

Ben looked for Ruth and winked at her. She managed a smile back.

'So finish your rockets. You have half an hour and then we can move onto the next section.'

Christopher risked sanction by speaking up, 'This is going to be impracticable. This isn't going to work,' he explained to his immediate neighbours. 'If we are to be rocket scientists then it will be all about teamwork, less rigid structure and we get the rockets built.'

Looking round the other teams as they settled into the process it looked like they had drawn the same conclusion. All the teams relaxed as the perception that they had been given an impossible task to finish the day on swept through the groups. The two exceptions were the Sir Lancelots who appeared to be working furiously and the Galahads where Joan was determined that 'impossible' wasn't in her vocabulary apart from when it had 'not' in front of it. Right enough twenty five minutes in, tempers frayed as it became clear that two incompatible types of launch system were being built. Aaron and Jana now talking at each other but neither was listening. Joan's 'Management by shouting' technique had reached new and quite painful heights.

'Rigid structure and driven personnel. It's an explosive mixture,' Ben said. Kevin was called in and there were some earnest conversations in hushed tones. Kevin looked angry.

'Ladies and gentlemen!' he shouted, 'Competition rules still apply so no talking please!' He looked pointedly at team Galadriel. Catherine looked pointedly back making it crystal clear that she wasn't bothered. 'Since none of you have managed to finish the rocket yet, we have decided to extend the time allowed by a further fifteen minutes.' Curious looks flashed around the teams. 'Though that may mean that we don't have enough time for phase two,' he looked darkly at Aaron. 'If we haven't reached a conclusion by then the team closest to completion will win this a particular game.

'Bugger,' Christopher said, 'does that mean we were meant to do it then?'

'Too late for that thought,' Ben had been observing Galadriel and Lancelot closely to try and gauge how many parts of the rocket both teams had built. What he had seen was that determination to finish that which could not be finished, was inflicting a terrible toll on the team members. Tears and tantrums and people stomping off meant that the crews were falling apart as he watched.

'Actually, it could be time for an intervention. Wouldn't you say Christopher, that given they are now down to six staff that Sir Lancelot are now in breach of the rules of the game? While Galadriel appear to have set up some sort of knitting circle in order to complete the task.'

Christopher looked away from his attempt at drawing a three dimensional model of the piping he needed, 'How right you are dear boy. In fact that is the Flight Engineer talking to Mission Control. Oi! Ref!' Christopher waved at Kevin, 'Foul!'

Ben and Ruth had time to go and get a drink and come back before the dust had settled. Christopher was obviously having an excellent time baiting Aaron and Jana with the charge of dishonesty. The team were using Kevin to try and gain some respectability which was clearly making Kevin himself wish that everyone would grow up. The growing sense of chaos infected the rest of the teams and work stopped, rockets lay abandoned and people started wondering if the game had actually come to an end. If it was a game. And if it had an end. Kevin, having to shout for the second time in less than twenty-four hours called proceedings to a halt. Scooped up all the score charts and stomped off towards the staff offices trailed by a concerned Jana. The sense of dissatisfaction was palpable.

'That's what I like about these motivational weekends,' Ben said.

Ruth looked much more like her old self as she responded, 'They're so motivational.'

'Couldn't put it better myself. Motivational. There was Tomorrow all in bits and feeling down, and now look at them. Motivated and bonded,' Ben screwed his face up in mock happiness.

The process of bonding, helped by the free wine, strengthened through the meal. By the time the presentations started, the spirit against Sir Lancelot was strong enough you could build oil rigs out of it. There was a curious silent argument between Aaron and Kevin which resulted in Kevin taking his name tag off and walking out into the shadows. Aaron was still talking to Jana as he absentmindedly turned on the mike too early.

'Probably still pissed about getting those T-shirts wrong,' Aaron looked out into the seething darkness. 'Hello?' he said hesitantly, 'I'm pleased to announce the results of the day's competition. Kevin should be doing this but I think he has to be somewhere else. So in reverse order, in third place, Galadriel with 27 points,' a curious high pitched roar went up from the back of the room. 'In second place Sir Gawain.' Gawain's cheering was drowned by the collective puzzlement of the staff and some of the Gawain team.

'Did they show up?' Christopher shouted.

'Yes they did,' Aaron, off balance, went for paternal but got patronising, 'they did very well with 29 points.' Someone coughed 'bollocks' from one of the front tables. Ben thought it might be Peter.

Aaron pointedly ignored the comment and launched straight in with what appeared to be sincere discomfort, 'Which means that in first place, and this is rather embarrassing, was Sir Lancelot. I'm sure you'll all join in with our celebrations. If the team would like to come up and collect their prize?'

'What about Sir Robin?' Ben shouted, there were catcalls from the rest of Sir Robin and those who had played Sir Gawain and won. Galahad radiated the fury of those who had suffered greatly for nothing. There was a furious amount of calculation re-calculation and comparing. So much so that Aaron's closing statement was lost completely.

Christopher looked furious, 'I can't believe the bastards would be so barefaced about it!'

Ben got up from the table and swooped up his lager, 'Christopher. Fuck it. Do you really care?'

'Yes I do! I care because those shits think we are too stupid to figure it out or too lazy to do anything about it if we did. And that isn't right.'

Ben paused for a moment thinking through what Christopher had said.

'I agree with you,' Ben pointed his glass at him, 'but shouting at them won't change anything.'

'I'll punch the weasel then.'

Ben smiled at that, 'Confrontation won't work Christopher, we haven't got the power. Might is right.'

Christopher was standing now too, his finger jabbing the table as he shouted above the background noise at Neville who was trying to back up onto the stage to collect his prize and not look like he was ignoring Christopher, which he clearly was. Ben and Ruth decided to be elsewhere. Christopher spotted them going.

'Is that it? Are you just going to walk away?'

'Live to fight another day,' Ben paused at the door. During the meal it had occurred to him that that the best opportunity to have a real chat with Aaron was before he announced whatever the new plan was. Was he really planning some kind of return to Hermione's ethos? Had Ben understood the significance of the rocket building correctly? There had been a moment when it had been Ben getting the briefings before anyone else, the little insights on future plans, the organisation charts. That didn't seem to be happening now. Had he failed some unspoken test? But he was sure he should try and talk to Aaron before anything went public, before it was too late.

Ben went back into the room but spotted Jana before he spotted Aaron. Actually he couldn't miss Jana. She was standing close to Aaron at the bar, talking earnestly, dressed in a Skydiver string vest that underlined the importance of pectoral muscle exercises. It was already too late. Whatever argument Ben had about the best direction of the company, it clearly wasn't going to matter one bit.

Chapter Twenty Six

The following morning was easier as at least they had remembered to close the door. Ruth was still sleeping off the free wine so Ben decided to go get breakfast. It was quiet, nobody seemed to be in a rush to get back to being spontaneous and motivated. Ben collected a set for himself, Ruth and their uninvited guest, but ran out of steam as he wandered outside where there were benches spread out, blurring the edge between the canteen and the forest. He watched the chaffinches working their way across the tables looking for French and Danish crumbs. One hopped onto his table and looked at him with alternate eyes.

'Big Issue?' Ben asked. He broke off some of his pastry and span it halfway down the bench. The bird skipped towards him, darting forward to get the crumbs one at a time. Ben sipped his coffee and took a bite himself. He lost minutes absorbed in the chaffinch's game of dare.

A scream echoed through the forest, quite close by. It was a horrible noise, nothing like the Hollywood version. The anger and pain were something that Ben couldn't ignore. He lurched to his feet, the chaffinch flew straight up to the nearest branch scattering the rest of the debris in his downdraft. There was a woman shouting, somewhere directly through the trees. She sounded angry rather than frightened. Very angry. Ben stuffed the remaining croissant into his mouth, picked up his coffee and pushed his way through the pines to the path on the other side.

Feeling rather like Mr Ben, he appeared beside Kevin who was standing with his arms folded, his face was a curious confusion of fear, anger and triumph. In front of them was an abandoned car with rather frightened looking children in the back seat. Kevin didn't seem to be interested in this flagrant flouting of Park rules. His focus was the middle aged woman standing in front of the car shouting at the villa front of her.

'Aaron! I know you are in there! Cody isn't well. Your phone was off so I went to your lodge but it was empty!' Ben couldn't see her face but he recognised the voice and the children had that same wide-eyed look which they had greeted him as a stranger to Fort Windsor. How they were coping being out here in Indian country?

'I panicked but this nice man said that you were probably here.'

Kevin jumped at that point and Ben offered him a fag. He lit them both off the same match.

'I don't understand. Why weren't you in your chalet? Why are you here?' she asked, her pleading tone made it clear that she had already guessed the answer. 'Is she in there with you? Is that why you're not coming out?' The headlights from the car illuminated her, adding an avenging angel glow to her shapeless fleecy top and grey leggings. Startled people were beginning to appear at the edge of the woods like nervous deer. The silence and the gathering crowd goaded her.

'You miserable little shit. I spend the night mopping up sick and you're here fucking her.' The woman stomped back to the car and stood by the open door, hand on the horn. Kevin took a step forward but she lifted her hand off and banged it on the roof in frustration.

'Come out!' she screamed. Suddenly she was at the back of the car hauling out children. The oldest looked about ten but Ben was guessing, he was aware there was a pre-adult stage but he had not had contact since he was one himself. The rest tumbled out like champagne after the cork. Four children stood looking lost and confused in the sudden publicity. She was still screaming incoherently at the villa as she bundled the last of them out. The villa remained so still and silent that Ben wondered if Kevin had gone American and picked the wrong house to hit with shock and awe.

'Aaron! You little shit!' she repeated, 'I am off to the hospital to look after your sick son.' There was no missing the emphasis there. Five kids - you wouldn't think Aaron had it in him. The Chrysler van thing lurched as she knocked it out of park. The back left door still open as she reversed away from Aaron's offspring and the tomb-like villa. Turning, she accelerated away the back door slammed into place. Ben's fag had just about burned down to the filter. He looked at it but it was Kevin that swore.

'I had no idea she would go off her rocker like that.' He had a Geordie accent when he wasn't in front of a mike. Vengeance hadn't been as good as he hoped, obviously.

Ben looked at him, frowning while he lit another fag, 'What the fuck else was she going to do? Hope somebody rescues those kids in a minute or it's me and you taking them to Captain Pete's Pirate Hideaway for buried breakfast treasure and some Corsair Colouring activities.'

Somebody must have heard Ben for the red door opened and Jana, a tight strained smile making her almost unrecognisable as she stepped out of the door,

'Buzz, Chip? Come in. Come in for a moment kids till we get things sorted. Your Dad's in here.'

The stunned collateral damage shuffled forward down the path past the bicycle holders and into the house. Ben caught a glimpse of Aaron hugging the oldest boy. Jana looked up and down the path looking for Tomorrow faces. Hell of a sense of awareness that girl. He'd already done the sweep and was pretty sure he was the only one. He'd thought of it too but then he hadn't just been called out by the wife of the man she'd just shagged in all senses of the word.

'He really is a useless fucker,' Ben pushed through the trees again back to the chaffinches. He heard Jana pull the door to, with a click that echoed in the forest. Ben refilled his cup and grabbed another bun. They were paid for and clearly going to waste otherwise and then he walked back to the Chalet. Ruth had got up, but in preparation of a repeat appearance by Christopher, had put on a dressing gown.

'You been gone a while, they haven't started have they?' she asked as tucked into her breakfast. 'You got any gossip?'

Ben thought of the Johnson clan broken and confused on the pine needle path. Their mum trying to rip the doors off cars and their Dad too frightened to come out and rescue them. Ben shrugged, 'I'm going home. Had enough.'

Ruth raised an eyebrow, 'Thought you were keen to play the game.'

'Seeing Jana...' Ben shrugged, 'well seeing her and Aaron made me think that the Tomorrow we were trying to build isn't going to happen.'

Yesterday, that was a game, this morning though, that was too raw for him to talk about. And then there was Neville in charge of sales, surely not. Ruth was watching him, trying to guess his internal monologue.

'I have had enough of rocket surgery.'

'Yes, I think I have had enough too,' she agreed. The drive back to Staines was a quiet but pleasant one.

'How would you like to go and see Runrig, they are playing in Cambridge next weekend?' Ruth peered over the top of her paper at Ben. Vick was still in bed so they effectively had they house to themselves for a few precious hours. Even the smell of warm croissants hadn't drawn Ruth's sister down.

Ben spread raspberry jam on the pastry to buy himself some thinking time, 'That's the band Davie was into. Are they from Orkney?'

'No Lewis. Top left, Orkney is top right. But anyway it's a good chance to catch up with some of the folk from Helensburgh,' Ruth said lightly.

Ben stopped mid-jam and looked at her, 'Anyone I know?'

'Judith you will remember. Chris? Quite a few of the St Mungo's gang ended up down here,' Ruth added. Ben wasn't sure what the clarification was for. Was it to remind him who Chris was or who he was related to.

'I didn't know you were still in touch? Hankering for the glens?'

'Have you not heard about the Scottish boomerang?'

'No.'

'You throw it away and it sings about coming back.'

Ben finished off the spreading and bit into the croissant. Why had he turned his back on Scotland? He really couldn't answer that question.

'You know what, that would be great. I could do with a bit of a blow out.'

As they drove across to Cambridge, Ben was trying to work out if he would be more sad if Clorinda was there or not. Ruth was staring out of the window looking north across the flat bits of Cambridgeshire, not giving any clue as to where her thoughts were. As they drove into the car park Ben finally came down on the side that hopefully Clorinda wasn't there. He and Ruth were in a good place, why risk it? Chris Ferguson was as tall and good looking as ever and didn't mention Clorinda as they caught up with the news. Chris's girlfriend Sarah looked a bit confused.

'You have all have gone really Scottish in the last ten minutes,' she commented, 'I can't understand you anymore.'

Ben, having got back up to the speed that English should be spoken, was struggling not to finish her sentence for her.

'Have, you, been, to, one of, these, before?' asked Ben slowly and deliberately. Well, you have to make allowances. Her reply was interrupted.

'Ben Williams!' A shout across the foyer. 'I thought you would be dead by now!'

Ben looked around nervously. To a man who had had grown accustomed to the dedicated anonymity of the South, all this meeting people he knew was proving a bit of a shock. He stared at the woman a full second, distracted by the metallic orange hair before he worked it out.

'Rae! Good grief. No, pleased to disappoint you.'

Rae looked round the rest of the faces not recognising anyone from St Mungo's until she saw Judith. She smiled in recognition but clearly not sure why. Judith laughed and introduced herself, 'I'm Miss Paterson's wee sister, Judith. You must be from the Academy?'

Rae nodded and chatted to Judith briefly before refocusing on Ben, 'I haven't seen you since those weird card games we used to play at school. I thought with all the drugs and stuff you would all be dead by now.'

'Don't believe the Government propaganda. Anyway stopped all that after I left school. Mostly,' Ben laughed. 'Rhino and Alison are doing well I hear,' he said, pointing at Judith.

'Yes. They are planning to get married now that they have had the baby. One thing at a time is Alison's view.'

'Amazing I never thought Rhino would be the first to be a Dad. How about Angus?' Rae asked Ben.

'Chris was saying earlier that he is now in Portugal. Got himself a beautiful wife and is now tuning up the pianos of the rich and famous in the Algarve.'

'And you're living here in Cambridge?'

'Slough,' corrected Ben. 'In Electronics now. Computers,' he added in an attempt to clarify. 'Working for an American company with Ruth. Who you might remember?' The two woman looked at each other and waived a greeting. Ben had been trying to remember the guy that played Nuclear War with Rae at school. 'And how about you and...'

'Sandy? Oh no we split up after Uni. I moved to St Albans and he went to Bathgate.' The pair looked round the room. 'This place is amazing,' Rae continued. 'I have seen so many people that I know here tonight. How did Tiny do in the end?'

'Last time I saw him was a couple of years ago in a bar in Helensburgh. He was just out. But he didn't look so good. I don't think anybody has heard from him since.'

'See Ben, drugs don't work. Lovely to see you. And I'm very glad that you are still alive,' Rae waived at everyone and disappeared back into the crowd. The band started and the group now numbering more than thirty, linked by friendships old and new, bounced the night away. At the end Ben and Ruth stood hip to hip singing the words to 'Loch Lomond' back to the band. It was all over too soon, the big lights came on and it was clear it was time to go home. Ben could see all the other large groups, catching up on news, laughing, talking about where to go next, the same sense of gathering mirrored in each group. He shook Chris's hand and hugged Judith.

'Great to see you all. Maybe try and sort something out for the summer?' On the way back home Ruth put on a Runrig tape she had borrowed from Davie and they sang all the way round the mist covered M25.

Chapter Twenty Seven

Two weeks after the weekend designed to bring motivation and bonding, it was clear that something was badly amiss. Neither Aaron nor apologies were apparent in the office and even the Management Meeting passed without an appearance. Joan was there bright and breezy as ever but when it came to the agenda and Key Performance Indicators Review, she didn't do her usual 'Voice of Aaron' bit. The meeting was wrapped up early as everybody had plenty of work to do. As the staff dispersed Joan seemed unsure which way to go.

'You okay?' Ben asked. When she smiled little creases appeared around her eyes like a badly ironed shirt. She looked tired.

'I'm all right thank you Ben. I hear you VTs are working closer than ever.'

Ben smiled at the deflection. The lack of subtlety was more eloquent than her eyes.

'Yes. I'm pleased to say we are.'

'She is a lovely girl. Very straight up and down.'

Something about the way that Joan made the comment made Ben sure this was genuine. Contact with the real Joan. She also seemed surprised at her candid comment and the pair stood in silence for a moment.

'She is. Joan?' Ben couldn't finish the question.

'Yes?'

'If I can help, don't forget we are all in this together. The teams I mean. I know sometimes things get a bit hectic. If I can help I'd be glad to.'

'Thank you,' Joan said. Confused by the sudden break out of humanity, both walked back to their desks.

Part way through the third week and Aaron still did not appear. The questions started to pile up. Ben couldn't join in properly with the idle speculation that occupied every fag stop and lunch hour since he knew the answers, or thought he did. Having Jana so pitch-perfect normal made Ben doubt that he had really seen anything at all. Ruth, though, was enquiring and concerned.

On the Thursday Aaron finally came in looking casual. Seeing the President of Global Business Development without his trademark suit and immaculate shirt, tie and sock combo was as much a shock as his unexplained absence.

'It sort of suits him,' Ruth commented, as the Value Trustees compared their internal and external goals and profiles for the month. 'He looks good for an older man.'

'He's not that old,' Joan said, 'mid-forties?'

'You two seeing him in a new light then?'

There should have been four in the meeting but as soon as Jana had seen Aaron she excused herself and positively ran to his office. The sales floor had stopped completely, heads tracking Jana as she flew through the door and closed it behind her. Ben could see her as she pressed back into the glass of the office. Ruth opened the entrance of the Leaders' room and shouted

'Oy!' As one, the office leapt back to their tasks.

'I thought that was Joan,' Ben said, looking with exaggerated confusion between the two women.

'Watch it Ben Williams. Any comments like that will not win you friends round here,' Joan was smiling like she used to. Ruth came back to her seat but the concentration had gone.

'Any idea what is going on?' she asked.

Ben let out a long breath, 'No.'

Joan frowned, 'I thought we had a new spirit of understanding?'

Ruth looked between Ben and Joan with a slightly hurt look.

Ben rolled his eyes up to the sky, 'We have. This isn't anything to do with the office.'

'So you do know what is going on then.'

'This is between us?' Ben asked, his hand indicating the three in the room.

'Of course.'

'No really, this is really bad stuff. Children's lives getting destroyed.'

Ruth looked shocked, Joan sat forward.

'You have my undivided attention,' Joan paused suddenly looking quite girly. 'And I promise not to tell anyone.'

Ben felt that he was making a mistake but that he had no choice but to continue. He talked about what he had seen in the Park. The headlights on the bracken. The image of the injured wife and the stunned children were still pin sharp in his mind's eye.

'On the bright side I'm pretty sure that I was the only Tomorrow person to see. I must have been, since I haven't heard a peep since.'

'Why didn't you tell me?' Ruth asked. Ben couldn't think of what to say. Was it as simple as Joan had asked the right question? It was what Joan was good at.

'I don't know it just seemed way too personal. It's not my story to tell.'

The three sat in silence looking at the closed door. It didn't give much away. Jana had stepped away from the frosted glass. The office had stopped again.

'I think the masses are wondering what they are missing,' Ruth closed her files and the three went back out, as though they had planned it, Ruth went to the uncollected faxes, Joan shouted at three people standing by the toilets and Ben pointed at the overhead phone queue which showed '16' in red. That sign meant there were sixteen people waiting to talk to Tomorrow. Clare, who had been watching the funfair, stepped back into the Marketing office without a comment.

'So ladies and gentlemen it feels like a very long time since I stood here in front of you, some of you, talking about the hopes of what we thought Tomorrow could be. About the great start that Hermione gave the company, its unique culture, its determination to succeed. But that wasn't all of it, Tomorrow is also about personal development and being all you can be. I think you can be proud of how far you have come.' The quiet West Coast voice kept the seventy-five or so Tomorrow people entranced as he spoke.

'But it's not just the people that have come a long way. We like to make money too,' he laughed and everyone laughed with him as though there was some surprise at the admission. 'Each of the UK managers here today have presented the strengths from their areas of responsibility and as we have seen, expertise. I'd like to thank them for the work they have put in over the last couple of years in not just coping but thriving in an atmosphere of constant change.' Aaron's smile washed over them all and they felt warm and wanted in the hotel function room they had hired for the day.

'Yes it's not just the people that have grown but the business. As you have seen today with the presentations that we have gone through, we have grown well beyond our original hopes.' He stepped out from the behind the lectern, 'Tomorrow, you, are uniquely positioned to dominate the electronic component industry in the UK. More than that it will become the headquarters for Tomorrow

Europe which will mean significant new investment in warehousing, in sales and in support staff.'

Spontaneous and quite possibly genuine applause broke out amongst the Tomorrow people.

'Now all of that means a lot of coordination between what goes in here in Europe and what we are doing back in Flagstaff. It's vital that the two parts of Tomorrow are acting in unison on this great third phase of our expansion. I'm pleased say that the Board have asked me to fill that role which I take as a great compliment, I really do. That coordination role will be based in Flagstaff which of course means that my time as a full-time member of the Slough team will have come to an end.'

Ben could see from his position at the front that the majority of the faces in the company looked shocked.

'And that's a real shame for me. This place gets under the skin. You can't work here, go through all those late nights and early mornings. Those times when we have worked through the weekend to make a deadline in getting a quote in or unpack the stock and go out that door unaffected. So I am genuinely sad to go and a few of you have been kind enough to say that they are sad to see me go too.'

Again a laugh, sadder this time, rippled round the room.

'This brings me to the last part of today's session which is about the organisation that will support you all through the next few years.' The management team, in its broadest definition, shuffled their chairs around so that they could get a first look at their future.

'I think we all agree that the current set up worked well.'

Since Aaron agreed, the rest of the company cravenly agreed.

'So the main aim here has been to minimise disruption,' he walked back and put the slide on himself.

Ben had the feeling he had been here before.

'So as you can see Clare and Arthur continue in their roles doing a superlative job. I think we have recognised that a better integration between the internal and external is essential. So we plan to divide sales into three teams. After a lot of thought we have decided to call them Team A- Scotland, Ireland and the North. Team B south west and central England. And Team C Eastern counties, London and the South East. Neville will get overall control of the sales force as Sales

Director. Underneath Neville we have Josh, John and Jeannette as Regional Sales Managers. We felt it was important to give some of the new guys an opportunity to show what they can do. Christopher retains specific responsibility for key accounts where his experience is really needed.

'Internally things have worked very well with the role of Value Trustee. Putting Jana, Ben and Ruth in charge of each of the teams has really paid off. Neville has suggested that the Value Trustees, embodying all that is good about Tomorrow, should have also have targets. I think this is a great way of showing how the VTs can lead Tomorrow in just the way we need them to.'

'Ah bollocks,' thought Ben. 'That's going to stuff us up very nicely.'

'Now this leaves a space for someone to bring all of the team together. It's a management role and will require some real team building skills.'

Ben felt sick. Was Joan really going to get the slot? She was beaming at the American for all he was worth.

'It's a pivotal role combining the sales, personnel and logistics. Above all it needs to be inspirational.' Joan looked like she was going to explode with pride. 'And that's why it's important that we don't rush into it. We have discussed the matter extensively here and back at Flagstaff and we have decided to put the matter out some of the best head-hunters in the industry to find the very best that we need to fill that slot.'

Ben was watching Joan very carefully and saw that this could be the moment when she stabbed Aaron through the heart.

'But the company is bigger than any one person and I'm sure in reality things will be fine with you all pulling together. This team,' Aaron addressed the back of the hall at this point, 'this team are so motivated and so empowered you really won't have any problems. And I'm sure that when that slot is filled you will go from strength to strength. I think the guys have put together a video of the last couple of years that should be ready now?'

The room darkened and a soundtrack that could only be Tina Turner started, slightly too loudly out of the speakers down each side of the room. Ben sat back watching the first pictures of the new office. Them setting up the first purple desks. A still shot of Hermione, then one of the whole team. Hells teeth they looked young. 'Simply the best' broke in where the starting vocals should have been. Shots of product getting shipped and packed. Video footage of the first fiche being moved around. He let the images roll over him. So many faces that had come and gone and the few that remained looking that little bit older each time they appeared. The video finished with a slow pan that they had taken this morning outside on the parched grass in front of the hotel. Very clever to include that on the same day.

The music and the video finished to thunderous applause and cheering. Everyone was on their feet smiling and cheering and shaking hands. Joan had gone forward and had a quick word with Aaron who showed her a chart. Ruth and Jana came over and gave Ben a hug.

'Looks like we have some interesting times ahead.'

'Any idea who is in each team?' asked Jana. Both Ben and Ruth shook their heads. Joan came over with a copy of the sheet that Joan and Aaron were looking at.

'Hello you three. I thought you would want to be the first to know who you have in each team,' she handed out three copies with her best and brightest smile. 'Could we get together later on this afternoon and go through things in a bit more detail?' All three nodded and Ben examined Joan walking away before he realised that he shouldn't. When he turned back though, Jana was still watching him but Ruth was concentrating on the paperwork. Joan finished with Aaron and was working her way through the management team shaking hands and congratulating as she went. Finally she sat back down with her hotel supplied pad, writing a few notes.

'I wonder what she is doing now. Aaron didn't mention that,' Ruth asked.

Jana looked at Neville's gift from the gods, studying all the small print.

'Vision Trustee role for all field sales. That's going to be tough. They would all rather die than embrace their Atlantean self. And if I understand Neville's nifty addition, that will make her responsible for their sales figures rather than him.'

Isolated in her chair, Joan got up, her walk to the exit took her past the clump of Value Trustees. She smiled at them and they smiled back but Joan kept walking.

'Good luck,' she mouthed and left the room which was emptying as people headed for the bar and lunch in that order. Ben walked over to where Joan had been sitting and saw that she had left her pad. There were a lot of notes. Quotes and stats jotted down in a typical Joan fashion. Implications and actions all carefully laid out. It was the comment at the foot of the page that caught his eye though. It read:

'three teams, ben, Ruth and jana reporting into Joan for VT. Field Sales VT!! The management team door closes.

Reps? Key Accounts!!!

bastards. They're all bastards. Smiley smiley all bloody day. Bastards. They're all out to get me'

Ben looked around the room. There were still enough people around that would be interested in Joan's views. People who would use her candid scribbling for maximum damage. Ben thought for a second about leaving the pad where it lay but then he ripped the page out, folded it, and put it in his pocket.

Chapter Twenty Eight

Ben and Ruth were up in Steve's old office as it had become thought of. There was a stack of Personality Profile Matrices that needed to get sorted. The pressure was on now that they were back in the sales game as well. Both Ruth and Ben had been lucky in breathing life into their old accounts. Ruth had been welcomed back to Better Meters with open arms and a £200k order to get things up and running. Ben had picked up a chunk of accounts that the reps hadn't wanted after Joan had given them a shake. Jana though was struggling, with no old accounts and only warm words from Neville that somehow failed to deliver, despite their apparent new found closeness.

However this was the week Jana's luck had turned. She had stepped in at the last minute to protect the North North West account. Apparently the quote had been completely messed up with the wrong stock, the buy prices had been put in instead of sell prices and they had even spelt the Purchasing Director's name wrong. Thank goodness Jana had been there to sort it all out. Even Christopher had said how grateful he was that she had been there to save the day. At least that's what Jana said.

The door to the office opened and Christopher, resplendent with pinstripe suit and Daffy Duck tie, looked round at the two, caught like pupils behind the bike sheds.

'Hello, I was told I would find you in here. 'The Team Leaders' room' they said to me. Took me a while to figure it out but I did eventually. I usually do,' he no longer saw the room but was looking somewhere else. 'Usually do. Thought I should say goodbye?'

'Goodbye?' the two Value Trustees chimed.

'That was easier than I thought,' Christopher turned for the open door.

Ben recovered first, 'Close the door Christopher, what the hell is going on?'

With a smile Christopher kicked the door to and pulled up a seat. He glanced at the spreadsheet and laughed, 'I see the North North West account is up there as won. Did Jana give you the good news?'

Ruth nodded, 'She came and told me Wednesday that we had the order and to start planning the stock and purchasing plan. That's what we have been doing this afternoon.'

'Got a fag Ben?'

Ben wordlessly handed over a cigarette and a box of matches.

'Thank you,' he blew out a long column of smoke and then stuck out his tongue looking disgusted. 'First one I've had for three years. I remember them tasting better than that,' he stopped as he saw the two sitting waiting for him to explain. 'What? Oh yes. When I phoned the order in on Tuesday I knew that something was up. Neville told me not to tell anyone about the order but to come into the office for a face-to-face. I think he said man-to-man but that would be absurd. Today was the first chance I had to get near the office.'

'I didn't see you come in.'

'I didn't. Neville and I met at that little restaurant round the corner. You know the comedy Italian bistro that Aaron and Jana used to go to?' Ruth and Ben both said 'no'.

Christopher settled into his seat, 'So the spineless wonder explains to me that they, whoever 'they' are, have great concerns over my ability to manage the account. In view of all the extra resources that had to be thrown at the opportunity at such a late stage to salvage anything at all from the debacle. His words obviously.'

'What did you say?' asked Ben.

'I think the little pipsqueak thought I would be careful what I would say in public. So I shouted as loud as I could that it was down to the relationship that I had built up over the last eighteen months that meant that when he and the company bicycle breezed in at the last minute with one of the most crass pitches the customer had ever seen or heard we still managed to win the business,' Christopher had drawn on the cigarette so hard that the filter was uncomfortable to hold. Barely half smoked it hissed as he dropped it into an almost empty coffee cup.

'I said that if he was determined to take the best account away from me then I would have to consider my position. He then said and get this,' Christopher slowed his voice right down from rant to very slow and deliberate. 'Get this. He said 'Jana thought you would say that and prepared this.' Neville then handed me my resignation letter. My own fucking resignation letter.'

It was Ruth that spoke first with genuine shock, 'I can't believe what they would do that.'

'Nor could I,' agreed Christopher.

'What did you do?' asked Ben.

'I signed the bloody thing. If they considered me of such little value. If they really believe that they will be able to manage North North West, then they have absolutely no idea of their own abilities and what the business requires.'

'Bingo,' thought Ben, but he did only think it. Christopher continued, 'Neville told me that due to my overreaction to the situation I wouldn't be required to work my notice. So I have come in to say me goodbyes and be off.'

Ruth threw her arms around Christopher and hugged him hard. She had tears in her eyes when she let him go, 'Stay in touch. We'll sort out a beer yeah?'

Christopher nodded looking slightly surprised.

Ben nodded, 'That we would be good Christopher, we need to send you off properly.'

'Yes,' Christopher said, 'I'd like that. A burning ship. Mourning maidens. Perhaps not. Right, no point in hanging around anymore. I've talked to all the people I thought were any good. A fairly short list I think you will agree? I'm off.'

Ben stood up and held out his hand, 'Good luck Christopher.'

Christopher shook his hand, 'You too love.'

And with that he was gone.

Ruth stuffed her belongings into her bag. 'Bastards!' she exploded. 'I've fucking had it.' She stomped to the door and slammed it behind her. The partition wall shook. Ben tidied up and came into the main office just as Ruth left Marketing and headed for the toilets. Catherine and Clare were watching from behind the magic marketing line that no malevolent sales spirit can cross. He saw Clare hand Catherine a ten pound note. Ben walked over. Clare stepped away, presumably to avoid being part of the conversation. As well as defensive magic Marketing were also good at plausible deniability.

'How did you know?' Ben asked Catherine.

'Didn't, honest. But Christopher didn't get the fact that it had to be Jana that brought in the order. He was trying all the harder to keep her out.'

'Do you blame him?' asked Ben.

'No. But that's not the point.'

'He got the order,' Ben stated wondering if they should be having this conversation in the sales floor.

'He lost his job. Which would you rather?' Catherine looked at him through cool brown eyes.

'Right now I'm not so sure. Sorry, this takes Fubar to a whole new level.'

Chapter Twenty Nine

'I enjoyed today.' Ben tried not to sound too sad when he said it. He was in Ruth's kitchen trying to make the pile of mini sausage rolls look artistic. It was an uphill battle. They had a couple of bowls of crisps and a box of biscuits. They had two pizzas to heat up later. Ben had also made a stack of sandwiches but was unsure if he should cut the crusts off. He looked into the living room as she kicked the Electrolux into silence. It was probably third hand and didn't really do much more than make a lot of noise while redistributing the dust.

'I was just saying I enjoyed it too. We should go into London more.'

Ben nodded agreement and brought in the plates of food. He had to hold them in the air while Ruth put a tablecloth out first. He watched the pastries take their chance to settle into a comfortable heap. It all felt very domesticated. Normal. Grown up. They had bribed Vick to stay away for the night. Ruth put on Woodface by Crowded House which had one outstanding feature- they both liked it.

'Plenty of space. And what could be nicer. The four Value Trustees of the company getting together to look at the company,' Ruth smiled and kissed Ben on the nose. 'What are you frightened of?' she asked.

'Both of them really,' Ben was surprised at his own answer but Ruth laughed and stepped to the window.

'Funny. Here they both are walking up the road together,' Ruth opened the door while Ben looked round the tiny living room trying to think of where he could hide. It was either under the table or back into the kitchen.

'I'll just check we have everything out of the oven,' Ben scurried off and washed the baking trays while he could hear high pitched laughter coming through the door. Ruth came through with a bottle of wine that looked like a giant perfume bottle.

Ben read the label, 'Mateus?'

'Open that will you? And then bring it in,' Ruth laughed at his face and went back into the living room. Ben managed to get the cork out and brought it into the room where Jana had nabbed the corner chair and Joan had already covered half the floor in files and loose sheets.

'Hello Ben. I thought I would bring everything I could find.'

'I did the same,' Jana said, pointing at a large cardboard box with the Tomorrow logo on it, but Ben could see it was half empty.

'I've got more in the car. Ben could you give me a hand please?'

'Why ask me?' Ben thought. 'Is she asking me because she already has Jana onside and needs to make sure I am the same to isolate Ruth. But that would be weird. Has Joan got some plan to get Jana and wants to make sure that Ruth and I are in on it? Or don't muck it up? Or possibly, just possibly they are quite heavy and she would like some help?'

'I'll go Ben. You finish off in the kitchen,' Ruth said, leaving Ben to wonder how many minutes he had been standing there, cheesy puffs in hand, trying to work out how he should respond.

'Good, yes I will get the sausages out and put the pizza in.'

Jana curled up in the corner with her box at her feet, 'I'm looking forward to seeing your sausages Ben,' she shouted through.

Ben hit his head on the grill door and swore quietly. He waited, he preferred that to the word 'hid' in the kitchen as long as he could and then came through with a full plate and put them in the centre of the table. Jana was smiling at him with the dial somewhere up around eleven, 'Don't look so worried Ben.'

'Why should Ben look worried?' asked Joan as she came back through the front door with Ruth behind.

'I just said I was looking forward to seeing Ben's sausage.'

Joan was looking at the cooling contents of the plate.

'They look a little small and wrinkled,' Joan chipped in. The three woman shrieked in a way that would have done the heaths of Forres proud. Ben felt his patient smile slip into pained very quickly. His appealing looks to Ruth failed and it was Joan that gathered them all back down to the earth.

'Right then ladies. And Ben. Let's see what we have then.'

The four sat round the table with their folders like a giant game of poker. It was quiet enough for 'Four seasons in one day' to be heard in the background.

'Jana, where are the files for your team?' asked Joan in the same cheery voice.

'I, eh,' Jana looked in the Tomorrow box, 'that's all I have.'

'But you must have a folder for each person. How else can you track their PPM's over time? Ben always struggled with this but even Ben has a folder each.'

Ben twitched at that but given the way the guns were pointing it was easier to keep quiet.

'I know I have got a little behind so your support in this would be amazing. The introduction of the targets has really thrown me.'

'Yes but that has only been for the last four months,' Joan pointed out. 'What have you been doing in your reviews?' she asked.

'I just kept notes in my diary when I did the reviews,' Jana said.

'Good. Well at least the diaries will give us a picture over time. That will allow us to rebuild the PPMs. Ruth, Ben you would help with that wouldn't you?'

Ben inwardly screamed- rebuild an entire teams' matrices for over a year! Good grief, are you mad!

'No, happy to help. I'm sure it won't take that long,' Ruth said.

'Er yeah,' said Ben.

'That would be great,' Jana beamed her thanks to all three.

Ben grunted in agreement, 'No problem, we are here to help. That is the whole point of having Value Trustees.' Everyone took a sip of their wine and Ben took advantage of the drop in tension to go and get the pizzas.

'We may have over catered. You guys need to eat some of this or Ruth and I are eating party food for a week,' he settled back down with a slice of Hawaiian to realise they were all looking at him.

'What?' he asked.

'Joan was just wondering if you could show Jana a historic matric.'

'Sorry I couldn't hear you over the noise of the pizza.'

Everyone laughed. Ben felt he should go find a red nose and some oversized shoes. 'Hang on,' Ben dug in the file, 'yes here you go.' Ben made a point of picking up the top file as if it was just the one at random. In fact the first five were spot on. He was hoping they would get bored before they counted to seven. Joan slid forward over the table to take the file off him. Her chest rolled forward against her bra like a wave slapping up against the harbour wall. Ben looked away but too late. Joan slipped back down beside Jana, apparently oblivious.

'So Jana if you get one of your diaries out we can start matching your notes to the fields that need to be filled on to get the PPM going, it really shouldn't take long at all.'

Jana's face was immobile. She stared impassively into Joan's face which was also frozen but in such a picture of angelic helpfulness that it should have featured in a nativity scene.

'I haven't got the diaries.'

'You forgot to bring them?' Joan asked her face collapsing into confusion.

'I don't know where they are. I couldn't find them.'

'I thought you were going to say the dog ate them Jana.'

Jana laughed but Joan didn't.

'This is very serious. We have Steve hospitalised and your best salesman has just walked out the door citing your mismanagement as the reason. I was hoping tonight to put some of those rumours to rest. But this is a mess Jana. You haven't done any of the Value management you are supposed to be doing.'

'I'm a team leader. I'm meant to be selling not this mumbo jumbo.'

'Your team has been missing their *sales* target Jana. You yourself haven't found any new business, even Neville's leads don't seem to have come to anything. So no sales and no management. What have you been doing with your time?' Joan asked looking very concerned.

'I-' said Jana.

'I'm not sure what to do with this, Jana. The new structure makes me responsible for the Value Trustee team of which you are a key part. Neville has overarching responsibility for sales. I think I need to talk to him and decide what to do next.'

Jana picked up her cardboard box, 'You do what you think you need to do.' She sounded angry.

'Are you going?' asked Ruth surprised.

'I need to go and see if I can find those diaries,' Jana said.

'Yes,' Joan said, 'that would be a good starting point.'

'Goodbye Ruth,' Jana hugged Ruth and Ben and she left. Crowded House asked 'How will you go?' to the silent room.

'Well,' Joan shrugged conspiratorially at Ruth and Ben, 'that was unexpected. Can I have a slice of pepperoni please Ben? I can't have a glass of wine and drive on an empty stomach.' Joan reached across the table to pick up the furthest away sausage. This time Ben was ready and already staring at the Artex as the tide came in. In the silence there was a discordant guitar note as the Finn brothers struck up 'I'm still here.'

Davie was not happy and said so.

'I'm not happy. The company is unravelling, our best sales guy dances off and nobody tries to stop him because all of the VT's are playing whose Ben sleeping with this week.'

'I didn't sleep with anyone. Well with one exception,' Ben protested.

'So you say. Most of the company says different,' he opened the window and lit a fag. 'I could slap the lot of you sometimes.'

The door opened and Davie threw the fag out before he realised it was Clare. The Chief Marketeer closed the door behind her.

'Have you heard the news?' she asked with a sense of drama and enthusiasm that would have done a Children's TV presenter proud.

'Depends,' Davie lit another fag and tossed the packet over for Ben and Clare. 'It better be good news because I've had enough bad news to last a lifetime.'

'Jana resigned this morning effective immediately,' Clare didn't put the quote marks round 'resigned' but she didn't have to. Davie laughed. Clare didn't say anything further only holding out her hand until Davie reluctantly deposited a ten pound note

Ben looked at the pair of them, 'Marketing does have a book on everyone.'

'Only on nominated Sales,' Davie answered, 'and you have to get the right quarter that they go in. Otherwise it would only be a matter of time. There would be no skill involved. I was sure she was safe for another quarter or two.' Davie rounded on Clare, 'So what made you so sure she was on her way out?'

'Neville started to have that edgy look around Jana. Suddenly she looked a bit exposed. As it were. With Joan shouting about how many mistakes she had made over the accounts, Steve, Christopher.'

'Wasn't that Neville's idea?' asked Ben.

'Not in hindsight,' Clare answered as if that explained everything.

'Where is she going?'

'PA job in town. Pays double, long hours but no two days the same apparently.'

'And what now here?' asked Ben.

'Consensus is we can't wait till Aaron comes back across. We need this sorted quickly with a minimum disruption. So there is a conference call tonight, we all agree and the plan is to get something out straight after that,' Clare bounced her half smoked fag off the glass and out of the open window. 'Better go. So many people to tell the good news too,' she laughed and left.

Chapter Thirty

There was a party in Bracknell. A full blown works party in Bracknell. It was a warm summer evening, the music was loud and to add variety, Joan and partner Richard had invited all the company to the metropolis of Hampshire. It was a great way for everyone to spend some time together out of the office, to restart the company. Ben should never have gone.

A celebration of the good business they had won and the good people that had been in Tomorrow before, during and after. When Ben turned up, it felt a little bit like his more random days at Brookside. There were people he knew and people he felt he should know and they were people he was fairly sure he had never met before in his life, but they clearly knew a lot about him. Ruth knew them all and was sucked into the party, leaving Ben in the garden feeling sober.

Ben took a bottle of Michelob from the ice-filled bin and took a deep swig, draining roughly half the bottle. Tonight he was in the mood to party. One of the Southern sales managers- Jane, Jean, Jeanette, the new policy seemed to be employ only field sales that started with 'J', cruised on up and poured herself a white wine.

'Hello Ben.'

With her dilated eyes and slurred speech his heart sank. He had a lot of catching up to do.

'Do you know what Ben?'

He necked the rest of the bottle and fished out another, 'I think I'm about to find out.'

'Do you know what Ben? Nobody is happy to see you when you're a rep.'

'Really.'

Half the beer gone.

'The customers all think you're lying, nobody believes you in the office. The suppliers all think you're trying to trick them about prices,' she downed the wine in one and smiled in a defocused way. 'Trust me I'm a rep.' She laughed. 'I'm going to find Clare and see how I can get into Marketing. Are you coming?' she asked.

Ben scooped up his third bottle, lit a cigarette and managed an enormous belch of beer froth and smoke, 'I think you have to bring them a Unicorn as tribute. Lead on!' As he dived into the crowded living room he saw Joan and her partner, Richard. Ben waved at them both. His initial reaction was to head in the opposite direction as fast as possible but he saw Ruth had already engaged them both heartily and circled round behind her.

'But the sales part of the role is just bloody bean counters,' Ruth was shouting against the background track.

Joan was nodding, 'They have to be.'

'The company lost its way. It's losing what makes us different.'

'It's losing its ideals,' Ben butted in.

Ruth nodded enthusiastically, 'That's right. You think of what it was like when we set up the company. That's the point. 'We set up the company.' It is vital that we get that sense back.'

Ben watched Ruth, her eyes bright with belief in the poorly lit room. Ben found himself carried along with the flow. There had been too many knocks recently.

'There are people, internally people, slagging off Tomorrow now.'

That got a vigorous nod from Joan. 'We need to find a way of changing the way that they behave. If we could get that old spirit back, imagine what we could achieve.' Joan was hitting the wine hard too. She seemed to staring only at Ben, even though Ruth was there.

'This is where you came in Ben. We need some others to lead the people. Get them motivated. Get them to believe in the company again.'

Ruth was nodding, 'Yes they need to believe. We need somebody to protect what the Value Trustees represent.' She paused trying the think of the word, 'The Values.' Ruth looked from one to the other for a response. There was a pause while Ben tried to tear his eyes away from Joan's. Shagging the boss? Well it had worked for Jana. Not in the end obviously but for a while it had.

'You are right. Everyone else is catching up with Tomorrow. We need to get back to what made us different at the start,' Joan said, she was back to normal now, sparkling at them both, Ben must have imagined it.

The talking got more heated and the drinking picked up pace as the discussion spread out amongst the Tomorrow people present. Ben started to lose chunks of the conversation. Time for some fresh air. Outside the grass had been carefully covered in bodies. Some, Ben noticed approvingly, had already been put in the recovery position. Others, in the less well-lit areas, appeared a little more active. Ben saw the reps lying together in a jumble. Their own kind was their only source of comfort. In the morning they would haul themselves on to rocks and wait for the sun to warm them so that they could begin to hunt again. Ben downed a whisky that appeared in his hand and headed back into the wall of noise.

The balance shifted then, from losing chunks, to only managing to hang on to a few lucid moments. He took up residence in the kitchen at one point. Ruth came to say goodnight.

'Don't go Ruth,' Ben held his arms out wide, smashing one hand into a wall. 'Stay here. Joan and Richard will put us up. They won't mind.' Unable to maintain thought and an upright position he sank to the floor wondering why his hand hurt.

'I have to go Ben,' Ruth patted him like a faithful hound, 'I promised Vick I would be back. You stay'

'You sure?' Ben asked.

'Yes, you stay and enjoy yourself.'

Ben was trying to work out if she meant that or if she meant that he should go with her in order to prove that leaving the party and being with Ruth would be enjoyable too. Which it would be, in a different way. It had been tricky ever since that night with the badly placed sausage and Joan's poorly supported chest; when Joan had distracted Ben with her womanly wiles and Ruth had noticed with her womanly ability to pay attention. And tonight, when Joan went all focused, what did that mean? By the time he had worked his way through that and decided that he should go after all, poof, Ruth was already gone. Ben struggled to his feet again. Davie came close enough to have sharp edges.

'She's gone,' Ben said in a sad voice.

'Aye the party is thinning out now.'

'Is it? Early yet,' Ben peered at his watch but there wasn't enough brain power to make sense of what it was saying.

Davie lit two fags and placed one in Ben's lips, 'It is four o'clock in the fucking morning Ben.'

'Shit. She's gone you know and I didn't tell her I love her.'

'Joan? No, she's next door I think. Scary. After all the denials I'm surprised you have come right out and said it.'

'Not Joan. Ruth. She's lovely. And I am her boyfriend,' Ben added proudly.

'Splendid. I'm very happy for you. I've heard you two do PPMs together in bed on a Sunday morning. Not entirely comfortable with that image. You all right Ben?'

'Fine and dandy my boy.'

'Good. I've been thinking about what you said. In fact I've been thinking about you all night.'

'Eh?' Ben tried to focus his smoke battered eyes. Joan not Davie.

'Give us a hug Ben. Those of us who started Tomorrow have got to stay together.'

Ben threw his arms around Joan. She was warm and soft. In that pink jumper the effect was like hugging a centrally heated marshmallow.

'What are you drinking?'

Ben looked blank and waved his arms in a slightly tighter arc.

'nything.'

Joan passed him a glass, 'I remember you saying that your favourite dream was kissing a woman when her mouth was full of Pernod.'

'Oh yeah man. It would be like-' he paused as he thought hard about the image, '- sex.' Ben was beginning to lose it. Consciousness had become an optional extra. Joan knocked back the glass she was holding and pulled his head down, her mouth already open, amber liquid lapping over her lower lip. It was like being a teenager again. Two mouths as wide as they would go. Chin and nose all included.

Ben came up for air, 'Is this a good idea? I mean like Richard's in the next room.'

'He is out cold,' she refilled the glasses and passed Ben one. 'There is no way he's going to get it up tonight anyway.' She dragged a finger round the outline of Ben's dick through his jeans, 'Not that you seem to have a problem that way.'

Ben drained the glass, and then thought he should go. Joan must have seen the look of fear. She pushed him hard against the fridge. Her crotch grinding against his, her hands shot up his shirt. Ben had decided; screwing the boss was a bad idea, really bad. He just needed to get her tongue out of his mouth.

'I really need to...' Ben's voice broke as he tried to shift sideways, 'Like go.'

She held his head in two hands, 'I want you Ben.'

He watched mesmerised she reached down scooping out the contents of her bra.

'Much bigger than I would have thought', managed Ben. Odd that, usually it's the other way round. With one arm supporting them like a tray, the other eased round Ben's neck and pulled him down to the point of suffocation.

'Fuck me, fuck me now,' she whispered. Ben's last thought slipped on the Pernod and fell, startled, into the darkness.

Chapter Thirty One

It's funny how something can act as a reset. Ben hadn't been that falling down drunk for a long time. As he sobered up the following day, he thought of all the people who had been at the party and those who had not. They all used to do everything together. When was the last time he had seen them outside of work? And it was then Ben realised he had never visited Davie since he split up with Steve. He checked the PPM, actually a year after he had moved out from Steve's. Time flies when it is always Tomorrow.

It was a warm clear evening. Ben left his Cavalier on the main road to Gerrards Cross and walked the last half-mile towards the housing association. Davie had been lucky to get a place in a housing association, he had been unlucky that it was in the Britwell. A lot of Britwell people were working hard at improving the place by themselves. They had to; the council's response to its decline into anarchy had been to seal it off and leave the poor white trash to their own devices, as long as they didn't kill anyone else, it wasn't a problem. Or at least it wasn't their problem. Self-help was working. Ben had heard that the buses had started going through the estate in daylight hours and that the police had adopted normal panda cars rather than the pair of armoured vans and the ground attack helicopter they had favoured up till then. Did they still call them pandas? Sounded a bit too friendly after the rise of the SPG. Jam butties. The road ended in a mass of high density housing, eighties style.

At some point it must have been fashionable to create homage to the New York skyline. A bustling, dynamic backdrop to inspire those suffering from a temporary setback and trying to get back on the first rung that there was something out there worth going after. The consequence was to create dangerous alleyways, poorly lit corners and a bleak outlook. The architect was doomed from the start though. Looming over all were the massive chimney and cooling towers of the Chocolate Factory. If the wind was in the right direction, it was like breathing chocky malty balls. The PPM said that Davie had lost a lot of weight, Ben was beginning to understand why. The broken block was a mass of vertical slits, like giant upended letterboxes. One of those narrow windows Ben was looking at was his, Davie's that is. Like he had said at the paintball. The banks had come down on him hard to get him to pay off the previous year's fast food, cars that had been fast in '76 and no women whatsoever. The housing association was the only way he was going to stay out of a cardboard box. It had, in that limited sense, worked. But a year of looking through a six inch wide window? That had to come at a cost. Davie must have spotted Ben shuffling slowly towards the Manhattan prospect because he came out, his hand outstretched. Ben shook it feeling faintly awkward.

'Good to see you man. Where's your car?'

'I, eh, left it just down the road. Seemed like a good idea,' Ben added weakly. Davie started walking back towards a dark close leading into the complex. He waved at the cars lined up to his left. The spare ground that made up the car park was dominated by Capris, Mantas and XR3is. The latter with obligatory red gaiters on the windscreen wipers.

'They're never touched here you know. I was really worried about it at first but I even forget to lock it sometimes. There are good people here. Come on in for a cup of tea.'

'Don't steal from their own,' Ben muttered as he followed Davie through the close and into one of the courtyards and then a large kitchen. Davie had already filled the kettle on his way out. The kitchen spread out into a large eating area with stairs leading up, assorted cupboards and a green door. It looked clean and moderately well maintained. Quite pleasant in the sunshine. There were earnest notes pinned to the notice board, majoring in consideration, tidiness, and help with the governing body.

'Not bad,' said Ben and he meant it. Davie looked around the place like it was the first time he'd seen it.

'Does the job. Once I learned to stop putting things in the fridge it was fine.'

He waved at the green door with his steaming cup, 'Through the green door,' he said in the style of Play School. Ben walked through to a four foot by eight foot hall with a bathroom ahead, a locked green door to his left and an open green door to his right.

'Me and the woman opposite keep this clean between us. Nobody else uses it,' he pointed towards the open door. 'At first I thought it was a shame that I was on the ground floor. I was worried that there would be a lot of people hanging around the kitchen and dining room and nipping into this loo. Nobody does. But above here they have four rooms per floor and the bathrooms are grim. It's impossible to control. Welcome to my abode.'

A double bed took up nearly half the room. A hi-fi and television took up the rest of the top half. The third quarter was taken up by a sink, cupboard and several stacks of paperbacks leaving the final quarter to stand in. A block of wood propped the thin window open, the little light it allowed to stumble in meant that the bare bulb hanging from its wire in the ceiling had a full time job.

'Compact.'

'Bloody tiny but it is giving me a chance to sort myself out. All my debts are paid off and I have even built up some savings again. I couldn't have got myself sorted out without this place. Catherine saved my life.'

Ben sat on the bed and Davie, the floor. He tossed a fag on top of the duvet. They both lit up and took a deep draw in.

'So what do you do for excitement round here?'

'There's the laundrette, see life in the raw there you know. Other than that,' He shrugged. 'I managed a work around on the cable TV security. I may live in a miserable hovel in the middle of a no go war-zone but I have the sixty channels of the financially solvent.'

'Bonus. You're looking well on it.'

That made Davie laugh. He rolled over to the cupboard and pulled out three packets of pasta and half a packet of bacon, 'Dried food only. Buy the meat and maybe a vegetable on the way back from work. Stir in some black bean sauce and you're sorted.'

'Filling and nutritious.'

'And it doesn't leave anything for the thieving bastards upstairs to steal,' Davie turned on the telly. He did something complicated with the box when it turned on and Sat-Eins started shouting at them in German. Davie looked slightly embarrassed. 'They seem to have a Benny Hill style fixation only all their clothes really do fall off. Anyway that wasn't what I was after.' He started cycling through till CNN came up. 'This is neat.'

'What is it?' Ben asked.

'It's just the news. That's all they do. It's sort of on a rolling loop but with the Kuwait war thing going on it is just compulsive viewing.'

Ben tried to make sense of the wash of information. At some point Davie went away and made another cup of tea for them both. An hour or so passed until they had seen the same video footage three or four times. Ben had seen nothing like it. Davie was right, this was compulsive viewing though it could do with some analysis as well as the commentary.

Ben stared out the window, gloom was beginning to gather around the base of the cooling towers. Davie stepped over to the window and hung a grey bath towel from two tacks, covering the long thin window. 'All the comforts of home,' Davie said sadly. He seemed to continue quickly before he had time to stop himself, 'after the party the question on everybody's lips is did you sleep with her?'

'I never slept with Clorinda,' Ben said distractedly.

'Is Clorinda one of the new reps? Bloody hell Ben,' Davie laughed half in horror, half in admiration.

'Not Clorinda. I meant to say Debbie,' Ben said, suddenly well aware of where Davie was going with this and not at all keen to follow him.

'Well I know that's not true. Everybody thinks she made that up but Helen and I know you managed it somehow.'

'The truth? I did sleep with her,' Ben admitted.

'Debbie? Thought so.'

'I was seduced, raped,' said Ben indignantly.

'Yup that tiny woman just overpowered you. Anyway you know I wasn't asking about Debbie or the mysterious Clorinda.' Davie paused to see if Ben would fess up. But no. 'Joan man, you two were getting awfully heavy when I left. Did you sleep with her?' Davie asked again.

'Absolutely not.' Ben stared Davie down keeping his mind completely blank, which matched his memories of that night.

'Okay. Nothing to do with me. Well it is. After the whole Aaron/Jana/Neville thing we thought we were all clear shitting on your own doorstep is a really bad idea. But nooo, everybody seems to have gone crazy apart from Steve who has a piece of paper which says he isn't. And Ruth, well, all the girls including me are wondering why the hell she left you at Joan's house.'

Bens face didn't shift a millimetre from his stare, 'Davie I did not sleep with Joan.'

'Okay. Nothing to do with me,' Davie repeated without conviction.

'Anyway I'd better be going. I didn't realise it was so late. It will be night soon,' Ben finished his cup and looked for somewhere to put it before handing it to Davie. The two walked in silence back through the kitchen, the courtyard and out in front of the cars. Davie handed Ben another cigarette. Somewhere above a couple started arguing. It was loud and vicious.

'Five floors up and you can hear every word. They'll be bonking in an hour. That's just as noisy and a lot more depressing,' Davie held out his hand again. 'Thanks for coming Ben. I've been here a year and you're the first one of the gang to visit.'

'No problem. It's not that bad.'

They both laughed at that, breaking the tension.

'Still if the Belgian things works out I am out of here! In a month or three.'

'Helen will be sad to see you go,' Ben said

'Helen?' asked Davie, slightly thrown.

'You two never seemed to quite get the timing right.'

'Eh. No. No we didn't. I think the getting the Belgian job might make her realise what she was missing.'

'Is it all sorted?'

'Neville can't agree the package. Or rather there is no package. In fact they can't even agree if the post is internal or external. I'll know I'm going when I'm on the ferry. We'll see what happens. There is nobody else that knows the market. They have to send me or they don't have a business. But then when has anything they've done made sense...' Ben was habitually noncommittal when it came to criticising the company.

'Thanks again for coming to see me,' Davie stood and watched Ben as he walked back along the road away from the chocolate factory. Ben picked up his pace wanting to get back to his car before sun set and the oompa loompa came out to play.

Chapter Thirty Two

It was a Monday. It was the Thermometer. A moment's reflection. Eyes closed, picturing themselves in their favourite safe place, a place to gather their thoughts and prepare to help motivate each other for another successful week. On the MV Captayannis the curtains of rain were so heavy that Ben couldn't see land in any direction. The hull shuddered with the weight of each giant wave that tried to drive the ship further into the sand. Even here at its highest point the sea's fingers hissed around Ben's feet before sliding back down the steel shore and into the seething mass of white water below. The bell sounded. Far away Tomorrow would be walking back to the meeting room in their minds eye. Ben left the storm battered ship on the Clyde behind and refocused on the blinking faces around him.

As a Value Trustee he had a notepad to make sure that everyone's contribution was focused and motivating. There was a big turnout today even though they had started the meditation at eight o'clock. As part of the 'Get Into Tomorrow' campaign, Ben and Ruth had really managed to get people to value the Thermometer again. Most people. Davie was sitting opposite with the people from his quad, some new bod, Helen and Catherine. The four were nudging each other and sniggering as usual. That new chap was never going to make a decent PPM score behaving like that. Joan at the end of the table looked at her watch, winked at Ben and gently put her nine part file and time manager on the table. At the signal the room hushed.

'Right. Hello everyone. It's lovely to see almost all of the company here again for the Thermometer, isn't it Ruth and Ben? Really is lovely. So I'm sure you all remember we are here to share our wishes, hopes and dreams with the rest of the company. I would like to start with some interesting news.'

Joan got up and went to the door to the meeting room and brought in Steve.

'I am really pleased to say that after a long period away Steve is able to join us again.'

Ben and Davie jumped to their feet, holding out their hands for Steve to shake, 'Good to have you back.'

Steve took the chair beside Joan smiling in recognition of everyone but looking rather shy.

'Steve will be joining us two days a week at first and we'll see how it goes from there. Won't we Steve?'

He managed a quiet, 'Yes. I'm sure it will all come back to me.'

Not all I hope, Ben thought. He remembered the night the hospital had rung saying that Steve had broken out and they thought he was heading for the Tomorrow Office. He had made it quite far that night before they had caught him, naked and on foot.

'I have some news,' Davie stood up. This was a first, Davie had tears in his eyes. Contributing and emotion. A double whammy. 'Some of you already know but this will be my last week with Tomorrow Slough. A week today I'll be opening the phones on Tomorrow Belgium.'

Although standing up he was really only looking at Helen and Catherine, 'I will really miss you all.'

'Especially Helen in her St Trinian's outfit.' That comment from Neville got a cheer. Helen had tears in her eyes too. Davie looked awkward now but was clocking all the faces.

'Anyway. I really will miss you. It's been a hell of a four years. Thank you,' he sat down again. People were taking the mickey out of Davie and Helen. Clare had gone to crouch beside Steve and was talking to him quietly. She held his hand for a moment.

'I've got some good news too,' Joan was sitting, radiant at the head of the table. Ben would swear afterwards that there was some sort of backlighting involved. 'As some of you may know me and Richard have been trying for a while.' Ben didn't like the way this was going, he felt a cold spot the size of Alaska settle on him. 'Some of have already guessed,' Joan shared a sisterly shrug with Clare, 'well I'm really pleased to say that I am expecting.'

In horrible slow motion Ben saw every head in the room turn as people wanted to see his reaction to the news. Eighty-four eyes fixed on his face, including two, shining like torches from the top of the table. He saw Joan's beaming face falter as she became aware of the focus shifting from her to Ben. Before Ben thought, he found himself on his feet facing Ruth.

'I have never touched her,' he looked round the faces. 'Clear? Never touched her. The baby is nothing to do with me.' Ruth crumpled in her chair as though someone had let her air out. It was as silent as a fresh snow dawn. Ben let his arm fall to the table with a thud. Joan looked for support from her nine part file. Neville coughed.

'Almost nine o'clock. Everyone to their desks. Very exciting start to the day.'

Ben sank back in his chair and rested his head on the cool table. He could hear mumbling belated congratulations to Joan as they all shuffled out. Others were commenting that Neville had got it wrong again and it was only twenty-five past eight and would this still count towards their Voluntary Extra Time? When it was quiet Ben sat back, pushing the hair out of his face. He looked around the empty meeting room.

'Well. That's fucked things up very nicely.'

He went back out to the office and sat at his desk. 'The entire bloody company thinks I shagged the boss. More to the point Ruth thinks I did.' His hand went out for a small purple box sitting on the top of his in tray. If ever he needed to lose some negative energy it was now. He thumbed the catch open and stared at the polished jewel within, black as coal. He looked up to see Ruth staring at the obsidian blade on its purple cushion.

'Overwhelmed by the darkness in your soul Ben. Why did I think you had changed?'

Carefully putting her phone off circuit she sat looking at him with the same expression she had that day in Helensburgh. 'Do you have any, any idea who I am?' she asked quietly.

'I don't understand.'

'Was I just a goal for you on your personal development plan? Get Ruth back on side to prove to yourself what a nice you guy you really are. Tick.'

'No. I l...' but the word stuck. Couldn't get past the 'L'. Ruth got up and walked to the toilet almost knocking over Davie as he came out of the men's bogs. He passed Ben on his way to the quad. Davie saw the crystal and laughed.

'I meant to say. Neville bet me that it wasn't light sensitive. I won. Bit of direct sunlight and foom. Black as the ace of spades.' Ben went to shout a reply but caught sight of Ruth walking out the front office door.

'You have no idea what you have done,' Ben went to hit Davie but decided against it.

'Ben!' It was Joan. 'My office now!' Ben spun.

'Really? Now?' he asked. When he looked back Ruth had walked past the toilets and down the stairs. By the time he had reached the bottom step Ruth's red Polo was already out the car park. It hurt so much he could hardly breathe.

Chapter Thirty Three

Ruth had gone. She had left the company. She had left him. In the months since Ben had danced his way round the rules, the regulations, the job, almost on autopilot as if thinking would break the magic spell and he would have to face the fact that Ruth really was no longer there. Joan's frustration with him finally boiled up to the point where Ben found himself in a meeting despite all his best efforts not to be.

'Are you paying attention to me Ben?' Joan was leaning over the desk while Ben was so far back in the seat as to be almost horizontal.

'Absolutely. Totally paying attention. Absolutely. How's Richard?'

'Richard is fine.'

'Good. Miss bowling with him. Splendid chap.' Joan winced. 'And you how are you doing?'

'I'm fine.'

'Can't be that long now till you're due? With the baby?' Ben added, having strayed well outside his normal vocabulary. He was well pleased with himself at not asking when she was meant to 'drop the sprog'. His smile, and the obvious internal conversation meant that Joan, having drawn breath for a reflex ten minutes on scans and water births, repeated, 'I'm fine thank you,' backed by a smile as sincere as a crocodile offering free passage to a slightly nervous wildebeest contemplating the Zambezi. She was looking pale, Ben thought. The lipstick a little more than scarlet. A chilli laid out on some raw puff pastry. She hadn't answered his question, looking uncomfortable under the scrutiny. Excellent. He couldn't resist turning the notch up again.

'Will Richard be there? Him being the father and all.'

'Of course he'll be there.'

If she put any more weight on that table it'll go. Ben pulled his long legs out from under the potential danger zone. He looked up and was surprised to see that she was really angry now.

'It's just that I had heard you were thinking of a birth partner,' he added lamely. At that point Neville burst into the room, the man always looked in a complete panic. Apart from the hair. Always together, in place. You can go far with hair like that.

'Sorry I'm late. I didn't realise you'd started. I was on the phone and then saw you in here with Ben and realised that you must have already. Started. The meeting.'

From Joan's face Ben wondered if she knew which useless man she was more angry with. Neville, Sales Director, sat down awkwardly at the end of Joan's desk. Joan waited till the roar of paper shuffling eased.

'Ben. I'm not happy with your performance.'

Ben was stunned. He sat back in his chair, formed his fingers in an arch and incautiously stretched his legs back to their previous position. The seconds passed in silence. Neville started shuffling his papers again, caught Joan's eye and stopped in mid-shuff.

'In what way?' Ben let the words go one at a time, flat and neutral, watching the reaction to each before releasing the next. He suddenly knew he had taken a wrong turning two minutes ago and he wasn't sure of the way back.

'It has been building up for months Ben. I've tried to address it before through the medium of the Thermometer but got nowhere. I don't seem to be able to get through to you at all Ben.' Her words were equally measured back. She leant back in her chair, the table allowing itself a small creak of relief, 'You have been a key member of the program. You have always put your heart and soul into the company...'

'Unlike Davie,' Ben interrupted, 'and he's got Belgium while I'm stuck here.'

Joan paused for a moment but saw the gambit for what it was and left it, gasping for air between them.

'We are not here to discuss Davie's performance but yours.'

Damn Ben thought. Passing up the chance to ritually curse the company doubter. Ben's mind contracted with fear, he failed to acknowledge Neville's comment 'Yes yours Ben,' until well past the appropriate time. The meeting was already lost. Meetings were always like this at Tomorrow, worse than a game of chess, always trying to figure out in any one room who was in on which game. Some were neutrals, often cruising through without even releasing what was going on. But Ben was an Atlantean. Self-development was the key. Believe in yourself and anything was possible. Be not just all that you can be, but pick who you want to be and be all that they could be too. Ben had known this was coming but hadn't felt able to do anything about it. He would be hung out to dry. 'Wonder what for?' he thought idly.

'I am unclear as to which part of my performance you have an issue with?' Pawn slides forward into the centre of the battlefield.

'I find incredible that you pretend that you don't know.' Knight leaps over the ranks and threatens Pawn. Real anger there. Ben looked to Neville.

'I'm really not clear.' Bishop out to support pawn

'It's about your sales figures.' Queen out into the centre. Neville scattering pieces as he goes.

'I have the best figures in my team. With Steve not coming back and Davie in a different country, there is nobody close to me.' Neville tried to pull his Queen back and Ben's Bishop slipped forward.

'Over the year Jeanette shows a better average figure,' Neville said without conviction. He never checked his details.

'All of Jeanette's business is based around one £500k customer. It's fine as long as it lasts. My customers are on better payment terms; bring in more margin and a far better risk spread.' Snick as the Queen falls. Maybe this wasn't going to be so bad after all.

'This isn't about your figures,' Joan's voice was cold fury as she managed to stare down Neville whilst still very clearly talking to Ben, 'it's about your attitude.' Ben looked down at his DMs, shining darkly from under the table and scratched the stubble on his chin. Both verboten in the new business dress recommendations. It must have taken all of thirty seconds after Aaron walked out the company to introduce that and a dozen other changes to keep Ben and the others Professional and Motivated. He watched his Bishop die.

'I-'

'There is no excuse. The new people look up to you Ben. Your role as Value Trustee means that they take their lead from you.'

'I thought that was the role of the Management Team.'

'The Management Team?' Joan was almost shouting now. Neville had faded out beyond peripheral vision. Ben's pieces were falling fast. 'The Management Team are worried about whether we meet our call rates and sales figures. I kept you and Ruth in the role of Value Trustee because I thought you would rise to the challenge. Here was an opportunity to make sure that the company still believed in what we are doing. You managed to force Ruth out of the company just when I needed her most. Just when the company needed her most. I went out on a limb for you Ben, and now I find you constantly undermining my position.'

He wasn't sure you could undermine a limb. Anyway that wasn't how Ben saw it and he said so.

'Listen to what I am saying Ben. You are damaging the moral fibre of the company.'

Ben realised his defence was in a mess, 'You're right. I should have put more effort in to the role. I probably didn't put enough emphasis on it. The last couple of months have been really weird. The whole Aaron Jana thing seemed to derail me more than it should have done. Then Ruth going, going...'

'I'm really pleased to hear you recognise that Ben,' said a voice from outside the tunnel between Ben and Joan. But Joan didn't look very pleased at all.

'It's not good enough. I am asking you to leave the company.' Draw not accepted then. Ben thought he might still be able to fight on.

'You can't do that Joan. We've talked about it often enough when going over the PPM. You have to give me a written warning. You are then required to give me an opportunity, usually three months' time and reasonable support to address the charges raised. I know I've made some mistakes recently but I can change. I let Ruth going get to me too. I can get my act together.'

Neville had already stood up with his papers dangerously close to freedom. Ben let a breath he hadn't realised he was holding. Draw. Eat humble pie. Keep his nose clean. Keep the sales coming in, the disciples in line and it's business as usual.

'I thought I'd made myself clear I want you out of the company now.' Pieces, board and table were crushed by a huge cartoon Harley Quinn hammer that Joan hefted out of nowhere. She sat back looking uncomfortable. It all clicked into place. Three months from now Joan would be up to her armpits in baby shit and vomit, worrying about sore nipples and sleeping in half hour bursts. Three months from now Tomorrow wouldn't remember why Ben had a warning on his record. Three months from now he would be home and dry. Only now Ben saw where Joan had been from the start.

'You have to leave now.'

'No way,' Ben said flatly. Neville looked at the door but apparently decided against making a run for it.

'Subject to Arizona law you're eligible for only three weeks salary. I'll make it four.'

Hard cash? Ben thought for a moment. She must really want me out bad. Desperate making that kind of offer in front of Neville. It had been done before but Ben had checked, all the long-termers had. They weren't subjects of Arizona but good old Blighty employment law. Slightly dog-eared after Thatcher but still obviously a damn sight better than the Colonies. He could bluff her out. There is no way sacking me now would be legal. Ben paused. What was he fighting for? He hated the place. Davie was in Belgium boring everyone with how happy he was now that he didn't have the thought police on him all the time. Ruth hated the company and him, all right mostly him, so much she had resigned on the spot without anywhere to go. Steve had left the company a month after announcing that Tomorrow was the root cause of him believing he was the Second Coming. If Ben stayed here, that could be him. Clothes off, howling at the moon and cursing Tomorrow for the rest of his life.

'Four months.'

'Two months. You walk out of here now. You don't come back. You don't tell anyone.'

'Four,' Ben repeated holding his hand out, which Joan shook. Neville came back in the frame now that hostilities were over, he looked really worried.

'Is this legal? Have you cleared it with Arizona?'

'Who gives a flying...' Joan caught herself, 'I'm doing this for the company. They'll see it when I have explained it to them properly. They always do.'

Rocket Surgery

After Tomorrow

CHAPTER THIRTY FOUR

It had been a surprise when Davie popped in to see him. New improved Davie with added glasses. A surprise because it was the first contact Ben had had from anyone at Tomorrow since he had left. Thinking about it, it was first contact with anyone at all for a while. It was also a surprise because Davie was meant to be some months into his two year secondment in Belgium.

'Hadn't worked out,' Davie talked as he exhaled the smoke, sitting on the floor against the far wall of the living room, 'the company. You know how it is.'

Ben agreed though he wasn't entirely sure with what. Davie seemed to be studying the beige flock wallpaper for answers, 'Have you heard from Steve?' Ben shook his head.

'He seems to be fine now. Moved to Brighton, got himself a nice fella. Turned out that that Thermometer meeting was all he needed to realise Tomorrow was not where he wanted to be.'

'Yes, it wasn't the most welcoming of Thermometer readings.'

'But it was fairly typical. Well. Steve is probably in better shape now than the rest of us although he still has that 'seen too much that others have not' look.' Ben thought of Tiny staring into the mirror in the Incapable. Davie continued. 'You should talk to him. When was the last time you actually sat down and had a chat with Steve where you didn't have a folder in front of you?'

'A very long time. I can't even think of when I stopped.'

'You should man. I'm sure he would be glad to, you know, just have a pint,' Davies voice brightened, 'Did you hear about Neville?'

Ben shook his head but realised that wasn't going to work with Davie determined to talk to the opposite wall, 'No?'

'New general manager after all the fuss about what Joan did when you left.'

Ben closed his eyelids slowly and smiled, 'Glad I did some good.'

'He has played it well Neville.'

'Are we talking about the same man? Blond, startled look, couldn't find his arse even with a map?' asked Ben

'You say that but when you think about it he got Sales Director by being the only Field Sales able to walk and talk at the same time. He was the one that suggested targets for Value Trustees. That pushed Jana into panicking and trying to take Christopher's accounts. That took out both Jana and Christopher, although it turned out Jana had Joan gunning for her already because of the thing with Aaron. Who was the one instituted notes for all meetings? Neville. And of course naturally he circulated the ones after your meeting with Joan because that's what he always did. That put paid to Joan's ambitions and indeed employment as a Tomorrow Person.'

'That is amazing. It all seemed so accidental. You sure it's really been a plan?'

'Without a doubt. Not the detail perhaps but he scattered ropes around the place so that people could hang themselves. To crown his achievement, they went on the New Management weekend course. Even Clare. It's funny now that Joan has gone they have decided that it wasn't the Atlantean philosophy that was evil, just Joan. Neville is really up for it all now. Do you remember I picked you up from one of them? I laughed so much I was crying that night.' Davie broke into song for a moment. 'I'd like to buy the world a coke'?'

Ben didn't get the reference but tried not to look blank.

'Anyway. So off they all go with renewed enthusiasm for the cause. This time, as an introduction, they were all handed a competition arrow, as in Robin Hood, and told to crush it, end on, with their hands.'

'As you do.'

'As you do. Of course, everyone is bleeding away like the faithful with stigmata by the end of the session. You'd think 'sharp, pain, I'll stop now'. But not this lot.'

'That's why you'll never make Management Davie,' Ben said, chain-lighting a new cigarette and tossed another one at Davie.

'So at the end of the weekend they are all so high on self-belief that when they are handed the arrows back and told this time they are going to put the sharp end against- what do you call this?' Davie stretched his neck and jabbed just above his collarbone.

'Epiglottis dear boy,' answered Ben.

'Aye well, that. So sharp end there, blunt end on the guru's chest. Of course all the arrows have been scored around the middle so that they collapse as each of the acolytes demonstrates her new found faith and walks towards the teacher.'

'Apart from Neville's'?'

'Apart from Neville's. Somebody forgot to make the switch. There he is, eyes all bright and shiny. Ready to shave off his hair and be at the helm of Tomorrow, takes a step towards a brave new future and instant do-it-yourself tracheotomy. Blood all over the shop,' Davie laughed.

Ben pointed the two fingers holding his B&H at Davie, 'Now that would be worth seeing.' They sat in silence sharing a smile and reflecting on the importance of good medical care.

'This place looks different.'

The two looked round the empty room as if its condition came as a surprise to the both of them. Ben sat in the solitary armchair with the lid from his B&H packet as an ashtray. The picture he was going for was the bit in The Wall when things aren't going too well for Bob Geldoff and he sits in his chair, unmoving, as the cigarette burns down to the filter leaving a perfect arc of ash. Ben's hands shook too much to pull this last part off. He thought that Davie had missed the reference anyway. Philistine. The curtains were drawn against the bright summer light.

'Susan sold her furniture and disappeared. Poof!' Ben spread his long fingers wide to match his eyes. 'Bye-bye. Gone.'

Davie looked round the room and nodded whilst also looking puzzled, 'I thought you were renting it from her?'

'I was but the bitch has got my deposit. I was really counting on getting that back. It's gone too, of course. Her sister was looking for her last night so the family are none the wiser.'

'She was all right as I remember. On the bright side, your costs are going to be low till she turns up, or they pull her out of the river,' His voice echoed off the bare walls.

'S'right,' replied Ben, 'but the bills are going start coming in soon. What the hell do I do then?'

'Owner sells the furniture and does a runner, leaving the Tenant-'

'And a chair,' Ben interrupted

'And a chair,' Davie agreed. 'Slightly odd isn't it?'

'Completely fucking mad Davie. This has been building up for months. You've been away. You've missed it but Susan was getting more and more tense. No idea what the spark was but she was losing it man. I'm telling you. She was losing it. I was one week late with the rent and it was like the world had ended. I went back home for a break and I came back to this?' Ben leant forward stabbing the side of his head with one finger, emphasising each word. 'Off her fucking head,' Ben sat back exhausted by the effort. Davie prised himself from the floor with difficulty. Ben wondered if Davie would be driving a Mexico in ten years' time while sporting a brown nylon shirt. He stood looking out the back window at the garden that had decided to go for the meadow effect over the summer.

'Where's the car?'

'I had to sell it. That's what's made up the rent money when I got back from Scotland. That and fag money for the last couple of months.'

'That's a damn shame. And Ruth, the Team Leader Trustee thingy. Splendid girl. I thought. None nicer. I heard that she had left the company too. Did you and her stay…?"

'Blew me out. Left Staines as well, a complete change.' Said Ben. Davie was quiet for a moment, his face screwed up as he tried to avoid saying something crass. 'Never trusted me about Joan. The baby.' Ben added.

'What was the truth there?' Davie asked.

'The truth! The truth? Who knows man. I seem to have lost mine somewhere between Garfield and a bloody totem pole. How can you know what's true? I thought the road to Atlantis was a way to get Ruth back and instead I lost her again. How about you and Helen? Did you ever go out with her?'

'No,' Davie was laughing, 'I've been going out with an Irish girl. Siobhan. You met her; she used to work at the company a couple of years ago. Decided we were all bloody mad. I bumped into her at a David Bowie concert in Milton Keynes about a year ago.'

Ben found himself mentally checking down Davie's PPM folder.

'I had you down as liking U2.' he said weakly.

'Me and Helen just kept everything going out of habit. Fun. It was useful for both of us as well,' Davie stated to Ben's puzzlement. Davie looked like a man who had to explain something he didn't want to. 'You guys spent so much time on your Personality Profile Matrix doo dah for each of us and stopped seeing us as people,' Davie's smile had left his eyes and he paused for a good twenty seconds before continuing. 'Friends. The PPMs meant the less we told you, the fewer buttons you could press,' he shrugged. 'Sorry dude but all that under the sea stuff works. You either evolved a coping strategy- something to stop the company squeezing every ounce of life out of you, or you ended up like Steve.

And I went a long way down with him. That Atlantean shit was too good. It didn't leave any space for us to be us. I think we all tried to reach you. Clare, Catherine, me, Helen but every conversation seemed to end up feeling like an evaluation. We all liked you, liked Ruth but...'

Ben was trying to catch up and Davie was looking uncomfortable at the way the conversation had gone. He changed the subject, 'And she split with the money?'

'Susan? Aye,' Ben struggled to speak. How had he missed so much?

'I better be getting back Ben. We should have stayed in touch. It's been too long. Good to see you and eh, sorry.'

'Not your fault. Sounds like it's mine. Good to see you too. Where are you staying now? You are working up in Buckingham?'

'That's right. It has all been a bit hectic. I'm stopping in Maidenhead, Catherine and Arthur-' Davie stopped and then started again. 'They are putting me up till I get myself sorted out. I think Lone Star Semiconductors should work out fine. I can't believe I have been lucky enough to get in. Neville nearly stopped them taking me on as well. That Lone Star was breaking its contract with Tomorrow by taking me on. Bastards. If they hadn't tried to stuff me in the first place I wouldn't have gone looking and then they try and...' Davie realised he was going over old ground and the anger left him. 'Bloody company. We're both better off out of it. You know out of all the Tomorrow people you were the only one to visit me in the Britwell? Are you going to be okay?' Davie asked.

Ben nodded and held out his hand and then remembered to take the fag out of it, 'Fine and dandy, Davie boy. Fine and Dandy. Keep in contact this time.'

Ben watched Davie as he climbed into a different Manta, now a black one with a tasteless gypsy cream interior. The car rolled slowly down the street and out of sight. 'Fine and Fucking Dandy,' Ben slapped the door shut and returned to the chair.

'Splendid girl. None nicer,' Ben repeated to the empty room. Davie was right. Twice now Ben had completely cocked up his life by making Ruth walk out of it. He washed his face with his hands. Davie had reminded him of all of the team, the way they had been. One by one they had moved away without leaving their desks. Ben paced the room trying to think of what to do. The chair called to him, begged to him to come back and sit down. Ben was frightened if he sat down he wouldn't be able to get up again.

'What to do?' he asked himself.

'Get Ruth back,' he was aware that he was talking to himself and made a conscious effort to stop. He was right though. Start there. He needed to see her, needed to explain what a dick he had been, although she probably knew that bit. No car, couldn't afford a taxi. Actually he hadn't been able to afford eating much for the last couple of days. The idea hit Ben. He could walk. He used to walk all over the hills round Helensburgh without thinking about it. Tomorrow he would walk to Ruth's. After that, start rounding up the gang again. Get it back like it used to be.

Chapter Thirty Five

Ben is excited; walking gives him time to think about what he is going to say to Ruth. He has memorised the route. It takes about thirty minutes in the car, average say of twenty miles an hour, so ten miles. Ten miles: that would be no longer than walking to Glen Fruin, so it shouldn't be a problem. When he does meet Ruth he should start with 'I'm an idiot.' And end with 'I love you.' But the cohesive argument to win her back in between eludes him. But Ben finds his spirits staying high as he walks alongside a choked stream of traffic. The roads are always busy here; even at three in the morning, there will always be at least one car in sight. Not so much a city that doesn't sleep, more an urban sprawl with apnoea.

Ben continues walking out of Slough. That in itself feels like progress. He looks at the houses he is passing - large semi-detached houses, old-style ones, with the halls and doors in the centre and a hint of mock Tudor around the gables. The Fifties' picture of successful living. It fascinates Ben the way a single building could so clearly have two owners. An old one on the left, untouched since it was built, leans up against its distant cousin and peeks enviously at the imitation lead-paned double glazing, the one-metre-square porch and the red tiles that stops so abruptly halfway across the shared roof. Why is there never enough money to finish off the garden?

There is a six-car pile-up on the elevated section of the M4, the car radios tell the drivers as they sit stationary in the heat, windows down, arms hang lifelessly over the doors, nodding heads mark absent time till the traffic news ends and the beat returns. The seizure has spread along the length of the motorway and down the contributing roads. Traffic lights lose their meaning as cars, unable to clear the contested space, rob others of their turn. Cars inch dangerously close to each other.

Ben walks by a beautiful woman in a cherry red BMW - roof down, she flicks a mass of blonde hair back with the leg of her sunglasses. Putting them back on, she gives Ben an open, confident smile. He has passed her twice now and is trying to work out if he should say hello when all the water he drank before setting off demands to make a reappearance. He realises he should have stopped for a slash back in the centre of Slough. Waist-high weeds behind an advertising hoarding provides the only shelter. As he comes back out from behind the sign -

noting that the future will be Orange - the traffic lurches and the BMW blats away down the road and off at the roundabout, blonde hair fans out in the breeze.

Bens legs are warm now and his easy, loping, stride keeps him ahead of schedule. He still doesn't have any ideas about his speech but feels thankful that Dr Marten had invented these boots. Ben can't resist a bad Alexi Sayle impersonation as he walks. In contrast Ben had scared himself last night with thoughts of Tiny. It is always tricky keeping things in proportion when the sun is down. The four of them had been so tight at the start of Sixth Year- Tiny, Rhino and Angus and himself. Inseparable even. Ben uses the time to think through his last year at school. When had they, in fact, separated? Was there a specific point at which Tiny had shifted categories from friend to 'mad bloke that I used to hang around with'? Ben finds himself distracted so although the shapes are familiar, the detail is new. Here is a land best seen from the car flashing to the Three Tuns or the Wheatsheaf. Only now is he aware of just how much distance lay between his house and those two pubs. Matter transportation has already happened and nobody has noticed.

It worries Ben, Tiny that is, because of what Davie said yesterday. Somewhere in Ben's life at Tomorrow had he changed from all round good guy, only occasionally being confused as an adult version of Odie, to the odd man in an empty house. He thinks his way back to the start of his time at Tomorrow. That is a lifetime ago. Hermione and the new way to run a company. Discovering Atlantis. Creating the Personality Profile Matrix. He mulls it over as he walks. Bens' head is splitting by the time he gets to a row of shops that look like they have gathered together for protection.

He pays for an apple and a can of Pepsi and sits on the wall outside the armoured off-licence munching a couple of paracetamol before he starts his lunch. He waits until the pain subsides a little. Lack of water? Lack of food? Or simply just thinking too much?

This walk is good. It feels like the first time he has really left Slough in a long time. Although he has left Slough many times, it has always come with him in his mind. Space folds in on Slough. You tended to forget that there is a whole world out there. Ben had met people who had never been beyond the town's boundaries. In their world, twinkling stars are replaced by the two counter-rotating stacks feeding the planes into Heathrow between Maidenhead and Reading. The wind doesn't carry the salt spray of the sea, or the freshness of country fields, only rubbish in little dirt devils that wander amongst the bombproof bins. Fields like these gasp their last between housing estates rather than the picture book of village life where it is the country that dominates the landscape. Ben has turned his back on somewhere very different. But the people here, with conurbation for ninety miles to the east and all the way to Reading to the west, assume that all the world is like this now. You can walk to the horizon four times and still not see the end. All the world, indeed.

His legs really hurt now. Tired, they just want to stop. Stop here, it would be fine, a couple of minutes' rest, that's all they need, then, as soon as Ben said, they promise they will be up and running again. Don't believe you, he tells his legs, almost there. They don't believe him in return. He is arguing with his legs. Surely that can't be a good sign.

With all the reflection on Helensburgh and Tomorrow Ben suspects his subconscious is trying hard not to let him think about Ruth. She had hunted him down, picked him out from the herd, made him hers. And then what, he had thrown her away! The idea makes him hurt inside.

'How could I have been so stupid?' Ben asks as he walks.

'So stupid three times,' Ben replies.

'Ah, no, because Debbie was before I met Ruth again. I think. Yes. Debbie doesn't count. At least not in this particular way.'

'So you only let down Ruth twice. And she dumped you for that?' Ben asks himself.

'I should have left the party with her. She knew it. I knew it.'

'But you stayed because of a twinkle in Joan's eye and you wondered what could happen.'

'Damn me,' Ben hasn't been aware that he has been talking out loud until a tired, pale woman looks up at him from the buggy she pushes, clearly wondering whether she should scream or smile. Ben smiles at her, but that seems to do little to reassure her. The strange man in the white T-shirt keeps walking, but glances back at the ghostly kid in the buggy, blankly staring out over a huge Mickey dummy, black ears framing his nose nicely. It has been sunny for five weeks, how can you stay that pale?

Ben is getting thirsty again. The can at lunch time picked him up for a bit but the afternoon is warm and the throbbing returns to his head. He has what is left of that pack of paracetamol folded in his pocket and has been holding out until he finds some more water. He rubs the sides of his head as he walks. Mind over matter. If he tries hard enough he can think his way out of this pain; or perhaps, not thinking would be wiser.

Ben reaches Ruth's house just after six. For some reason he expects a fanfare of trumpets as he takes the final step onto the drive. Perhaps a heavenly choir to underline the supreme effort for true love that today represents. Instead an ageing Nova blows a raspberry as it accelerates past, with a backing track of a sound system that must weigh more than the car. Ben sits down on the wall beside the door, out of sight of the window. This is the trickiest part of the plan: find Ruth, and say something wonderful, witty and winning. Ruth then realises where her true future lies, and she and Ben walk off into the sunset, only not too far, his legs point out.

Ben thought that he would plan his speech on the trek, inspired as he walks for love. But now that he is here the muse is not so much eluding him as gone on a refreshing holiday in the Bahamas and sent him a postcard saying 'I can let you have something in a month'. And he hadn't appreciated how mind-numbing the sheer physical work of the walk would be. All he really has so far is, 'I'm sorry about that night, whatever you've heard isn't true, and I love you.' But the 'sorry' bit seems to contradict the 'isn't true' bit, and both bits just detracts from the important 'I love you' bit. And whilst it is true, and despite the fact that it will be the first time he will say it to anyone outside his immediate family, Ben can't help feeling that just saying 'I love you' scores poorly on originality and impact.

'I love you, but we only have fourteen hours to save the earth?' No. 'I love you and I'm stupid enough to walk all this way to tell you,' he says out loud to the garden. He decides to wing it - seeing Ruth's beautiful face will draw poetry out of him — he knocks on the door. He knocks again. He leaves it a bit and knocks one more time, more loudly, in case she can't hear the door over the sound of complete silence emanating from the house. So. It looks like Ruth is out. Well, her car isn't there, which is a clue. He will never make Detective.

Ben checks his watch again; yes, still just after 'too'. He wanders round the back of the maisonette, trying to look like somebody who is waiting for somebody rather than somebody who is waiting for nobody. On the patio, in the corner where the kitchen extension meets the back wall, there is a standing pipe with a tap. Ben kneels down and drinks as much as he can. He is certain that is the wrong thing to do but bollocks to that, he is thirsty. She is out then. That is all right. He will just wait for her to come back. He has a steady water supply and nine fags.

Ben chews a paracetamol and looks round, trying to pick the coolest place to be discovered. He pulls over a squashed roll of spare carpet from the other side of the patio, shapes it and sits on it, his back into the corner by the tap. He feels like he has never sat on anything so comfortable. The sun has gone off for its evening counselling session leaving the sky to settle into a shapeless orange dome. He can't see the aeroplane stacks from here, but with his eyes closed he can imagine them as enormous bees droning above the English country garden of brick and tarmac that he has just walked across. The air is cooling rapidly, as is Ben now that he isn't walking. Shame he doesn't have his flying jacket anymore. He looks at the carpet and wonders how he could use it to keep warm until Ruth turns up.

Ben was standing on the hill with no name. The Ancient Kingdom of Strathclyde was at his feet. The air so clear he could see every detail of the trees of the forest, the rocks on the shore, the big cranes in Greenock. Out in the glittering Clyde the sugar boat Captayannis lay on its side beneath a perfect blue sky, two contrails recreated the cross of St Andrew above. He could feel the warmth of the sun right through his body. Ruth was beside him pulling him to the blanket spread out on the heather. They had planned to go for a walk up the Hill and now here they were, brilliant.

A piano was playing somewhere in the background, the same refrain going round and round. Neither of them appeared to have any clothes on, which was handy. With only the piano for sound Ruth held Ben close. Her kisses deep, her body held close to his as they rolled across the blanket. It felt so good but it wasn't Ruth any more it was Clorinda. She looked fantastic as she always did. But Ben didn't want to be with Clorinda no matter how great she looked. Ben closed his eyes and thought really hard about Ruth. He opened his eyes only to see Joan smiling at him, licking him from chin to forehead. The smell of Pernod was overpowering. Her legs clamped round his buttocks. This was all wrong but he couldn't stop. An orchestra and bass guitar had joined the piano in the same hypnotic tune.

Joan ran her fingers threw his hair and then stretched out her arms into the heather above her head. Ben tried to lift himself up, scrub scratching at his knees. Those tits really were huge. He watched them rise and fall in time to the music, in time with them copulating, making love didn't really cover it. Joan squeezed him tight. Ben knew he was going to come. Her hands were in his hair again.

'Not yet Ben,' Joan whispered. The piano was back on its own now, everything else was hushed. She began to twist his head. With a jerk the top half began to unscrew. Ben was still humping away for all he was worth. 'First I'm going to fuck with your mind.' With a clunk the top half of his skull fell to the ground, discarded pink and white amongst the heather. Long nailed fingers scraped over the bloody bone lip, his brain slopping back and forth in time with Joan's chest. The nails flashed down.

'Bloody hell!' He is shouting, awake, alive, intact. Tightly bound in the dark Ben is sweating. The panic passes, rolling himself up in the rejected carpet hadn't been such a good idea. He frees his arms, shakily lighting a fag and uses the lighter to illuminate the watch. Just after 'Be' in the morning. He swears again. Slightly quieter this time. Stars are out above the maisonettes night filled backyard. That really wasn't nice.

Ben unravels himself completely to get a drink from the tap. He shivers half at the memory of the dream and half at the night chill beyond that carpets warm embrace. Ben rubs his bare arms, squinting against the smoke in his eyes. He strolls round to the front of the house to make sure that Ruth's car hasn't turned up while he played a rather disappointing Cleopatra. Nothing.

It is dawn now. Ben goes for a slash in the corner of the yard, steam rises from his piss in the cold air. He drinks as much as he can from the tap, lights up a cigarette and blows the smoke out of his nose. The last twenty four hours have got him thinking, thinking about things that he has not considered for a long time. Too long.

'The only person who has fucked your life up Ben is you. Not your friends, not your boss and certainly not Ruth. Just you.' Ben puts his watch on the wall by the patio window. He walks out on to the street in front of the house and stretches like a cat. He points back down the long straight road.

'It'll be that way then. Next time I do this I'm going to bring a jumper.'

He laughs. Ben holds his arms out wide to the excited new dawn. 'Next time?' He starts off, limping slightly as his weary legs complain. He tells both of them to be quiet and he picks up the pace. A metallic blue Renault 25 drives slowly past, the driver is peering cautiously at the early morning interloper through the still misted windscreen. Heading in the same direction Ben begins to sing:

Rocket Surgery

'I've got a job waiting for my graduation
Fifty thou a year -- buys a lot of beer
Things are going great, and they're only getting better
I'm doing all right, getting good grades
The future's so bright, I gotta wear shades'

Also by DJ Gilmour and available on Amazon-

REMNANT KINGS

Arthur, the Undying King, still dominates Europe in 1625. With the death of James VI, Scotland faces an uncertain future as Arthur reasserts his ancient right to rule and Vampires return to the streets of Edinburgh.

Remnant Kings is the story of two Scots from the same village in Argyll caught up in the tragedy and turmoil of a country riven by politics, religion and fear. A place where old certainties are lost and new ideas may have a greater impact than anyone realises

'Wonderful story and setting! Includes interesting interlude in Sweden, possibly my favourite part. The pace is good but the real strength of this book is its fantastic world building, there's a feeling of a large and lived-in world here. Eagerly awaiting next instalment to see where these characters are heading. Would recommend.'

A Edwards

'Remnant Kings is a colorful and at times graphic representation of a Scotland gone by, fighting off the marauding English with one hand and, in a touch of fantasy/horror, vengeful vampires with the other. It portrays the battles for power between kings, countries, nobility and common people alike and the unwillingness of many to acknowledge the dangers in their midst. A colorful cast of characters all share 1 common trait : a love of Scotland.

Time is needed at the outset to become familiar with the period, setting and people but the plot rapidly gathers pace culminating in fierce battles and a medley of not always favorable outcomes for the entire cast and intrigue as to how this unique and enjoyable representation of Scottish history could evolve in the future. I look forward to any sequels.'

R Cyphus

A spellbinding mix of, presumably, some historical accuracy (I'm not well up on the events in Scotland in 1625), and fantasy/horror. D.J. Gilmour skilfully blends the two in such a way that I was almost inclined to believe in some scenes that the vampires and other dark forces at large across the well-invoked Scottish landscape, were really there at that time. The power struggle between rival factions, both mortal and supernatural aspects, is well captured and builds into a fascinating read as we follow the fortunes of wide-ranging, believable characters.

Much of the action takes place in Edinburgh, depicting the often inhospitable climate and conditions, even in the castle. The graphic description of life in the taverns and on the streets, along with particularly bloodthirsty battles, reveal Gilmour to be a talented writer, and I look forward to reading more of his work.

S Bint

'Not my genre at all but it was recommended to me so I thought I would give it a go. Lots of characters to learn about and to understand their journey but lots of action happening to keep the pages turning. The vampire involvement was an interesting twist but fitted in well with the other characters and kept an edge to the plot. An enjoyable read.'

K Matlock

'A gripping tale of how ordinary people fight for political reform against an autocratic King in league with vampires. Set in Scotland in the 1600's there is both historical context and vivid imagery of Edinburgh. One of the characters Amanda becomes an extraordinary heroine and is pivotal to the story.

Remnant Kings is full of plots, twists, romance, drama and tension. I could not put the book down and it left me hanging right till the end as to whether good or bad would prevail. For the first time ever I found one of the baddies endearing. I very much hope it leads onto another book.'

K Yates

Printed in Poland
by Amazon Fulfillment
Poland Sp. z o.o., Wrocław
19 September 2023

8e7ab398-4cab-4088-8cbe-16640ef154a0R02